# IMAGES OF JUDAISM
# IN LUKE-ACTS

# Images of Judaism
# in Luke-Acts

by

JOSEPH B. TYSON

UNIVERSITY OF SOUTH CAROLINA PRESS

Copyright © 1992 University of South Carolina

Published in Columbia, South Carolina, by the
University of South Carolina Press

Manufactured in the United States of America

Library of Congress Cataloging-in-Publication Data

Tyson, Joseph B.
    Images of Judaism in Luke-Acts / Joseph B. Tyson.
        p.      cm.
    Includes bibliographical references and index.
    ISBN 0–87249–794–1 (alk. paper)
    1.  Jews in the New Testament.      2.  Judaism—Relations—
Christianity—Biblical teaching.      3.   Christianity and other
religions—Judaism—Biblical teaching      4.  Bible.    N.T.    Luke—
Criticism, interpretation, etc.      5.   Bible.    N.T.    Acts—Criticism,
interpretation, etc.      I.   Title.
BS2595.6.J44T97    1991
226.4'08296—dc20                                                        91–34519

# Contents

# Preface

Within the last several years a number of scholarly works have been written on the understanding of Judaism in the New Testament. Scholarly interest in this subject has not arisen simply out of concern for antiquity, but to a large extent it has been influenced by recent history. In particular, the Holocaust of 1933–45 has awakened an interest in exploring the roots of modern anti-Semitism. Some scholars find the roots of modern Christian anti-Judaism in the New Testament itself, while others defend the ancient books against these charges. Luke-Acts has been at the center of much of the controversy, and interpretations of these documents have been wide ranging.

This book is an attempt to read Luke-Acts in a new way, utilizing some of the concepts that have come from reader-response criticism. In particular, the concept of the implied reader, i.e., the reader in the text, is employed as a control device on the varying possibilities of reading. Chapter 2 is a survey of the knowledge that is assumed to be in the possession of the implied reader, and a profile of this reader is drawn. The result is that the implied reader is similar to those characters in Luke-Acts who are termed Godfearers, i.e., Gentiles who are attracted to Judaism but not fully committed to it. In chapters 3–8, we examine the ways in which Luke and Acts lead this implied reader to think of the Jewish people and their religious life.

The images of Judaism for which we will search are, of course, verbal images. Since we have recently learned to think of first-century Judaisms rather than first-century Judaism, there will be a particular interest in the basic conception of Jewish religious life and thought that is expressed in Luke-Acts. We need to be sensitive to the ways in which the implied author speaks to the implied reader about various aspects of Jewish religious life, including individual and social piety, the scriptures, the traditions, the institutions, and the people. And since Luke-Acts is a narrative, it will be important to be sensitive to changes in these images that result from narrative developments.

This book may be characterized as a study in ambivalence since the images embedded within the text of Luke-Acts are not all of one kind. Indeed, what results from this study is an impression of a complex ambivalence in these documents. Luke-Acts is both pro-Jewish and anti-Jewish and both in profound ways. An appreciation of this fact is essential for understanding the ways in which these texts work and in assessing their role in the development of Christian attitudes toward Jews.

In chapter 6, I have incorporated revisions of some material that originally appeared in my article "The Gentile Mission and the Authority of Scripture in Acts," *New Testament Studies* 33 (1987): 619–31. I am grateful to *New Testament Studies* and Cambridge University Press for their permission to use this material.

Portions of chapter 8 originally appeared, in a different form, in my article "The Problem of Jewish Rejection in Acts," reprinted from *Luke-Acts and the Jewish People,* by Joseph B. Tyson, copyright © 1988 Augsburg Publishing House. Used by permission of Augsburg Fortress.

Unless otherwise noted, scripture quotations are from the New Revised Standard Version Bible, copyright 1989 by the Division of Christian Education of the National Council of the Churches of Christ in the United States of America. Used by permission.

Transliteration of Greek follows the guidelines of the Society of Biblical Literature's "Instructions for Contributors," *Journal of Biblical Literature* 107 (1988): 579–96. Abbreviations of biblical books also follow these recommendations.

I have learned many things from a number of scholars and consulted directly with some during the preparation of this book. In particular I want to thank the members of the Society of Biblical Literature's Group on Acts. It was my pleasure to chair this group from 1986 to 1990 and hence to become acquainted with the work of an impressive and talented group of scholars. They will recognize their own influence in various parts of this book. I want especially to thank Susannah Heschel, my colleague at Southern Methodist University from 1988 to 1991. She has read the entire

manuscript and has shared with me insights that come out of a
perspective and heritage quite different from my own. Although
she bears no responsibility for the book, her comments and suggestions have enriched it and helped to clarify it at a number
of points.

# Abbreviations

| | |
|---|---|
| AB | Anchor Bible |
| AnBib | Analecta biblica |
| *ANRW* | *Aufstieg und niedergang der römischen Welt* |
| BBB | Bonner biblische Beiträge |
| BETL | Bibliotheca ephemeridum theologicarum lovaniensium |
| *Bib* | *Biblica* |
| *BTB* | *Biblical Theology Bulletin* |
| *BZ* | *Biblische Zeitschrift* |
| CBC | Cambridge Bible Commentary |
| *CBQ* | *Catholic Biblical Quarterly* |
| EBib | Etudes bibliques |
| *ETL* | *Ephemerides theologicae lovanienses* |
| *ExpTim* | *Expository Times* |
| *HeyJ* | *Heythrop Journal* |
| HKNT | Handkommentar zum Neuen Testament |
| HNT | Handbuch zum Neuen Testament |
| HTKNT | Herders theologischer Kommentar zum Neuen Testament |
| *HTR* | *Harvard Theological Review* |
| *IB* | *Interpreter's Bible* |
| ICC | International Critical Commentary |
| *Int* | *Interpretation* |

| | |
|---|---|
| *JAAR* | *Journal of the American Academy of Religion* |
| *JBL* | *Journal of Biblical Literature* |
| *JES* | *Journal of Ecumenical Studies* |
| *JR* | *Journal of Religion* |
| *JSJ* | *Journal for the Study of Judaism in the Persian, Hellenistic and Roman Period* |
| *JSNT* | *Journal for the Study of the New Testament* |
| JSNTSup | Journal for the Study of the New Testament—Supplement Series |
| *JSOT* | *Journal for the Study of the Old Testament* |
| *JTC* | *Journal for Theology and the Church* |
| LCL | Loeb Classical Library |
| LXX | Septuagint |
| MNTC | Moffatt New Testament Commentary |
| *NedTTS* | *Nederlands theologisch tijdschrift* |
| NICNT | New International Commentary of the New Testament |
| NIGTC | The New International Greek Testament Commentary |
| *NovT* | *Novum Testamentum* |
| NovTSup | Novum Testamentum Supplements |
| NRSV | New Revised Standard Version of the Bible |
| NT | New Testament |
| NTD | Das Neue Testament Deutsch |
| *NTS* | *New Testament Studies* |
| *Numen* | *Numen: International Review for the History of Religions* |
| OBT | Overtures to Biblical Theology |
| OT | Old Testament |
| 11QMelch | *Melchizedek* text from Qumran Cave 11 |
| *RB* | *Revue biblique* |
| *ResQ* | *Restoration Quarterly* |

| RSV | Revised Standard Version |
|---|---|
| *RTP* | *Revue de théologie et de philosophie* |
| SANT | Studien zum Alten und Neuen Testament |
| SBLDS | Society of Biblical Literature Dissertation Series |
| SBLMS | Society of Biblical Literature Monograph Series |
| *SBLSP* | *Society of Biblical Literature Seminar Papers* |
| *SecCent* | *Second Century* |
| SJLA | Studies in Judaism in Late Antiquity |
| SNT | Studien zum Neuen Testament |
| SNTSMS | Society of New Testament Studies Monograph Series |
| S. P. C. K. | Society for the Promotion of Christian Knowledge |
| *ST* | *Studia theologica* |
| Str-B | H. Strack and P. Billerbeck, *Kommentar zum Neuen Testament* |
| THKNT | Theologischer Handkommentar zum Neuen Testament |
| *TS* | *Theological Studies* |
| *TZ* | *Theologische Zeitschrift* |
| UBSGNT | United Bible Societies Greek New Testament |
| WMANT | Wissenschaftliche Monographien zum Alten und Neuen Testament |
| *ZKT* | *Zeitschrift für katholische Theologie* |
| *ZNW* | *Zeitschrift für die neutestamentliche Wissenschaft* |
| *ZTK* | *Zeitschrift für Theologie und Kirche* |

# IMAGES OF JUDAISM
# IN LUKE-ACTS

# 1

# Introduction

Among ancient writers of gospels, Luke is alone in extending his narrative beyond the time of Jesus. Although in many respects the Gospel of Luke is comparable with other gospels, especially Matthew and Mark, the book of Acts reveals an interest that goes far beyond the chronological limits of other gospels. Luke's interest in history requires some explanation but has been understood in widely different ways. It is frequently maintained that he was interested in the period after Jesus because he was aware that earlier apocalyptic expectations had not been fulfilled and that he wrote in order to dampen any remaining or reviving enthusiasm about a pending end to present historical circumstances. It is argued that in Luke's view those expectations that might have been popular among the earliest followers of Jesus could no longer be sustained. To put the matter in theological terms, Luke believes that God has stretched out the time so that one should no longer entertain hopes for an immediate end. Rather, one should settle down to a long future, and the story that Luke records in Acts is intended to provide a model for living in that extended time.

Hans Conzelmann has propounded this view most forcefully.[1] Conzelmann's emphasis on *Heilsgeschichte* is based on an understanding that Luke sees the action of God in three historical periods: that of Israel, that of Jesus, and that of the church. This perception of Luke's work allows us to understand how he can distinguish between the conditions and theological problems that pertain in the different ages. Conzelmann writes:

> The period of Jesus and the period of the Church are presented as different epochs in the broad course of saving history, differentiated to some extent by their particular characteristics. Thus Luke can distinguish between those commands of the Lord which were meant only for

1

the contemporary situation, such as the directions concerning equip-
ment given when the apostles are sent out, which in Luke xxii, 35–7 are
explicitly annulled for the period to follow, and those which are permanent, such as in the Sermon on the Plain. Therefore he cannot simply project present questions back into the time of Jesus. His aim is
rather to bring out the peculiar character of each period.[2]

Conzelmann states that Luke devotes attention to the period of the
church as an extended period of time because he recognizes that
the eschatological expectations of an earlier age have not been fulfilled in his time and are not to be fulfilled in the near future. The
force of Conzelmann's interpretation of Luke's eschatology is represented in the original German title of his *Theology of St. Luke (Die
Mitte der Zeit)*.[3] In Conzelmann's analysis of Luke's thought, the
time of Jesus formed the middle period of history, not the last.

   In an article on Paul and Luke's treatment of him, Ernst
Käsemann expanded Conzelmann's view of *Heilsgeschichte* and
claimed that Luke provided the grounds for *Frühkatholizismus*,
early Catholicism.[4] Luke's picture of the church, his interest in its
leadership, its preaching, and its exercise of authority, and in particular his alignment of Paul with the apostles, suggest that he has
in mind providing a model for the Christian community, a model
that would serve in the development of a triumphal Christian
institution.

   For both Conzelmann and Käsemann, the problem of a delayed fulfillment of eschatological hopes serves to explain the interest in the post-Jesus history displayed in the book of Acts. But
not all scholars have found his interpretation satisfactory, and
some have looked for other explanations. Several decades earlier,
in fact, Henry J. Cadbury stressed the apologetic motifs discernible
in Luke-Acts.[5] Cadbury acknowledged that Luke's motives in writing were probably varied, but he nevertheless was impressed with
the stress in Luke on the political innocence of Jesus and with the
numerous statements in Acts about the innocence of the heroes.
The problems that engulfed the apostles and Paul are sometimes
pronounced to be issues relating to Jewish customs and, hence,
not of interest to Roman governors. Paul, like Jesus, is regarded as
not guilty of breaking any Roman law. Thus, Cadbury urged consideration of the view that Luke-Acts was motivated largely by in-
terests in political apologetic.

   Paul W. Walaskay presents an interesting twist on the view
that Acts is a political apology.[6] He admits that the delay of the

parousia was a problem among Luke's readers, but he claims that one of the major reasons Luke wrote was to commend the Roman empire to a Christian audience. Walaskay argues that Luke "held a positive view of the empire which was shared by several of his literary contemporaries and which he imparted to his reading public. Luke was less concerned about the political stance of the church than he was to defend the imperial government to the church."[7]

Recently Richard I. Pervo has maintained that, although Luke had other purposes in mind in writing Acts, entertainment was a primary one.[8] Pervo claims that there is more in common between canonical Acts and the apocryphal Acts than is usually perceived, and he understands the genre of both to be that of the historical novel. David E. Aune has called attention to significant similarities between Luke-Acts and Hellenistic histories and has classified it as general history.[9]

Neither the explanation of Luke-Acts as an answer to a delayed parousia, nor its characterization as apology, historical novel, or general history pays sufficient attention to a significant aspect of these texts, that is, the concern that is devoted to relations between Jesus and his followers on the one hand and non-believing Jews on the other. The narratives reveal a passion to say something not only about those Jews (and Gentiles) who accepted Jesus but also about those Jews who did not. In this respect Luke-Acts displays a remarkable imbalance, for there is no comparable interest in Gentiles who rejected Jesus and his followers. Story after story in both the gospel and Acts tells of Jewish acceptance or rejection of the message of Jesus, the apostles, and Paul. In addition, verbal images of Jewish people, institutions, piety, and religious practices add color to the narratives. The interest in Jewish religious life is remarkable, especially in Acts, and, despite the author's sympathy with the mission to the Gentiles, there is no corresponding interest in Gentile religious life. What little there is pales into insignificance when compared with the rich detail about Jewish traditions. This interest in Jewish religious life forms a major part of the story that Luke tells, and attention to it may help to uncover the reasons for his interest in the history after the time of Jesus.

If Luke is writing, as most scholars contend, after the Roman destruction of the Jewish Temple in 70 CE and after the surrender of the Jews to the Romans at the end of the first rebellion, i.e.,

73–74 CE, he must be acutely aware that the situation of the followers of Jesus with respect to Jewish life, thought, religious practices, and institutions is not what it was in the time of Jesus, or Peter, or Paul. Although it is misleading to talk about a formal break between Christianity and Judaism in the first century CE, the first decades after the war must have been a time when these two increasingly independent communities gave serious consideration to their own identities.[10] Jewish rabbinical schools engaged in the development of traditions that led to *Mishnah*, first at Jamnia and later in Galilee. At the same time, there was an increase in the production of Christian literature. The letters of Paul were, of course, written before the war but were probably not generally known until late in the first century. The beginning of the composition of gospels almost surely dates from the last decades of the first century. Intellectual and literary activity in Christian communities was pursued in increasing independence from Jewish communities, but Christian writers, nonetheless, continued to hold a deep interest in Judaism. The Gospel of Luke and the book of Acts reveal the depth of this interest on the part of one such writer.

The people whom Luke considers to be Jewish, both individuals and groups, are significant characters in the gospel and in Acts, and aspects of Jewish religious life form parts of the fabric of many narratives. If we concentrate on the activities, experiences, and conflicts involving the chief characters in Luke and Acts, we observe that many of them involve questions of Jewish religious observance and call attention to issues that tend to separate Jesus and his followers from other Jewish people and their leaders. Within Acts, some of the narratives that deal explicitly with conflict and problems supposedly internal to the Christian movement involve questions that have implications for relationships with Jewish communities. These relationships are among the fundamental concerns revealed in Luke-Acts, and the author's attitudes toward the Jewish people and Jewish religious life inevitably shape the narratives in these texts.

Furthermore, there are images of Jewish religious life embedded within these texts—images of individual and social piety, religious institutions, groups, leaders, special observances, leading beliefs and practices, revered history, and sacred scripture. A study of these images should produce a firm basis for forming an impression of Judaism and the role of the Jewish people in our texts. In view of the significant attention paid in Luke-Acts to Jews, such a study may have implications for understanding Luke's historical interest and for explaining his purpose. Thus, the focus of attention in the chapters that follow will be on various images of Judaism to be found in Luke and Acts.

Questions about Luke's portrayal of Jewish religious life are not simply of interest to the historian of antiquity. They also have contemporary social significance. Although she was not the first to do so, Rosemary Radford Ruether has forcefully claimed that there is a connection between a form of anti-Judaism to be found in the NT and modern forms of anti-Semitism.[11] Since the publication of Ruether's work in 1974, a number of treatments of the subject have appeared, but there is a sense in which she set the agenda for a discussion of anti-Judaism in the NT.[12] A summary of Ruether's work and the responses to it should demonstrate the significance of investigating Luke's images of Judaism.

Ruether traces the history of anti-Semitism from ancient times to its most unspeakably tragic expression in the Holocaust of 1933–45. Although she is aware of the complexities of those events during which some six million Jews were among those who were exterminated, she nevertheless maintains that there is a connection between the concepts that failed to prevent such events and their roots in early Christian writing and theology. Her conclusion is that in ancient, classical, and modern expressions, Christian belief in the person and work of Christ has carried with it a condemnation of those who rejected this belief, notably, the Jews. Thus Christology and anti-Judaism have travelled hand in hand through the Christian centuries. The more insistently Christians have proclaimed their Christological creed, the more damning has been their rejection of the Jews. She writes:

> Our theological critique of Christian anti-Judaism, therefore, must turn to what was always the other side of anti-Judaism, named Christology. At the heart of every Christian dualizing of the dialectics of human existence into Christian and anti-Judaic antitheses is Christology, or, to be more specific, the historicizing of the eschatological event. Realized eschatology converts each of the dialectics we have examined—judgment and promise, particularism and universalism, letter and spirit, history and eschatology—into dualisms, applying one side to the "new messianic people," the Christians, and the negative side to the "old people," the Jews.[13]

Ruether then asks, "Is it possible to say 'Jesus is Messiah' without, implicitly or explicitly, saying at the same time 'and the Jews be damned?' "[14] In her concluding section, she lays out some proposals for doing just this.

It is of interest to observe that much of the response to Ruether's suggestions has come, not from Christian theologians, whom she supposed herself to be addressing, but from NT scholars. What Ruether wanted to do, presumably, was to initiate a dialogue on theological questions, specifically on the question of the possible separation of Christology from anti-Judaism. But in tracing the history of Christian anti-Judaism, it was necessary for her to go back to the foundation documents, the NT writings, and to analyze them in terms of their contributions to that history. It is this analysis that has received the attention of NT scholars, and so it is necessary for us to look at this section of her work in some detail.

Ruether begins her study with an examination of attitudes toward Jews in paganism. She finds there an ambivalent attitude.

> On the one hand, their exclusiveness was decried as an absurd misanthropy and a pretension to superiority in a foreign people whom the educated Greek regarded as superstitious "barbarians." Their various customs, such as circumcision, abstinence from pork, and Sabbath leisure, were regarded with amused contempt, rather than hatred. On the other hand, there was the traditional Greek philosophical curiosity and Roman political practicality that created cultural assimilation and administrative accommodation.[15]

Against this background, Christian anti-Judaism is new, not a continuation of pagan attitudes. Although there were negative attitudes to be found among Greeks and Romans in the Hellenistic period, it was not feasible for Christians to take over these particular attitudes. "Since the pagans objected to Judaism primarily because of its exclusiveness and its condemnation of all other religions as idolatry, these objections could not be taken over by a Christianity which shared the same Jewish attitudes of intolerance."[16] In summary, "it was the distinctively religious hostility of Christianity to Judaism that provided the constant drive behind a polemic that was to transform itself in Christian civilization into social anti-Semitism."[17]

After describing the Pharisaic retracing of the Jewish tradition in reaction against Hellenism and apocalypticism, Ruether turns to the rejection of the Jews in the NT. It is here that one finds the major turn from pagan negativity toward Jews to Christian anti-Judaism.

Ruether finds the origin of Christology in the "decision of faith made by the circle of Jesus' disciples in response to the trauma of the crucifixion."[18] Significantly, she does not see either a shaping of Christology or anti-Judaism in Jesus' life or teaching, which was not materially or formally different from that found in leading Pharisaic schools. But there was a messianic-apocalyptic element in the ministry of Jesus, and the disciples refused to see in the crucifixion a negation of Jesus' messianic mission. Their decision required them to embark on a new exegetical task, that of finding within the scriptures some justification for understanding Messiahship in a fashion that was not paralleled in contemporary apocalyptic circles. For these purposes, the writings of Isaiah were most useful in supporting the concept of a suffering Messiah. But the traditional apocalyptic message was not forgotten either in its sense of immanence or in its triumphalism. Thus, the early Christian community coupled its proclamation of Jesus' Messiahship with a condemnation of those who refused to recognize it. The condemnation also found support in passages from the prophets that condemned recalcitrance and unbelief in Israel. Ruether compares early Christian preaching with that at Qumran:

> Like the Qumran community, it claimed to represent the true Israel of the last era of world history, over against the apostate Israel of the official tradition. It demanded a conversion to its interpretation of the tradition as the means by which Jews must enter the community of salvation. Like the Qumran community, Christianity vilified the Judaism outside its converted community as apostate, sinful, worse than the Gentiles, and even of the devil. It regarded the others as fallen outside the true covenant and ranked with the enemies of God.[19]

Particularly in its conflicts with the Pharisees, this preaching hardened, and adherence to Christianity came to be perceived as an alternative to Judaism, and an exclusive one at that:

> Christianity confronted Judaism with a demand for a conversionist relation to its own past that abrogated that past, in the sense that that past itself no longer provided a covenant of salvation. Christianity did not ask Judaism merely to extend itself in continuity with its past, but to abrogate itself by substituting one covenantal principle from the past for another provided by Jesus.[20]

The result of this confrontation was, according to Ruether, the synagogue leaders' explicit rejection of Christian preachers.[21] That was not surprising. What was surprising, however, was that the more Christians were barred from synagogues, the more they found a ready response among Gentiles. Although conservative figures such as James attempted to hold the line against a progressive gentilization of the church, the more radical wing, led by figures such as Paul, abandoned such requirements as circumcision for Gentile converts. The result of this process was that, in time, even Jewish Christianity became obsolete. This historical development brought with it yet another exegetical tradition, which "added the idea of inclusion of the Gentiles to the idea of apostate Israel."[22] Thus the Christian evangelists stress the contrast between Jewish rejection and Gentile acceptance, even as they tell the story of Jesus. They not only transfer the responsibility for Jesus' death from Gentile to Jewish government but they also transfer it from political to religious authority. The same is true in the case of Jesus' disciples in Acts. Thus, the reader of the gospels is impressed that the blame for these deaths is squarely on the head of the Jewish religious leaders. Christians had reached this position even before Paul wrote his first letters. Ruether concludes her analysis of the gospels and Acts by claiming that "the anti-Judaic tradition in Christianity grew as a negative and alienated expression of a need to legitimate its revelation in Jewish terms."[23]

Despite the fact that a major section in Ruether's second chapter—entitled "The Growing Estrangement: The Rejection of the Jews in the New Testament"—is devoted to the Synoptic Gospels and Acts, she does not intend to provide a systematic reading of these texts. Her procedure rather is to trace the history of early Christianity as this history may be found embedded in these documents. Only occasionally do we find a remark about the tendencies of individual documents. Nevertheless, she leaves the reader with a clear impression about the gospels and Acts taken together, namely, that the early Christian preaching about the Messiahship of Jesus carried with it a condemnation of the unaccepting Jews.

In responding to Ruether's challenge about the Synoptic Gospels, Douglas R. A. Hare distinguishes three kinds of anti-Judaism.[24] Prophetic anti-Judaism is "a hallowed tradition in Israel."[25] It may contain powerful invective, but it is essentially a condemnation from within Judaism. Hare claims that it is to be expected that this form of anti-Judaism should be found within Christianity, since the movement itself began as "a conversionist sect within Judaism."[26] The preaching of Jesus, or of the other early Christians, was no more involved in Christological beliefs than were the prophetic proclamations in the Hebrew Bible. The second form of anti-Judaism is termed Jewish Christian, which Hare describes as making the following claims: "Israel manifests its apostasy not only by failing to repent and return to God in ways prescribed by the prophet Jesus, but also by refusing to acknowledge the crucial importance for salvation history of the crucified and risen Jesus."[27] But the key point is that this Jewish-Christian preaching maintained the possibility of repentance for Israel and never claimed that it had been rejected. The third kind of anti-Judaism is called "gentilizing." "Gentilizing anti-Judaism takes over prophetic and Jewish-Christian forms of anti-Judaism, but adds thereto the conviction that Israel's apostasy is incurable and that God has finally and irrevocably rejected his people."[28] Hare finds this form of anti-Judaism only in Matthew. In general he finds only prophetic anti-Judaism in Luke-Acts: "It is clear that the picture Luke wishes to present is not that the mission to Israel has proved a total failure, but rather that it has produced schism within the Jewish community."[29] The conclusion to Acts (28:25–28) constitutes Luke's attempt to justify the Gentile mission, and it explains the refusal of the majority of Jews to accept Paul's preaching, but it is not, according to Hare, an example of gentilizing anti-Judaism. Hare admits that Luke's frequent pejorative use of the expression "the Jews" in Acts "verges on gentilizing anti-Judaism."[30] But he emphasizes the basic thrust in Luke-Acts that "is still optimistic concerning the possibility that at least a minority of Jews will continue to respond positively to the gospel."[31]

In his analysis of anti-Judaism in early Christianity, John Gager, for the most part, follows the work of Hare.[32] He adopts the three levels of anti-Judaism that Hare had proposed and works through the various layers of gospel material in order to determine the extent of these polemical levels. In general he finds prophetic anti-Judaism, which he prefers to call "intra-Jewish polemic," in the oral pregospel traditions in Q and Mark. Matthew and Luke include this intra-Jewish polemic but add other passages that express gentilizing anti-Judaism. Gager is more ready to find gentilizing anti-Judaism in Luke-Acts than is Hare, and he explicitly differs with him in his assessment of the ending of Acts, which, according to Gager, announces the permanent close of the Pauline mission to the Jews.

Despite their differences both Hare and Gager tend to support Ruether's major contention. Hare provides helpful distinctions that enable one to address the problem of anti-Judaism in early Christianity in sophisticated ways. He insists, however, that Christology was not the sole cause of Christian feelings against Jews. Even more basic was the Jewish nonacceptance of the Christian message. Gager agrees, but also points to the inner connection between Christology and Jewish rejection and shows that Ruether is supported even by Hare's objections, "But inasmuch as the claims about Jesus were undoubtedly the basic issue of dispute between followers of Jesus and other Jews, Ruether's assertion is actually supported."[33]

Ruether has successfully called attention to a certain stream in Christian thought that finds its origin in the writings of the NT. Among these writings, Luke-Acts constitutes a particular problem, a problem noted by Lloyd Gaston, who once observed that "Luke-Acts is one of the most pro-Jewish and one of the most anti-Jewish writings in the New Testament."[34] Whether this assessment of Luke-Acts is accurate or not, the polarities that Gaston noted seem to represent the approaches taken by NT scholars in the period after World War II.

Indeed, Luke-Acts has become once again something of a "storm center" in NT scholarship.[35] Along with questions about Luke's theology and the literary genre of Luke-Acts, questions about the author's attitude toward Jews and Judaism have been widely debated. Whatever we may decide about the literary genre of these writings, the Acts of the Apostles has given its author an opportunity to express judgments about different patterns of religious life and about optimal relationships between them.

The contemporary discussion of the understanding of Jews and Judaism in Luke-Acts was initiated by Jacob Jervell.[36] Although Jervell's most formative essays dealing with this subject were written before Ruether's book was published, they nevertheless serve to address some of the same problems that she later raised. This is especially the case with Jervell's essay entitled "The Divided People of God: The Restoration of Israel and Salvation for the Gentiles."[37] Here Jervell quite intentionally challenges what he perceives to be the consensus interpretation of Luke-Acts, which he describes as follows: "Luke describes the rejection of the Christian proclamation on the part of the Jewish people. Only after and because Israel has rejected the gospel, and for that reason has itself been rejected, do the missionaries turn to Gentiles."[38] The consensus view finds in Luke-Acts an anti-Jewish tendency, which accuses the people as a whole of obduracy and condemns them as forever rejected by God. As the major proponents of this consensus, Jervell cites Ernst Haenchen and Hans Conzelmann, but the roots of it go back to Franz Overbeck and F. C. Baur.[39]

Jervell's view springs from three fundamental theses about the work of Luke. First, he claims that Luke does not think of the Jewish people as totally rejecting the Christian message. Rather, the Christian proclamation served to divide the Jewish people into two groups: the repentant and the obdurate. Second, Luke does not think of the church as the new Israel. Rather, according to Jervell, the term *Israel* is used only for the repentant group of Jews, that is, Christian Jews, and not for Gentiles or non-Christian Jews. Third, the necessity of the Gentile mission is made clear from the very beginning of Luke's writing, and it is presented by the author as the fulfillment of scripture. To support these theses, Jervell calls attention to passages in Acts in which the Christian mission to Jews meets with amazing success. He reverses the usual explanation of the Gentile mission: "One usually understands the situation to imply that only when the Jews have rejected the gospel is the way opened to Gentiles. It is more correct to say that only when Israel has accepted the gospel can the way to Gentiles be opened."[40] Jervell calls attention to the theme of division among the Jewish people even at the end of Acts, where Luke states that some Roman Jews accepted Paul's message while others disbelieved (Acts 28:24). This ending, says Jervell, is not to be understood as the beginning of the Gentile mission, despite Paul's proclamation, "Let it be known to you then that this salvation of God has been sent to the Gentiles; they will listen" (Acts 28:28). That mission had begun long ago and had been authorized in scripture. Paul's words here do, however, announce the end of the mission to the Jews. Israel has been purged of unbelievers, and the believers have been gathered. The Christian Jews constitute Israel, and there is no conception that the group will be enlarged: "Strictly speaking, Luke has excluded the possibility of a further mission to Jews for the church of his time because the judgment by and on the Jews has been irrevocably passed. . . . The unbelieving portion of the people is rejected for all times.[41]

Jervell's work has influenced a number of scholars, who have seen here a potential for addressing the problem of early Christian

attitudes toward Jews in new and creative ways. Robert C. Tannehill, for example, drawing on literary-critical theory, understands
the narrative in Luke-Acts in terms of tragic irony.[42] Tannehill calls
attention to the many references to unfulfilled promises about the
restoration of Israel that appear in Luke-Acts and to passages that
show Jesus weeping over the projected fate of Jerusalem and to
tragic reversals. In contrast to Jervell, he de-emphasizes the initial
success of the Christian mission among Jews, claiming that this
cannot mean for Luke a genuine fulfillment of God's promise. Also
unlike Jervell, Tannehill finds in the ending of Acts some hint of a
hope for Jewish salvation. But his answer to claims about anti-
Judaism in Luke-Acts is to stress the tone that he finds in these
texts. For Tannehill, the author of these documents regards his
narrative, which includes an emphasis on Jewish rejection of the
gospel, as a tragedy. He writes: "The emotions of anguish, pity,
and sorrow aroused by tragedy are not the same as the hatred of
anti-Semitism, nor does the negative stereotyping of anti-Semitism
fit the emphasis on the great hopes and honors of the Jews, which
is essential to Luke's tragic story."[43]

Jack T. Sanders occupies a position almost directly opposite
that of Tannehill. He probably has become the most outspoken
proponent of the view that Luke-Acts is an anti-Jewish writing.
Sanders has worked out his approach to Luke-Acts in a number of
articles but most fully in a recent book, *The Jews in Luke-Acts*.[44] He
finds the underlying motive for this negative attitude toward Jews
in a crisis in Luke's own church over the inclusion of Gentiles. The
crisis, Sanders thinks, was precipitated by opposition by Jewish
Christians to a mission to Gentiles. Thus, for Luke there is little
difference between Jewish Christians and non-Christian Jews, and
his treatment of Pharisees in the gospel and Acts has largely been
affected by his attitude toward these Jewish-Christian opponents.
The Pharisees are, in effect, symbols in Luke-Acts, standing for
Jewish Christians. Sanders gives credit to Étienne Trocmé, who re-
vived some explanations derived ultimately from the Tübingen
school. Sanders writes that Trocmé "may well have laid his finger
on the issue that gives coherence to Luke's hostility towards both
non-Christian Jews and Jewish Christians; for is not, in fact, the
Jewish opposition to and hostility toward Christianity and Jesus,
as Luke presents the matter, from first to last over the issue of the
inclusion of Gentiles?"[45] Thus Sanders claims that for Luke it was
the Temple authorities who carried out Jesus' crucifixion and that

apart from the "Jerusalem springtime" described in the early chapters of both Luke and Acts, Jerusalem is the scene of hostile confrontations with Jews. The "Jerusalem springtime" has an important function in Luke-Acts, however, in connecting Christianity with Judaism. "By emphasizing that connection, Luke makes two points for his Gentile readership: one, that Christianity has not broken with the ancient Israelite religion, and that, rather, a direct line of continuity runs from Moses and the Prophets to the church; and, two, that it is not Christianity that has rejected Judaism, but Judaism that has rejected Christianity."[46] Sanders points out that after Acts 6, "the time of Jewish conversions in Acts is over and the time of Christianity's separation from Judaism and of eternal enmity between the two religions has arrived."[47]

These recent discussions of Luke-Acts reveal deep disagreements among Lukan scholars on some fundamental issues and suggest that the meaning of these documents is far from clear.[48] The major question in controversy is the nature of Luke's treatment of the Jewish people, whether it should be judged as pro- or anti-Jewish and whether Jewish rejection of Jesus is viewed with sorrow or presented as an act deserving God's punishment. If there is anti-Judaism in Luke-Acts, there is the additional question whether it is to be understood, to use Hare's terms, as a version of prophetic, Jewish Christian, or gentilizing anti-Judaism.

Beneath these issues there is a host of additional related questions that have not been adequately addressed. Among them are the following: What for Luke-Acts constitutes Judaism? How is it defined? How are Jewish life and faith related to Christian life and faith? How do the Hebrew Scriptures function and what authority do they have in Luke-Acts? What is the role of the Jewish Christians in Acts?

These questions basically ask about the images of the Jewish people and their religious life in Luke-Acts. Despite their major contributions to the study of Luke, scholars who have been interested in questions about Judaism in Luke-Acts have not concentrated on these images in a systematic way. Focusing attention on them holds the promise of giving us a firm basis for drawing conclusions about the author's attitudes and for explaining his interest in history and his purposes in writing.

Several major problems meet us at the outset. One is that of selecting those words, phrases, and concepts in Luke-Acts that might constitute clues about Jewish religious life and thought. It may seem appropriate to start this process by searching for references to Judaism and related terms, but there are few of them. Another procedure may be to look for references to Israel, but the term has a fundamental ambiguity, as Augustin George and others have shown.[49] It may refer to the political dimensions of a certain people and carry only the connotations that are proper to these dimensions. Or, as George claims, it may represent an ideal people, Israel as the people of God. Clearly, consideration must be given to Luke's use of terms such as *Israel*, but it would not be profitable for us to confine our attention to such references or even to begin our consideration with an analysis of them. A similar ambiguity adheres to Luke's use of such terms as *the Jews* and *ho laos* when used to refer to the Jewish people. An approach that begins with a word study, either of Judaism, or Israel, or the Jews, runs the risk of neglecting important dimensions of Luke-Acts.

Rather than confining ourselves to a few major terms and phrases, we should be sensitive to a significant number of clues that in context suggest something about Jewish religious life. Such clues would include technical terms that refer to Jewish religious institutions, groups, and observances, names of Jewish persons and Hebrew worthies of the past, references to the Hebrew Scriptures and to acts of individual and social piety. The portrait of Judaism in these books can only be drawn by examining all of these aspects, and an analysis of them would contribute toward our understanding of the ways in which the portrait provides information about Jewish religious life and thought.

Another problem is that Luke-Acts may not represent a simple and self-consistent portrayal of Judaism but may rather exhibit something like fluctuating images. Indeed, the narrative character of these books suggests that there is no flat background against which the main lines of action may appear. Jewish religious life may rather be a rich ingredient in the narrative that shows up in different ways, depending on changes in the plot and relationships to various characters in the narrative. If, for example, there is a description of some pre-Christian aspect of Jewish life, it is likely that it will carry a different value from one that explicitly describes a negative Jewish reaction to the Christian message. Additionally, we should be open to the possibility that different aspects of Jewish religious life and thought may carry different values in our texts. Jewish concepts about God, for example, may be more highly valued than certain Jewish institutions.

Thus, in order to maintain sensitivity to the context and to trace developments in our narrative, our procedure will be to analyze specific sections of Luke-Acts in terms of the images of Judaism and the Christian challenges to it. Although we shall work through Luke-Acts in a straightforward fashion, what follows should not be thought of as a commentary, for no attempt will be made to analyze every sentence or even to cover the major issues that usually are faced in a commentary. Our questions are specific and limited, and what does not have a bearing on these questions will simply not be addressed.

Yet another problem is that of outlining these texts. The Gospel of Luke and the Acts of the Apostles have been outlined in a number of widely divergent ways, and no single outline will be acceptable to all scholars of these books. Outlines, despite claims that are sometimes made, are less skeletal presentations of an author's concepts than they are devices that we as modern readers create for managing texts. In creating such devices, we should avoid putting our own stamps upon them by supplying supposed theological themes or concepts to describe the various sections. Nor should we, in the case of the Gospel of Luke, draw up an outline in terms of an alleged source of Luke, be it Mark, or Q, or Matthew. Although comparisons between Luke and the other two Synoptic Gospels may be of interest and value, the state of our knowledge about the use of sources by Luke is such that we cannot make defensible and meaningful observations on the basis of a supposed source theory.[50] The source problems for Acts are even more serious. It is more meaningful to give full weight to the narratological movements in the texts. These movements are also generally accompanied by changes of chief characters or locations, which signal the reader of breaks in the narrative. Thus, our outline of Luke-Acts should follow perceived breaks in the narrative and should, so far as possible, avoid other considerations. The broad outline to be used here follows, and in the succeeding chapters more detailed observations will be made about these major sections.

1. The Lukan Infancy Narratives, Luke 1:1–2:52.
2. Jesus in Galilee, Samaria, and Judea, Luke 3:1–19:44.
3. Jesus in Jerusalem, Luke 19:45–24:53.
4. The First Christians in Jerusalem, Judea, and Samaria, Acts 1:1–12:25.

   5.  The Pauline Mission, Acts 13:1–21:14.
   6.  Paul in Jerusalem, Caesarea, and Rome, Acts 21:15–28:31.

   A final problem to be faced before we can begin the actual
study is that of defining the point of view from which the reading
is to be made. This problem, essentially that of describing the
reader of the texts, involves significant literary-critical issues and
will be dealt with in chapter 2.

   Chapters 3 and following are written in the conviction that
certain verbal images of Jewish people and Jewish religious life are
embedded in Luke-Acts and may be discerned by a close reading
that makes a conscious search for them. Chapters 3–5 consist of a
reading of the Gospel of Luke, and chapters 6–8, a reading of Acts.
Chapter 9 will state the conclusions and implications of the study.

   Even though there are almost certainly sources behind both
Luke and Acts, these texts will be treated in their present form,
without respect to their supposed sources. The justification for this
procedure has been set forth in a number of articles and mono-
graphs and need not be repeated here.[51] Suffice it to say that recent
source-critical studies of the Synoptic Gospels have questioned the
legitimacy of assuming the two-document hypothesis and making
use of it in redaction-critical work.[52] As yet, however, no rival hypothesis has supplanted it. At the same time, literary-critical studies have shown the utility of approaching a document as a whole
rather than breaking it up into its supposed *Vorlage*. While form-
critical and source-critical studies are certainly valuable, it is also
worthwhile to study NT documents in something approximating
their final shape.

NOTES

   1.  See *The Theology of St. Luke*.
   2.  Ibid., 13.
   3.  The original German edition was published in Tübingen by J. C. B. Mohr,
       1957.
   4.  Ernst Käsemann, "Paul and Nascent Catholicism." Käsemann emphasizes that
       Paul himself affirmed and documented his independence but that Luke, in
       Acts, began the process of domesticating Paul by bringing him into line with
       the apostles. Käsemann at this point stands in a tradition that leads back to
       certain Tübingen theologians, e.g., Jülicher, Bruno Bauer, Ritschl, Overbeck,
       Holtzmann, et al. For references and a discussion of these views, see J. C.
       O'Neill, *The Theology of Acts in Its Historical Setting*, 172–85.

5. Henry J. Cadbury, *The Making of Luke-Acts*, 299–316. O'Neill, *Theology of Acts*, revives the conception of Acts as political apology but also claims that Luke-Acts was written as an evangelistic appeal to the educated Roman citizen.

6. Paul W. Walaskay, *"And So We Came to Rome": The Political Perspective of St. Luke*.

7. Ibid., 67.

8. Richard I. Pervo, *Profit with Delight: The Literary Genre of the Acts of the Apostles*.

9. See David E. Aune, *The New Testament in Its Literary Environment*, 77–157.

10. See E. P. Sanders, ed., *Jewish and Christian Self-Definition*.

11. Rosemary R. Ruether, *Faith and Fratricide: The Theological Roots of Anti-Semitism*. Jules Isaac was among the first to draw a connection between ancient Christian teaching and modern forms of anti-Semitism, but he was careful to state that Christian anti-Judaism is not to be found before the establishment of the state church at the time of Constantine. See Jules Isaac, *Jesus and Israel*, first French edition, 1948; *The Teaching of Contempt: Christian Roots of Anti-Semitism*, first French edition, 1962.

12. Among recent studies, see Alan T. Davies, ed., *Antisemitism and the Foundations of Christianity*; John G. Gager, *The Origins of Anti-Semitism: Attitudes Toward Judaism in Pagan and Christian Antiquity*; Peter Richardson, David Granskou, and Stephen G. Wilson, eds., *Anti-Judaism in Early Christianity*.

13. Ruether, *Faith and Fratricide*, 246.

14. Ibid.

15. Ibid., 27f.

16. Ibid., 29.

17. Ibid., 31.

18. Ibid., 66.

19. Ibid., 74.

20. Ibid., 80.

21. On the historical evidence for excommunication of Christians from synagogues, see J. Louis Martyn, *History and Theology in the Fourth Gospel*, 37–62, 156–57. For a contrary view see Reuven Kimelman, "Birkat Ha-Minim and the Lack of Evidence for an Anti-Christian Jewish Prayer in Late Antiquity."

22. Ruether, *Faith and Fratricide*, 84.

23. Ibid., 94.

24. Douglas R. A. Hare, "The Rejection of the Jews in the Synoptic Gospels and Acts."

25. Ibid., 29.

26. Ibid.

27. Ibid., 29f.

28. Ibid., 32.

29. Ibid., 37.

30. Ibid., 37f.

31. Ibid., 38.

32. Gager, *The Origins of Anti-Semitism*, esp. 134–59.

33. Ibid., 143.

34. Lloyd Gaston, "Anti-Judaism and the Passion Narrative in Luke and Acts," 153. Gaston would account for this paradox in part by separating Luke's source materials from his editorial work.

35. The phrase "storm center" was first used by W. C. Van Unnik in a well-known essay, "Luke-Acts, a Storm Center in Contemporary Scholarship." Van Unnik had in mind the scholarly attention that was paid to the theology of Luke. More recently, Richard I. Pervo used the phrase "the eye of the storm" in the title of the first chapter of his book, *Profit with Delight*. Pervo refers to recent discussions on the literary genre of Luke and Acts.

36. See especially Jacob Jervell, *Luke and the People of God: A New Look at Luke-Acts*.

37. Ibid., 41–74. This essay first appeared in *ST* 19 (1965).
38. Ibid., 41.
39. Cf. Conzelmann, *Theology of St. Luke;* Conzelmann, *Acts of Apostles.* Ernst Haenchen, *The Acts of the Apostles: A Commentary;* Franz Overbeck, *Kürze Erklärung der Apostelgeschichte;* Ferdinand C. Baur, "Über Zweck und Veranlassung des Römerbriefs und die damit zusammenhangenden Verhältnisse der römischen Gemeinde."
40. Jervell, "The Divided People of God," in *Luke and the People of God,* 55.
41. Ibid., 64.
42. Robert C. Tannehill, "Israel in Luke-Acts: A Tragic Story." See also his *The Narrative Unity of Luke-Acts: A Literary Interpretation.*
43. Tannehill, "Israel in Luke-Acts," 81. More recently, Robert L. Brawley has published a study of Luke-Acts that is generally sympathetic to the views of Jervell. See his *Luke-Acts and the Jews: Conflict, Apology, and Conciliation.* David L. Tiede, *Prophecy and History in Luke-Acts,* claims that Luke's approach is modeled on the ancient prophetic denunciations of Israel. In a more recent article, " 'Glory to Thy People Israel': Luke-Acts and the Jews," Tiede stresses the perennial character of God's dealings with Israel.
44. See Jack T. Sanders, *The Jews in Luke-Acts.*
45. Ibid., 316.
46. Ibid., 33. Sanders notes that the phrase "Jerusalem springtime" was first used by Gerhard Lohfink, *Die Sammlung Israels: Eine Untersuchung zur lukanischen Ekklesiologie,* 55.
47. Sanders, *Jews in Luke-Acts.*, 244.
48. For a fuller discussion of a variety of views on the subject of anti-Judaism in Luke-Acts, see Joseph B. Tyson, ed., *Luke-Acts and the Jewish People.*
49. See Augustin George, "Israel dans l'oeuvre de Luc."
50. On the Synoptic problem see below, p. 16.
51. For references on the problem of sources for Luke see the massive bibliography on the Synoptic problem compiled by Thomas Richmond Willis Longstaff and Page A. Thomas, eds., *The Synoptic Problem: A Bibliography, 1716–1988.* See also Arthur J. Bellinzoni, Jr., ed., *The Two-Source Hypothesis: A Critical Appraisal.* For a brief analysis of the ways in which source criticism, redaction criticism, and literary criticism impinge on the study of Luke-Acts, see Joseph B. Tyson, *The Death of Jesus in Luke-Acts,* 3–28.
52. The futility of depending on the two-document hypothesis was perhaps most forcefully stated by Charles H. Talbert, who wrote, "Employing Mark as a control today is about as compelling as using Colossians and Second Thessalonians to describe Paul's theology" ("Shifting Sands: The Recent Study of the Gospel of Luke," 393).

2

# The Implied Reader
# in Luke-Acts

$O$ur major task in this book is to identify certain images of Jewish religious life that seem to be embedded in Luke-Acts. There is no way to eliminate totally the ambiguity involved in this task, which is an act of interpretation, that is, an effort to determine the meaning of the text. An act of interpretation is the work of a reader, and Luke-Acts has had many different kinds of readers. Despite frequent claims of objectivity, there is no consensus in regard to the ways in which these and other biblical texts should be interpreted. Indeed, there seems to be no way to control the number and kinds of readings that might be produced.

Although it may not finally be possible to remove all traces of subjectivity from attempts to read ancient texts, perhaps especially biblical texts, some clarity may be achieved by defining in advance the perspective from which Luke-Acts is to be read in the following chapters. Modern literary theorists, whose work has not been primarily directed toward biblical studies, have long maintained that it is not possible to determine with any precision the thoughts of flesh-and-blood authors as they wrote the words that form the texts that we wish to examine.[1] In this sense, conceptions of an author's intention are inevitably misleading. Attempts to discover the intention of an author are based upon a failure to recognize not only the inadequate ways in which intention and act are related but also the symbolic nature and ambiguity of language itself. The depth of the problem can be seen by an author who, in rereading her own previously published work, is impelled to wonder about her intention in the writing of these words. This experience is common enough to suggest that there is no necessary congruity between a person's intentions and words. As John Ellis observed, people do not always say what they mean, nor do they always mean what they say.[2] Words do not necessarily or adequately convey intended meaning. Further, because of the symbolic nature of language, an unambiguous determination of meaning is, in any given case, unlikely. Thus, to approach Luke-Acts in an effort to determine the intention of the flesh-and-blood author will almost certainly not be fruitful.

But is there any way to avoid a reading of Luke-Acts that is nothing more than one person's, perhaps idiosyncratic, opinion about its meaning? In sorting out images of Judaism that seem to be embedded in these texts, am I simply calling attention to things that seem *to me* to be there?[3] Perhaps there is no way finally to avoid an idiosyncratic reading of a text, but clear definitions of the task and method of interpretation at least provide some controls. If the task is to determine images that seem to be embedded in the text, I must define the reader to whom these materials seem to be embedded. But I do not want to choose any flesh-and-blood reader, since this kind of reading depends on a whole host of particular variables, including the reader's linguistic competence, literary experience, historical knowledge, and quality of critical judgment—in the end, the reading of one particular reader.

A discussion of some concepts of reader-response criticism may be helpful at this point. Reader-response critics have developed an extensive literature about the role of readers in interpreting texts. Judgments about this role range widely from those that emphasize the intratextual encoding devices that serve as signals for reading to those that emphasize the creative act of interpretation involved in the process of reading. Perhaps the most helpful terminology that has been developed in the effort to understand the act of reading is that that distinguishes between various readers. Robert Fowler's lucid essay "Who is 'the Reader' in Reader Response Criticism?" provides a helpful summary of some of the more technical discussions.[4] Drawing primarily on the work of Seymour Chatman, Wayne Booth, and Stanley Fish,[5] Fowler distinguishes between flesh-and-blood readers and the implied reader. He maintains that the two have nothing to do with one another. The implied reader is a fiction embedded within the text that serves as the counterpart to the implied author. Similarly, the implied author is not to be confused with the actual, flesh-and-blood author; rather the implied author is the one who is revealed through the text. All we can know about an author is what is embedded within the text. From another perspective, the implied author is the *persona* that the real author uses in the act of composition. The implied reader, therefore, is the audience addressed by the implied author. It should also be noted that there may also be a narrator that is to be distinguished from the implied author and the real author and a narratee to be distinguished from the implied reader and the historical reader. But narrators and narratees are not always explicit in a narrative. In Luke-Acts, as in the other NT narratives, the story is told by the implied author, and explicit narrators and narratees are lacking.

The work of Wolfgang Iser is seminal in any discussion of the implied reader.[6] He defines the implied reader as follows: "He embodies all those predispositions necessary for a literary work to exercise its effect—predispositions laid down, not by an empirical outside reality, but by the text itself. Consequently, the implied reader as a concept has his roots firmly planted in the structure of the text; he is a construct and in no way to be identified with any real reader."[7] Iser claims that meaning results from the interaction of text and reader and that the implied reader in the text serves as a benchmark by which all other readings may be judged.

> The fact the reader's role can be fulfilled in different ways, according to historical or individual circumstances, is an indication that the structure of the text *allows* for different ways of fulfillment. Clearly, then, the process of fulfillment is always a selective one, and any one actualization can be judged against the background of the others potentially present in the textual structure of the reader's role. Each actualization therefore represents a selective realization of the implied reader, whose own structure provides a frame of reference within which individual responses to a text can be communicated to others.[8]

Iser and other literary theorists have made it clear that concepts of reader-response criticism are related to the study of the modern novel. Iser himself illustrated his method of reading by reference to a number of such novels, and in working through these interpretations one is impressed with the sophistication and subtlety of the texts, especially as compared with biblical narratives such as Luke-Acts. Clearly the method of interpretation developed by modern literary theorists suits the eighteenth- and nineteenth-century novels in ways that may not be appropriate for other kinds of literature.

Another potential problem occurs when we consider the probable fact that ancient biblical authors did not write with a reading public in mind. Recent studies have demonstrated the probability that the Christian gospels were composed for a listening audience and that in the first instances they were in fact read aloud to a group of listeners.[9] If this is the case, the aural reception of a gospel would appear to involve processes that are quite different from those employed by readers of eighteenth- and nineteenth-century novels.

Despite these problems it would seem useful to attempt a cautious application of some concepts from modern literary theory and to take the implied reader/hearer as the one to be examined in the text of Luke-Acts.[10] Neither the relatively unsophisticated character of these texts nor the fact that they were composed for hearers prevents us from using this approach. Regardless of the differences in communication, one may speak of the reader or hearer in the text to whom the narrative speaks. The reader or hearer in the text thus becomes the benchmark against which other readings may be judged. With a profile of this reader in mind, we will be able to search for images of Judaism that such a reader would immediately grasp. This way of going about the task has the merit of avoiding misleading statements about the intentionality of the flesh-and-blood author and of moving beyond idiosyncratic readings of flesh-and-blood readers.

A growing number of twentieth-century biblical scholars have found the work of Iser and others useful in interpreting the ancient texts. Of particular interest at this point is the work of Alan Culpepper on the Gospel of John.[11] Although he would not classify this gospel as a novel, Culpepper nevertheless has found it useful to employ some of the methods of what he calls "secular literary criticism" in his study of the Fourth Gospel. His analysis of the implied reader is particularly helpful in pointing toward ways in which this reader can be described.[12]

Culpepper explains the ways in which a portrait of an implied reader (or narratee) may be drawn:

> We may begin by making the simple and perhaps overly wooden assumption that the character of the narratee can be drawn from the narration by observing what is explained and what is not. We will assume further that the narratee knows about things and characters that are alluded to without introduction or explanation but has no prior knowledge of things, persons, events, and locales which are introduced by the narrator. By the nature of the evidence we can say with more certainty what the narratee does not know than what he or she does know. By gleaning the relevant data from the voice of the narrator throughout the gospel, a portrait of the narratee can be drawn.[13]

Culpepper then proceeds to examine the narratee's knowledge of persons, places, languages, Judaism, and events, and he concludes that "the intended [sic] readers are not Jewish, but their prior knowledge of many parts of the gospel story shows that the intended audience is either Christian or at least is familiar with the gospel story."[14]

Culpepper's study quite consciously goes beyond a strict application of reader-response criticism. As this form of study is usually understood, it is necessary to regard all elements within texts as strictly intratextual. Characters, places, and events exist only within the text. But Culpepper is aware that some of these entities did exist outside the text, and he thus maintains that unexplained references to them necessarily require extratextual knowledge on the part of the implied reader. Since the literature Iser deals with is the novel, a medium that in many ways differs from such texts as the Christian gospels, this adjustment in approach is justified. Thus it seems legitimate to proceed, as Culpepper does, on the premise that an implied author makes some assumptions about the intellectual capacity of an implied reader. The modern interpreter may identify some of the assumptions about the implied reader by being attentive to allusions that appear in the text, characters that are not fully identified, references that require geographical knowledge, events that are not fully explained, as well as indications of language, customs, and literary competence.

Culpepper has shown how a profile of the implied reader in the Gospel of John may be constructed, and his method ought to produce similarly useful results for Luke-Acts. But the wider-ranging character of Luke-Acts requires some amplification of the list of items to be surveyed. Our own study will consider the implied reader's knowledge of locations, persons, languages, events, measurements and money, religious practices, and literature.

In the prologues to Luke (1:1–4) and Acts (1:1–2), the implied author speaks directly to the implied reader. He describes himself as one who has followed certain events for some time and is aware of other writings that deal with this history. Moreover, the narratee is named: it is Theophilus (Luke 1:3; Acts 1:1). But Theophilus is not identified or described within the text, unless the adjective *kratiste* (most excellent, Luke 1:3) implies his noble status. The fiction of direct address by implied author is used again in the so-called "we" sections of Acts (Acts 16:10–17; 20:5–15; 21:1–18; 27:1–28:16). But elsewhere in Luke-Acts, the implied author does not

speak directly to the implied reader. Theophilus never appears
outside the prologues, and although the possibility that he is to be
identified with the implied reader cannot be excluded, we need a
great deal more information about the implied reader in order to
proceed with a reading of these texts. Such information as we can
gather about the implied reader's knowledge follows.

## LOCATIONS

The implied reader must know something about the geography of
a wide area of the eastern Mediterranean world, for geographic locations are numerous in Luke-Acts and accompanying explanatory
notes are often imprecise. Typical of the references to Galilee, Samaria, and Judea are the following: "a town in Galilee called Nazareth" (Luke 1:26); Mary went "to a Judean town in the hill
country" (1:39); Joseph went up "from the town of Nazareth in Galilee to Judea, to the city of David called Bethlehem" (2:4); "all the
region around the Jordan" (3:3); "Capernaum, a city in Galilee"
(4:31); "a town called Nain" (7:11); "the country of the Gerasenes,
which is opposite Galilee" (8:26); "a village of the Samaritans"
(9:52); Jesus "was going through the region between Samaria and
Galilee" (17:11); "when he had come near Bethphage and Bethany,
at the place called the Mount of Olives" (19:29); "the place that is
called The Skull" (23:33); "a village called Emmaus, about seven
miles from Jerusalem" (24:13);[15] "they returned to Jerusalem from
the mount called Olivet, which is near Jerusalem, a sabbath day's
journey away" (Acts 1:12); "the towns around Jerusalem" (5:16);
"the [or a] city of Samaria" (8:5);[16] "many villages of the Samaritans" (8:25); "toward the south to the road that goes down from
Jerusalem to Gaza" (8:26); "in Judea and in Jerusalem"(10:39).

One may note that there is some variation in the ways in
which these geographic references are described. Some, such as
Luke 24:13 and Acts 8:26, are unusually precise, as if the implied
author is compelled to supply the needed information, while others, such as Luke 7:11; 17:11; Acts 8:5, are vague and presume that
the implied reader understands. It is also notable that there is a
tendency to locate cities and towns in terms of the surrounding regions (Luke 1:26; 2:4; 4:31; 9:52; Acts 8:5; 8:25).

Judean towns are often located with reference to the city of Jerusalem. The centrality of Jerusalem in Luke's geographic scheme
has often been noted, and this centrality seems apparent from the
perspective of the implied reader as well.[17] While Luke is rarely

exact in his settings, there seems to be some effort to explain the relationships of certain places in their proximity to Jerusalem. Emmaus, for example, is said to be sixty *stadia* from Jerusalem (Luke 24:13), and the Mount of Olives is a sabbath day's journey from Jerusalem (Acts 1:12).[18]

While it would not be necessary for our implied reader to know the exact locations of all the towns and villages mentioned in Luke's writings, it seems as if there is an assumption shared by implied author and reader that the travels of Jesus and the narratives about the apostles (not including Paul) are limited to those areas most closely associated with Jewish people, especially the city of Jerusalem. Further, it would be nearly impossible to read Luke-Acts without associating this city with Jewish religious life and institutions.

The many narratives in Acts that are set in predominantly Gentile territories frequently carry explanatory notes that are similar to those listed above. Consider, for example, the following: "Lystra and Derbe, cities of Lycaonia" (Acts 14:6); "the region of Phrygia and Galatia" (16:6); "Philippi, which is a leading city of the district of Macedonia and a Roman colony" (16:12);[19] "the region of Galatia and Phrygia" (18:23). As in the Palestinian references, cities and towns are located with reference to their region or province, but many references carry no explanations. Only in the narrative of Paul's voyage to Rome is there a group of precise geographical notes: "Under the lee of Cyprus" (27:4); "under the lee of Crete off Salmone" (27:7); "a place called Fair Havens, near the city of Lasea" (27:8); "It [Phoenix] was a harbor of Crete, facing southwest and northwest (27:12); "under the lee of a small island called Cauda" (27:16). Notable also are the references in connection with Paul's approach to Rome: Puteoli (28:13); the Forum of Appius and Three Taverns (28:15).

It is probable that our implied reader would need to have a rudimentary knowledge of the eastern Mediterranean world and of the larger and more significant Roman provinces in order to make sense of Luke-Acts. There does not seem to be an assumption that the reader would be familiar with specific towns and cities, except Jerusalem, Athens, and Rome, but some familiarity with provincial divisions may be necessary. References to towns and cities as being in Galilee, Galatia, Pamphyhylia, Pisidia, Lycaonia, Asia, and Achaia would seem to presuppose some knowledge about these areas. Beyond that, our reader would need to associate Judea and Galilee with Jewish people but would also know about Jewish communities in the Diaspora. The implied reader would be a generally well-educated person, not unfamiliar with the eastern Mediterranean world.

PERSONS

In his study of the Fourth Gospel, Culpepper assumed that the implied reader knows those characters in the text who are not identified or whose roles are not otherwise explained. If this assumption should hold good for Luke-Acts as well, we should conclude that the implied reader needs to have almost no extratextual knowledge of the characters within the text. Almost all of those persons in Luke-Acts (and the number of characters is great) carry some identification. Zechariah is of the division of Abijah, Elizabeth is a descendant of Aaron (Luke 1:5), and Mary is a virgin betrothed to a man whose name is Joseph, of the house of David (1:27). As Luke's story unfolds we meet a tax collector named Levi (5:27), Mary, called Magdalene, from whom seven demons had gone out (8:2), Joanna, the wife of Chuza, Herod's stewart, and Susanna (8:3); Jairus, who was a ruler of the synagogue (8:41), a man named Zacchaeus, who was a chief tax collector and rich (19:2), Barabbas, a man who had been thrown into prison for an insurrection started in the city, and for murder (23:18–19), a man named Joseph from the Jewish town of Arimathea (23:50). Acts likewise is peopled with characters who are identified in such a way as to indicate that the implied reader needs no information except what is in the text: "a Levite, a native of Cyprus, Joseph, to whom the apostles gave the name Barnabas (which means 'son of encouragement' )" (Acts 4:36); "a Pharisee in the council named Gamaliel, a teacher of the law, respected by all the people" (5:34); "a certain man named Simon had previously practiced magic in the city and amazed the people of Samaria" (8:9); "an Ethiopian eunuch, a court official of the Candace, queen of the Ethiopians" (8:27); a prophet named Agabus (11:27; 21:10); "a maid named Rhoda" (12:13); "Blastus, the king's chamberlain" (12:20); "a certain magician, a Jewish false prophet, named Bar-Jesus" (13:6); "Judas called Barsabbas, and Silas, leaders among the brothers" (15:22); "a disciple named Timothy, the son of a Jewish woman who was a believer; but his father was a Greek" (16:1); "a Jew named Apollos, a native of Alexandria" (18:24); "a Jewish high priest named Sceva" (19:14); "a man named Demetrius, a silversmith who made silver shrines of Artemis" (19:24); "a young man named Eutychus" (20:9); "Mnason of Cyprus, an early disciple" (21:16); "a centurion of the Augustan Cohort, named Julius" (27:1); "the leading man of the island [Malta], named Publius" (28:7); and many more.

Even Jesus has an impressive identification in Luke 3:23: "Jesus was about thirty years old when he began his work. He was the son (as was thought) of Joseph son of Heli," etc. Then follows Jesus' genealogy. This identification is somewhat surprising, coming as it does after the birth narratives, in which Jesus has been well introduced.[20] In any event it does not suggest that the implied reader is required to have extratextual information about Jesus.

To be sure, some public figures are introduced without explanatory notes, although Luke frequently includes titles or other forms of identification. Witness, for example, Herod, king of Judea (Luke 1:5), Quirinius, governor of Syria (2:2), Pontius Pilate, governor of Judea (3:1), Herod, tetrarch of Galilee (3:1; cf. 3:19; 9:7), Philip, tetrarch of the region of Ituraea and Trachonitis (3:1), Herod the king (Acts 12:1), the proconsul Sergius Paulus (13:7), Gallio, proconsul of Achaia (18:12), "his Excellency the governor Felix" (23:26), and Agrippa the king (25:13). But Roman emperors can be mentioned by name only: Caesar Augustus (Luke 2:1), Tiberius Caesar (3:1), Claudius (Acts 11:28; 18:2).

For the most part the essential information about characters in the text is given at the point at which the character is first mentioned. But information about Simon, who is later called Simon Peter and finally simply Peter, is given piecemeal. He is first introduced to the reader as Simon, with no additional identification (Luke 4:38), perhaps suggesting an assumption that he is known to the implied reader. Indeed, in Luke 4:38–39, it is the mother-in-law of Simon who, with Jesus, is the chief character. Jesus enters Simon's house and heals his mother-in-law of a high fever. Simon next appears in Luke 5:3, as the owner of a boat from which Jesus taught. In 5:8, the reader learns that this character is named Simon Peter, and in 5:10 that he has partners in the fishing business, James and John, the sons of Zebedee. In the list of the twelve, in 6:12–14, it is said that Jesus gave the name Peter to Simon, but there is no explanation of the meaning of the new name. It is certainly possible that the implied reader is expected to have some extratextual knowledge about Peter, but in the process of the narrative enough is given to portray an understandable character.

There is no clear suggestion that extratextual knowledge about Simon Peter is required, but the way in which the information is
given suggests a particular interest in this character as central to
the plot.

The information about Saul/Paul is given in similar fashion.
He is mentioned quite unexpectedly in Acts 7:58, as a bystander at
the execution of Stephen, and a few verses later, in 8:3, as a persecutor of the church. The theme of persecution is then picked up
in 9:1, where the first narrative of his conversion begins, and here
we have a fuller description of his persecuting activity. His Christian preaching in Damascus (Acts 9:20–25) and Jerusalem (9:26–30)
is described, but not until after several stories featuring Peter does
the narrative return to Saul (13:1). Important facts about him, such
facts as are usually given with the first introduction of a character,
are withheld until near the end of Acts. It is only in Paul's defensive speeches, which begin in Acts 22, that we learn of his place of
birth and education (22:3) and his identification as a Pharisee (23:6;
26:5). As with Peter, the piecemeal way in which Saul/Paul is explained to the implied reader does not require extratextual knowledge but suggests a continuing interest in him and the central role
he plays in the narrative as a whole.

Luke's tendency is to provide for the implied reader brief identifications of the characters within the text and to do so at the point
at which the character is first introduced. The information contained in the identifications is usually minimal and strictly necessary for a proper understanding of the accompanying narrative.
Little or no extraneous information appears in these identifications. Thus, except in the case of the most prominent public figures, we may not assume that the implied reader is required to
bring to the text any knowledge about characters within the text;
the text contains almost everything one needs to know about the
characters within it.

There is, however, a notable exception in the case of a secondary character, James. Several persons by this name appear in Luke-
Acts, one of whom is a member of the twelve, the brother of John
and son of Zebedee (Luke 5:10; 6:14; 8:51; 9:28; 9:54; Acts 1:13; 12:2).
Another James, the son of Alphaeus, is listed among the twelve in
Luke 6:15 and Acts 1:13. Others are mentioned only as relatives of
certain characters in individual narratives (Judas of James, Luke
6:16; Mary of James, 24:10). But there are three references to one
James, who is not otherwise identified (Acts 12:17; 15:13; 21:18) and

who seems to be differentiated from others mentioned in Luke-Acts. Certainly he is to be distinguished from James, son of Zebedee, whose death was reported in Acts 12:2, that is, before the first reference to this other James. In the first reference, Peter has just escaped from prison and reported at the house of the mother of John Mark. He describes his escape and then says, "Tell this to James and to the believers" (Acts 12:17). The second reference occurs in Luke's report of the so-called apostolic conference. The conference, apparently called to settle questions about the requirements for Gentile Christians, began with Peter's report about his experiences among them. After Barnabas and Paul spoke, James, citing a passage of scripture from Amos, makes a determination (15:13–21). The third reference occurs in connection with Paul's last appearance in Jerusalem. The day after his arrival, "Paul went with us to visit James; and all the elders were present" (Acts 21:18). As a result of this meeting, Paul purified himself and saw to it that four men were able to fulfill their vows. In all three of these references, the figure of James is treated as one with formidable authority, a person to whom both Peter and Paul must, on occasion, report. The lack of identifying notes of any kind contrasts markedly with Luke's normal habit and strongly suggests that the implied reader is expected to know who this person is.[21]

Our analysis of references to persons in Luke-Acts indicates that the implied reader is expected to be familiar with a few public figures, notably the Roman emperors. The references to Peter and Paul do not require extratextual knowledge but signal acute interest in them as characters within the narrative. The treatment of James, however, seems to suggest some prior knowledge of him as a person of authority within the primitive Christian community. Surprisingly, although extratextual knowledge about Jesus cannot be excluded, the narrative does not seem to require it.

## LANGUAGES

It goes without saying that the implied reader must understand Greek. Knowledge of Aramaic or Hebrew does not seem to be required. In four passages in Acts, Aramaic or Hebrew words are used and translated into Greek. In Acts 1:19, the field that Judas bought is called "in their language Hakeldama,"[22] and it is obvious that the language intended is Aramaic. But 'Hakeldama' is then translated as *Chōrion Haimatos*, field of blood. In Acts 4:36 the reader is introduced to Joseph called Barnabas, which means *huios paraklēseos*, Son of Encouragement. Similarly, in Acts 9:36, the reader meets a certain disciple named Tabitha, which, in Greek, means Dorcas, or Gazelle. Despite a certain lack of clarity in Acts 13:6–8, some information is given in Greek about the meaning of a foreign name, i.e. Bar-Jesus means Elymas, or magician.[23] Note, however, that other Aramaic names are given without translation, among them Barsabbas in Acts 1:23; 15:22.

Occasionally our author calls attention to the fact that a character in the text speaks a foreign language. At Pentecost the apostles speak languages other than their own (Acts 2:4,8). In Lystra, the crowds praise Barnabas and Paul in Lycaonian (Acts 14:11). Paul is able to speak Greek (Acts 21:37) but addresses a Jerusalem crowd in the Hebrew language (Acts 22:2). But in all these cases of reported use of a foreign language, the accompanying speech is given in Greek. In this regard it is interesting to observe the use of the term *barbaroi* for residents of Malta (Acts 28:2,4). This characteristically Greek way of designating persons who do not speak Greek tends to confirm our impression about the assumed linguistic capabilities of the implied reader.

These indications suggest that the implied reader is not expected to know any language other than Greek but that he ought not to be uncomfortable with foreign terms and names, the most significant of which require translation into Greek.

### EVENTS

Culpepper makes the point that the implied reader of John's gospel has some acquaintance with certain events connected with the life of Jesus, namely his crucifixion and resurrection.[24] Culpepper's judgment is influenced by the various anticipations of the passion in the Fourth Gospel. In common with Matthew and Mark, the Gospel of Luke also has a series of predictions of Jesus' passion (9:22; 9:44; 17:25; 18:31–33). But the reader needs no extratextual knowledge in order to understand these predictions. Indeed, the literary function of the predictions is not only to provide anticipations of coming events but also to equip the reader to understand the events surrounding the death of Jesus. Another such anticipation occurs in Luke 9:31, where Moses and Elijah speak with Jesus about his exodus, "which he was about to accomplish at Jerusalem." If there were nothing else within the text of the gospel that pointed toward Jesus' death, Luke 9:31 might be said to require some external knowledge. But coming as it does after the first prediction of the passion (9:22) and just before the second

(9:44), it functions instead to heighten the reader's sense of anticipation.

Similarly, in the story of Paul in Acts, in four key passages the reader is led to anticipate Paul's fate in Rome. In 19:21, Paul announces his intention to go to Rome. In 20:25 he shares with the Ephesian elders the news that they will not see him again. In 23:11, the Lord himself appears to Paul to say, "Keep up your courage! For just as you have testified for me in Jerusalem, so you must bear witness also in Rome." And in 27:24, Paul reports that an angel has told him that he must stand before Caesar. Although in the immediate context there is a partial fulfillment of the announcements of Paul's abandonment of the mission to the Jews and taking up the mission to the Gentiles (Acts 13:46; 18:6; 28:28), these anticipations serve a literary function in Acts similar to that of the predictions of Jesus' passion in Luke. None of these anticipatory devices requires any special knowledge on the part of the implied reader.

There are, however, a few incidental notes in Luke-Acts that seem to presuppose some extratextual knowledge. There are seven such notes that constitute references to supposedly historical events that might have been matters of public knowledge:

(1)  A reference to "the first registration . . . taken while Quirinius was governor of Syria" (Luke 2:2). Despite the historical problems in identifying the precise time for this supposed census, the implied author seems to expect the implied reader to be acquainted with it.

(2)  The execution of some Galileans by Pilate (Luke 13:1).

(3)  The accidental death of eighteen persons when the tower of Siloam fell (Luke 13:4).

(4)  The insurrections led by Theudas and Judas the Galilean (Acts 5:36–37). Although Luke has these in the wrong historical order, there is an expectation that the reader will understand the references.

(5)  A famine in the days of Claudius (Acts 11:28).

(6)  The exile of Jews from Rome by Claudius (Acts 18:2).

(7)  An insurrection by an Egyptian supported by four thousand assassins (Acts 21:38).

Although it may not be necessary to suppose that the implied reader is expected to have extratextual knowledge about all these events and their significance, there are enough such incidents to indicate that some assumptions about public events are operative. Although some events would be generally well known, it is notable that several of them would be of greatest concern to persons in the Levant. The famine (Acts 11:28) is said to be worldwide and thus supposedly known to any reader. The census (Luke 2:2) may be understood as empirewide but seems to have a Syrian provenance due to the mention of Quirinius. One might presume that the exile of Jews from Rome (Acts 18:2) would be best known in Rome, but surely such an event would concern Jews throughout the eastern Mediterranean as well as those Gentiles who had significant contact with Jewish communities. The other events (Luke 13:1; 13:4; Acts 5:36–37; Acts 21:38) would appear to have a predominantly Galilean or Judean provenance.

The study of the implied reader's knowledge of events suggests a readership that is knowledgeable of public affairs, both historical and current. In addition, the implied reader is expected to have some knowledge of and special concern about certain events that occurred in Galilee and Judea. To be sure, references to these regions are to be expected in a narrative that takes place there, but the fact that the references are not self-explanatory argues for the presumption that the implied reader has extratextual knowledge about them.

### MEASUREMENTS AND MONEY

Although a number of the measurements of time and distance in Luke-Acts were probably in general usage in the ancient Mediterranean, it is notable that references to money are exclusively Greek and Roman. Measurements of time, given in multiples of three, probably represent customary practice. Luke mentions the sixth hour of the day (Luke 23:44; Acts 10:9) and the ninth hour (Luke 23:44; Acts 3:1; 10:30). Marking time by watches of the night, in Luke 12:38, betrays the influence of the Roman military. But references to days of the week are, at least in point of origin, Jewish— the Sabbath (numerous references); the first day of the week (Luke 24:1; Acts 20:7). One measurement of distance is Jewish: the Mount of Olives is said to be a Sabbath day's journey from Jerusalem in Acts 1:12; but the reference to *stadia* in Luke 24:13 is Greek.

In order to understand references to money, our implied reader would probably be expected to know both Greek and Roman systems of currency. Among Greek coins we have references to *drachmas* (Luke 15:8, 9), *mnas* (Luke 19:13, 16, 18, 24, 25) and *lepta*

(Luke 21:2). Among Roman coins are *dēnarioi* (Luke 10:35; 20:24) and *assarioi* (Luke 12:6). Jewish coins are never explicitly mentioned, although the Aramaic term, *mammon*, meaning wealth, appears in Luke 16:9, 11, 13.

Such knowledge about measurements of time, distance, and money as is required for Luke-Acts would probably be found among most ancient eastern Mediterranean peoples, including Palestinian Jews. But the references in Luke-Acts do not require that the implied reader be a Palestinian Jew.

### RELIGIOUS PRACTICES

The two volumes of Luke-Acts contain a wide range of references to Jewish practices and institutions, with little or no explanation. It seems to be assumed that the reader knows about the Sabbath, the Temple, and the scriptures, as well as about a significant number of figures of Jewish history—Abraham, Moses, David, Solomon, and more. These stand without explanation until we come to the speech of Stephen in Acts 7. Here for the first time a reader who is ignorant of the history recorded in the Hebrew Scriptures receives a summary of part of it. A similar summary is found in a speech of Paul in Acts 13:16–22.

But our implied reader seems to require some explanations about intra-Jewish groups. The note about Sadducaic beliefs in Luke 20:27 is in fact necessary for understanding the pericope about the resurrection life. To know that Sadducees deny that there is such a thing as resurrection is to know the reason behind their asking Jesus about the seven brothers who married the same woman. In Acts 23:8, the Sadducaic denial of resurrection, as well as angels and spirits, is reaffirmed and is contrasted with the Pharisaic acknowledgement of all three items. Here again the explanation is necessary for understanding the conflict that ensues between Pharisaic and Sadducaic members of the council. That the Sadducees are associated with the high priest is noted in Acts 5:17. In Acts 26:4, within a speech of Paul, the reader learns that the Pharisees comprise the strictest party among the Jews.[25] The Feast of Unleavened Bread is explained as the Passover, in Luke 22:1, and the day of Unleavened Bread is said to be the day on which the Passover lamb had to be sacrificed. But contrast the references to the Day of Pentecost, without additional explanation, in Acts 2:1; 20:16. In addition there is a certain distancing between the implied reader and the synagogue that is suggested in expressions such as

"their synagogues" in Luke 4:15, "the synagogues of the Jews" in
Acts 13:5, and "the Jewish synagogue" in Acts 14:1.[26]

References to non-Jewish religious practices and institutions
are rare in Luke-Acts. The only one of note is in the story of the
protest against Paul in Ephesus (Acts 19:21–40). Here the implied
reader needs to know something about religious practices connected with the worship of Artemis. He is told that Demetrius
made and sold silver shrines of Artemis (Acts 19:24), that all Asia
and the world worships her (19:27), and that Ephesus is keeper of
her temple and of "the statue that fell from heaven" (19:35). Some
of this information is provided by a character within the narrative
rather than the implied author acting as narrator. Nevertheless, it
is important to observe that it is provided.

Certain fundamental aspects of Gentile religious life are condemned by Luke's heroes. In particular there is the condemnation
of the worship of manufactured deities and an implied condemnation of polytheism in Paul's speech at Athens (Acts 17:22–31). The
worship of human beings produces divine displeasure in the case
of Herod (Acts 12:21–23) and is explicitly condemned when Lyca-
onians worship Barnabas as Zeus and Paul as Hermes (Acts 14:11–
18). The implied reader is expected to share these negative
judgments.

In contrast to the paucity of information about Gentile religious life, the material about what we would call Judaism is rich
and deep. Although many Jewish institutions and practices are not
explained, some significant ones are, as we have seen. Thus, our
implied reader would appear to be someone who has a limited
knowledge of both pagan and Jewish religious practices, as well as
an aversion to polytheism and the worship of humans. By contrast
the reader seems to have an attraction to Jewish religious life but
not an easy familiarity with all aspects of it. In terms of the implied
reader's knowledge of religious practices, we can describe him as
sympathetic with some significant Jewish beliefs and practices but
not a full-fledged participant nor a fully integrated member of a
Jewish community.

### LITERATURE

Although Paul, in his speech at Athens, quotes from pagan authors (Acts 17:28), by far the larger number of quotations and allusions in Luke-Acts are from the Hebrew Scriptures, quoted in
Greek. This fact is obvious and needs no demonstration here. In
terms of attempting to draw up a profile of the implied reader of

Luke-Acts, however, it is the status and interpretation of these scriptures that is of interest.

It seems clear that the implied author and the implied reader are in agreement about the authority of the Hebrew Scriptures. When the word *graphē* is encountered, it connotes a sense of authority. In his post-resurrection appearance to the two disciples on the way to Emmaus, Jesus assumes the role of the authoritative interpreter of scripture and shows that it was necessary for the Christ to suffer. "Beginning with Moses," he interprets "all the scriptures" (Luke 24:27; cf. 24:32, 45). It is scripture that makes the suffering of the Christ necessary (Luke 24:26). Although used in specific reference to Judas, Acts 1:16 appears to embody the principle that must be shared by author and reader: "The scripture had to be fulfilled." The debates between the devil and Jesus in Luke 4:1–13, with quotations from the scriptures on both sides, show that the authority of these documents is recognized. The phrase that introduces these and other quotations in Luke-Acts, "It is written," appears tantamount to saying, "God has said." In one place a quotation from scripture even serves to condemn an action of Paul (Acts 23:5). Paul himself seems to represent the Lukan point of view when he says to Felix, "I worship the God of our ancestors, believing everything laid down according to the law or written in the prophets" (Acts 24:14).[27]

These passages demonstrate a concern to provide for the reader a controlling method of interpreting scriptures that are regarded as authoritative. In terms of literary experience, it is clear that the implied reader has not only a familiarity with the Hebrew Scriptures in their Greek translation but that he also acknowledges their authoritative status. It is the interpretation of the scriptures as fulfilled in Jesus that requires defense, not their authority.

### THE IMPLIED READER AS GODFEARER

Analysis of locations, persons, languages, events, measurements and money, religious practices, and literature results in a complex profile of the implied reader in Luke-Acts. Such a profile would be based on the following observations about the implied reader.

1. Our reader is a generally well-educated person with a rudimentary knowledge of eastern Mediterranean geography and a familiarity with the larger and more significant Roman provinces.

2. The implied reader is familiar with some public figures, especially Roman emperors. He has some knowledge about James and his position within the primitive Christian community. It is

not possible to be certain about his extratextual knowledge of Jesus.

3. The implied reader is not expected to know any language other than Greek but is comfortable with some foreign terms and names.

4. The implied reader is knowledgeable about public affairs, especially those that are of concern to Levantine and Jewish communities.

5. The implied reader has a working knowledge of common Greek and Roman measurements and coinage.

6. The implied reader has a limited knowledge of both pagan and Jewish religions, an aversion to some pagan practices, and an attraction to Jewish religious life. But he is probably not Jewish and is not well informed about certain significant aspects of Jewish religious life.

7. The implied reader is familiar with the Hebrew Scriptures in their Greek translation and acknowledges their authoritative status but is not familiar with those methods of interpretation that find the fulfillment of the scriptures in Jesus.

It is difficult to situate the implied reader with precision, but we can say that he or she would need to be a literate person, reasonably well informed about the history, geography, and political situation in the eastern Mediterranean world, a person who is interested in Jewish culture and literature but probably not attracted to certain pagan practices. The most significant aspect of this profile is the claim that the implied reader is familiar with the Hebrew Scriptures and knowledgeable about some fundamental Jewish concepts but is probably not to be identified as Jewish.

In major respects, this reader is similar to those characters in Acts that are called "Godfearers."[28] For the most part, Godfearers are described as devout Gentiles who are attracted to Jewish religious life. In Acts they are often grouped with Jews. In some cases they probably should be perceived as proselytes, who nevertheless are not the same as Jews. Note, for example, the phrase in Acts 13:43, *polloi tōn Ioudaiōn kai tōn sebomenōn prosēlytōn*, "many Jews and devout converts to Judaism." It is not clear that Godfearers have made a public renunciation of pagan religion, nor that they have accepted key Jewish rites such as circumcision (see, e.g., Acts 16:14; 17:4; 17:17; 18:7). They are not described as Paul is, in terms of a particular sect of Jews, nor is it said that they have kept the law. They may be found either in Palestine or in the Diaspora, but when they are found they are in some way connected with Jews. The principle that operates in Luke-Acts seems to be enunciated in Acts 10:35: "Among all Gentiles, the person who fears him [God] and adheres to justice is worthy of him [my translation]."

Two centurions, one in the gospel (Luke 7:1–12) and the other in Acts (10:1–11:18), fit the image of the Godfearer particularly well and may stand as intratextual representations of the implied reader. Indeed, centurions as a group seem to be favorably treated in Luke-Acts. As representatives of Roman power and justice, one of them attests to the innocence of Jesus (Luke 23:47), and others help to protect Paul on more than one occasion (see Acts 21:32; 22:25–29; 23:17; 23:23; 27:43). Still other centurions may not go out of their way to support or protect Paul, but they are not unfriendly (see Acts 24:23; 27:1; 27:6; 27:31). Only in Acts 27:11 do we have a centurion presented in the role of an opponent of one of Luke's heroes.

But the centurions in Luke 7 and Acts 10–11 are paradigmatic of Godfearing Gentiles. About the centurion in Luke 7, it is said that he loves the nation, that is, the country of the Jews, and that he built the synagogue in Capernaum (Luke 7:4). His status among Jews is signified by the fact that Jewish elders speak to Jesus on his behalf. He is so well regarded by Capernaum Jews that they are willing to intercede for him with the healer, and even Jesus says about him, "Not even in Israel have I found such faith" (Luke 7:9).

Cornelius is described as "a devout man who feared God (*eusebēs kai phoboumenos ton theon*) with all his household; he gave alms generously to the people and prayed constantly to God" (Acts 10:2). Clearly the alms are designated for the Jewish people, and his prayers are directed to the Jewish God. Because of the character of his life, Cornelius experiences a visitation from an angel, who directs him to make contact with the apostle Peter. His emissaries describe him in words reminiscent of those used of the centurion in Luke 7, as "an upright and God-fearing man *(anēr dikaios kai phoboumenos ton theon)*, who is well spoken of by the whole Jewish nation" (10:22). Cornelius' conversion is an event of major significance in Acts, a model for the conversion of Gentiles.

These two centurions may thus stand as intratextual representations of the implied reader in Luke-Acts.[29] They are righteous Gentiles who are acquainted with and attracted to Judaism. They are generous to the Jewish people, and they pray to the Jewish

God, but they continue to live as Gentiles. It may be that the implied author expects the implied reader to conclude, as does another centurion in Luke 23:47, "Certainly this man [Jesus] was innocent."

To be sure, Luke's portrayal of the two centurions does not include all the items in our profile of the implied reader. We are given no information about their historical and geographical knowledge, and, above all, we know nothing about their acquaintance with the Hebrew Scriptures. There is, however, another character in Acts who, to a significant extent, fits the profile of the implied reader. This is the Ethiopian eunuch (Acts 8:26–40), a Gentile who goes to Jerusalem to worship (elēlythei proskynēsōn eis Ierousalēm, Acts 8:27), is familiar with at least one passage from the scriptures, and regards it as authoritative but in need of interpretation. He is reading from Isaiah and requests Philip to interpret the passage (Acts 8:26–40).

These considerations would allow us also to include Theophilus (Luke 1:3; Acts 1:1), as a "lover of God," among the intratextual representations of the implied reader. As a lover of God, he should be understood as a Gentile who is favorably disposed toward Jewish religious life. In addition, Theophilus must know something about Christianity, as Luke 1:4 shows. He has been informed about some things but does not know the truth about them. This statement conforms with that part of our profile that showed that the implied reader has a limited knowledge of Christianity, perhaps including an acquaintance with the figure of James. From Luke's perspective, such knowledge would need amplification and correction. Perhaps the figure of James requires some explanation that would correct the image held by such a lover of God. We may thus take Luke's address to Theophilus quite seriously without finally being able to say anything specific about his social or political position or his existence outside the text. As the narratee in the prologues, who has some of the same characteristics as the implied reader in the rest of Luke-Acts, Theophilus would be described as a well-educated Gentile who is acquainted with paganism, Judaism, and, to a limited degree, Christianity. He has been attracted to Judaism but has as yet made no commitment and continues to live as a Gentile. The implied author thus leads the implied reader to a positive commitment about Jesus, a commitment similar to that of the centurion in Luke 23:47.

Such a reader as is pictured here—represented in the text as a Godfearer, a centurion, an Ethiopian eunuch, and a Theophilus—

would be in a position to make sense of the text of Luke-Acts. Our own search for images of Judaism should be an act of reading over the shoulder of the implied reader. What picture of the Jewish people and Jewish religious life would this kind of reader develop in the process of reading Luke-Acts? This is the question to be addressed in the chapters that follow.

NOTES

1. See especially I.A. Richards, *Principles of Literary Criticism;* W. K. Wimsatt, Jr., and Monroe C. Beardsley, "The Intentional Fallacy"; Monroe C. Beardsley, "Textual Meaning and Authorial Meaning"; John M. Ellis, *The Theory of Literary Criticism.*
2. Ellis, *Theory,* 104–8.
3. Some proponents of reader-response criticism would claim that the reader is the only one who can create meaning and does so in the act of reading the text. Stanley Fish once defined the informed reader as "neither an abstraction nor an actual living reader, but a hybrid—a real reader (me) who does everything within his power to make himself informed" *(Is There a Text in This Class? The Authority of Interpretive Communities,* 49). The essay in which this quotation appears was originally published in 1970. In his most recent writings, Fish has emphasized the role of the informed community in determining meaning.
4. Robert M. Fowler, "Who is 'the Reader' in Reader Response Criticism?" See also Willem S. Vorster, "The Reader in the Text: Narrative Material," in *Semeia* 48, ed. by Edgar V. McKnight (Atlanta: Scholars Press, 1989), 21–39; Wilhelm Wuellner, "Is There an Encoded Reader Fallacy?"; Wolfgang Schenk, "The Roles of the Readers of the Myth of the Reader."
5. See Wayne Booth, *The Rhetoric of Fiction;* Seymour Chatman, *Story and Discourse: Narrative Structure in Fiction and Film;* Fish, *Is There a Text?.*
6. See Wolfgang Iser, *The Implied Reader: Patterns of Communication in Prose Fiction from Bunyan to Beckett; The Act of Reading: A Theory of Aesthetic Response.*
7. Iser, *Act of Reading,* 34.
8. Ibid., 37.
9. For a discussion of the relationship between orality and the Christian gospels, see Werner Kelber, *The Oral and the Written Gospel: The Hermeneutics of Speaking and Writing in the Synoptic Tradition, Mark, Paul, and Q.*
10. In what follows it should be understood that hearers as well as readers are intended, even if for the sake of simplicity I only use the term *reader.*
11. See R. Alan Culpepper, *Anatomy of the Fourth Gospel: A Study in Literary Design.* See also Jeffrey Lloyd Staley, *The Print's First Kiss: A Rhetorical Investigation of the Implied Reader in the Fourth Gospel,* whose approach to the question of the implied reader is quite different from that of Culpepper.
12. Culpepper, *Anatomy,* 205–27.
13. Ibid., 212. Culpepper later observes that there may be objections to his profile of the implied reader in John. The possible objections are: "(1) that the evangelist was careless or inconsistent in his comments and explanations, (2) that the explanatory comments from which we have inferred ignorance on the part of the intended reader have a different purpose . . . (3) that many of the comments and explanations are late additions to the narrative and reflect a change in the intended audience, or (4) that different writers working on this gospel

made different assumptions about the audience" (224). Culpepper insists that
the coherence of the profile that he has found for the Fourth Gospel argues for
its validity. It should also be observed, however, that the objections actually
have no force if the interpreter consistently follows methods laid down by Iser
and others. Objections (1) and (2) are based on assumptions about an author's
intention, which lies outside the text. Objections (3) and (4) do also, and in
addition they require the interpreter to break up a text into supposed components or layers, which are assumed to have been at one time independent. In
general, reader-response criticism brackets questions about an author's intention and respects the integrity of the text under examination.

14. Ibid., 224.
15. See textual variants.
16. For a discussion of the textual problem, i.e., the presence or absence of the def-
    inite article, in this verse, see Bruce M. Metzger, *A Textual Commentary on the
    Greek New Testament*, 355f.
17. In a well-chosen phrase Joseph A. Fitzmyer speaks of Jerusalem as the "pivot"
    of Luke-Acts; see *The Gospel According to Luke (I-IX)*, esp. 164–71.
18. On the two spellings of Jerusalem in Luke-Acts, see Adolf Harnack, *The Acts of
    the Apostles*, 76–81. For a more recent discussion of this issue, see Michael Bach-
    mann, *Jerusalem und der Tempel: Die geographisch-theologischen Elemente in der lu-
    kanischen Sicht des jüdischen Kultzentrums*.
19. See textual variants. See also the discussion in Metzger, *Textual Commentary*,
    444–46.
20. The Proto-Luke hypothesis, associated with the names of B. H. Streeter and
    Vincent Taylor, finds some support at this point. Luke 3:23 is an appropriate
    introduction of the main character in the Gospel of Luke only if it comes near
    the beginning. Proto-Luke, in this hypothesis, began at what is now Luke 3:1.
    The birth narratives, as well as the Markan material, were added later. See
    B. H. Streeter, "Fresh Light on the Synoptic Problem"; *The Four Gospels: A
    Study of Origins*, 201–22; Vincent Taylor, *Behind the Third Gospel: A Study of the
    Proto-Luke Hypothesis*. See also below, pp. 42–45.
21. Adolf Harnack came to the same conclusion about James. In a discussion of
    five persons of secondary rank in Acts, namely Stephen, Philip, Barnabas,
    James, and Apollos, he writes: "St. James, the fifth personality of this series,
    occupies a peculiar position. It is presupposed that the four others are un-
    known, while it is assumed that he is known. The readers evidently knew—
    though this is nowhere stated—that he was the Lord's brother, and that he had
    become the head of the Primitive Community after the Twelve had quite given
    up the leadership, which had already been limited by the appointment of the
    'Seven' " Harnack, *Acts*, 122.
22. See the discussion of the different spellings in Metzger, *Textual Commentary*,
    287f.
23. For a discussion of the textual problems, see ibid., 402f.
24. See Culpepper, *Anatomy*, 222f.
25. Although this information comes from a character within the narrative rather
    than directly from the implied author, Paul may at this point be regarded as
    acting as a reliable narrator, and the inclusion of the information here suggests
    that there is no assumption that the implied reader is in possession of it from
    extratextual sources.
26. The expression in Luke 4:15 may, however, be taken in the context of the verse
    to mean the synagogues of Galilee.
27. There are, however, some qualifications to the implied author's conception of
    scriptural authority. See Joseph B. Tyson, "The Gentile Mission and the Au-
    thority of Scripture in Acts"; "Scripture, Torah, and Sabbath in Luke-Acts."

28. On Godfearers, see A. Thomas Kraabel, "The Disappearance of the 'God-Fearers' "; "Greeks, Jews, and Lutherans in the Middle Half of Acts"; Jacob Jervell, "The Church of Jews and Godfearers"; P. W. Van der Horst, "Jews and Christians in Aphrodisias in the Light of Their Relations in Other Cities of Asia Minor."

29. It is important to emphasize their intratextual character. It would be methodologically invalid to identify the reader in the text with persons outside the text. But associations between the implied reader and other textual entities do not create confusion between the world of the text and the world outside the text.

3

# The Lukan
# Infancy Narratives

(Luke 1–2)

The Gospel of Luke as we now have it begins with a statement in the first person (Luke 1:1–4), in which a narrator addresses a narratee to explain his qualifications for writing and purpose in doing so. The narratee is in fact addressed by name, Theophilus, a name that, as we have seen, suggests a person who has some of the characteristics of a Godfearer. Studies of Luke 1:1–4 have shown convincingly that it is a conventional preface or introduction, in which the implied author explains his reasons for writing, defends his qualifications, and announces his purposes.[1] The narratee is told what to expect ("a narrative"), in what ways the narrator is qualified ("after investigating everything carefully from the very first"), and the purpose of the narrative ("that you may know the truth concerning the things of which you have been instructed"). In addition there is a kind of dedication ("most excellent Theophilus"), and a reference to previous similar works ("since many have undertaken to set down an orderly account of the events that have been fulfilled among us"). Never again in the gospel does a narrator speak directly to a narratee, either by using the first person or by using the name. Not until Acts 1:1 does a narrator speak again.[2]

Following the preface or introduction, there is a group of Lukan infancy accounts. Although Matthew has an account of the birth of Jesus at essentially the same point in his narrative, Luke's version is unique. The structure of Luke's account is similar to that of a diptych, in which the birth, naming, and circumcision of John the Baptist and Jesus are shown in parallel panels.[3] Both births are miraculous; each is announced ahead of time by angelic messengers; each is accompanied by poetic expressions of devotion and expectation; each is accompanied by miraculous signs; each is concluded by a statement about the growth of the child.

Although birth and infancy accounts seem perfectly appropriate in narratives such as Luke's and are frequently found in Hellenistic biographies,[4] serious questions have been raised about the original location of these narratives in the text of Luke. A number of NT scholars, operating from varying perspectives, have cited evidence that has led them to conclude that the infancy narratives were not originally a part of the Third Gospel.[5] Indeed, it has become almost commonplace to speak of Luke 3:1 as the original beginning of the gospel, even if one does not think that it ever appeared in public without the first two chapters. Clearly, the elaborate scene-setting device in Luke 3:1 constitutes some disjunction in the narrative. If it is not the original beginning of the gospel, it marks the start of a new section.[6] And there are suggestions that, even in the mind of the author, the real beginning is at 3:1. Acts 1:1, which contains a brief description of the gospel ("all that Jesus did and taught from the beginning"), seems to suggest that the infancy narratives are not included. The requirement for apostleship ("one of the men who have accompanied us during all the time that the Lord Jesus went in and out among us, beginning from the baptism of John until the day when he was taken up from us," Acts 1:21–22) serves more plausibly as a description of Luke 3–24 than of 1–24.[7]

But compelling reasons can be given for including the birth narratives in an attempt to interpret the Gospel of Luke in its present form and thus for regarding these narratives as integrally related to the rest of the gospel. Moreover, as an interpretive strategy for canonical Luke, the exclusion of the birth narratives is indefensible. Whatever the prehistory may have been, some conscious mind has put this book together in its canonical form, and the task of interpretation surely includes that of interpreting this finally achieved form.

In addition, there are significant connections between themes in the infancy narratives of Luke 1–2 and other parts of Luke-Acts. Elsewhere I have called attention to the theme of conflict.[8] There is a great deal of material in both the gospel and Acts that is devoted to the description of conflict between Jesus and Pharisees, Jesus and priests, the apostles and Jewish leaders, and between Paul and his various opponents. Although the birth and infancy

narratives do not contain explicit descriptions of conflict situations, and although their dominant tone is pacific, the narratives
are not without anticipations of conflict. The Magnificat speaks
of a reversal of social conditions, a reversal that implies social
conflict:

> He has brought down the powerful from their thrones,
> and lifted up the lowly;
> he has filled the hungry with good things,
> and sent the rich away empty.
> He has helped his servant Israel,
> in remembrance of his mercy (Luke 1:52–54).

In these verses, the expectation of a reversal of social and political
conditions is accompanied by anticipated conflict: the powerful
and the powerless exchange places, as do the hungry and the rich,
and Israel and its enemies. In the Benedictus, Zechariah speaks of
deliverance "from our enemies and from the hand of all who hate
us" (1:71). And in Luke 2:34–35, Simeon describes Jesus as "destined for the falling and rising of many in Israel." Not only do
these verses contain notes of social reversal and conflict, but they
also connect closely with themes that work themselves out in the
later parts of the gospel and Acts.

J. K. Elliott has called attention to another connection between
the birth narratives and later sections of Luke.[9] The narrative of
Jesus in discussion with the leaders in the Temple (Luke 2:41–52)
appears to be a kind of foreshadowing of the longer section in
Luke in which Jesus teaches for several days in the Temple (Luke
20:1–21:38). In that long section Luke calls attention to the location
of Jesus. At night he is at the Mount of Olives, and during the
day he is in the Temple (Luke 21:37). In the Temple he is constantly
engaged in teaching the people under the suspicious eyes of the
priests, who watch for a chance to arrest him in the absence of
the supporting populace (22:2). Although Luke 2:41–52 does not
have a dominant menacing tone, it nevertheless serves more than
one function. To be sure, it serves as a typical story of the preco-
cious child and foreshadows his future career as a teacher. But the
location of the discussions in the Temple and the presence of the
Jewish leaders is significant as well.

Significant connections may also be seen in the theme of the
throne of David. In Luke 1:32, the angel Gabriel proclaims that the
son of Mary will be given "the throne of his ancestor David." In

Acts 2:30, Peter reminds his audience that God promised to David
"that he would put one of his descendants on his throne," and in
2:35–36 he announces that it is Jesus to whom this promise has
come. Paul preaches a similar message in Acts 13:23, 34, when he
states that Jesus is the heir of the promises to David.

Indeed, the setting of the birth narratives as a whole involves
a connection with other parts of Luke's two-volume work. The author's literary artistry may be seen in his geographical settings, in
particular the place of Jerusalem and the Temple in these settings.
It has been frequently observed that the Gospel of Luke both begins and ends in Jerusalem, specifically in the Temple. In the
opening narrative a faithful priest is shown in the course of fulfilling his duties (Luke 1:8–9). At the end of the gospel the apostles
of Jesus are in the Temple joyously praising God (Luke 24:52–53).
In succeeding chapters we shall observe the role of the Temple in
Luke-Acts as a whole, but it may suffice simply to note here that it
has an ambivalent role, one that may be appreciated fully only by
taking into account the setting of the infancy narratives.[10] Not only
do these narratives present the reader with a picture of pious Jews
in the joyful performance of their ritualistic duties, they also point
to the centrality of the Jerusalem Temple and to its significance as
a point of contention. Both its centrality and its controversial role
are anticipated in the birth narratives in general and in the story of
the twelve-year-old Jesus in particular.

Thus, because canonical Luke includes infancy narratives and
because of the thematic connections between them and other parts
of Luke-Acts, it seems right to conclude that Luke 1:5–2:52 should
be taken as integral to and (with 1:1–4) the proper beginning of the
Gospel of Luke, and our study of images of Judaism in these texts
begins with these chapters.[11]

### IMAGES OF JUDAISM IN LUKE 1–2

The infancy narratives in Luke 1–2 present us with images of Jewish piety unlike any other descriptions in early Christian literature.
Indeed, although, as we have seen, these chapters contain themes
that connect with the rest of Luke-Acts, the portrait of Jewish religious life to be found here contrasts markedly with material to be
encountered later. The infancy narratives give the author a chance
to describe the quality of Jewish religious life in what is conceived
to be its pre-Christian phase. Elsewhere, Luke-Acts will focus attention upon conflicts and contrasts between the message of Jesus

and his followers on the one side and Judaism on the other. But here we have a description of Jewish piety as the author sees it working apart from the Christian message. We learn of the importance of the Jewish Temple, about its ritual and priesthood, and the significance of sacrifices. Here are angelic messengers, miraculous births, and predictions of future greatness. Here are righteous people living lives of quiet devotion and hopeful expectation.

The influence of the LXX on Luke is most obvious in the infancy narratives. Not only is there a multitude of quotations and allusions to a wide variety of texts from the Hebrew Scriptures in their Greek translation, but the linguistic style itself appears to be a conscious imitation of Septuagintal language. Henry Cadbury called attention to the striking contrast between the style of the preface (Luke 1:1-4) and that of the rest of Luke 1-2. The style of the preface, he said, may be favorably compared with that which is characteristic of Hellenistic historical writing. Cadbury described Luke 1:1-4 as "a single long sentence, well balanced, periodic, with some choice Greek words and inflections."[12] By contrast, the infancy narrative proper consists of "a string of co-ordinate clauses with many unidiomatic phrases."[13]

The use of LXX style and substance would have a subtle effect on a reader. In these chapters the implied author transports the implied reader back into the world of the ancient Hebrew writers and prophets. The characters in this part of the narrative are portrayed against this background, and their lives are governed by the values of the Hebrew Scriptures. Their piety is pictured in nearly idyllic terms.

The extent to which Jewish religious life, as pictured in Luke 1-2, centers on the Temple is notable. In these narratives the implied reader learns that the Temple is the scene of important rituals, some apparently occurring daily, and others, such as circumcision and purification, occurring at significant points in a person's life. There are also annual observances, such as Passover (2:41). The reader learns that there is a priesthood and a routine of priestly service attached to the Temple. Not only is the Temple the cultic center of Jewish religious life, it is also the setting for prophetic proclamations.

The rituals associated with the Temple are means of fulfilling certain religious duties prescribed in "the law of Moses" (2:22), "the law of the Lord" (2:24, 39), or "what was customary under the law" (2:27). In most cases the material about Temple rituals is referred to but not described, as if the implied reader were expected to have some familiarity with such things. Circumcision is mentioned as a matter of course, something that is regularly done for an eight-day-old Jewish male (1:59; 2:21). But the treatment of the purification of Jesus' mother is accompanied by an unusual amount of detail. "When the time came for their purification according to the law of Moses, they brought him up to Jerusalem to present him to the Lord (as it is written in the law of the Lord, 'Every firstborn male shall be designated as holy to the Lord'), and they offered a sacrifice according to what is stated in the law of the Lord, 'a pair of turtledoves or two young pigeons' " (Luke 2:22–24). There would seem to be a conflation of two separate rites at this point, a rite of purification for the mother, in accordance with Lev 12:1–8, and the presentation of the first-born son, as required by Exod 13:2, 11–16.[14] Luke's narrative does not clearly associate the sacrifice of the turtledoves or pigeons with the rite of purification, and *auton* in Luke 2:22 suggests that purification was required not only for the mother but for either the husband or the son as well.[15] Bo Reicke made the attractive suggestion that Luke intends to convey the idea that Mary and Joseph used the occasion of the purification of the mother as an opportunity to present Jesus to God in the Temple and that the presentation was exceptional, since there is no mention of a redemption of the first-born son that is allowed in Exod 13:13.[16]

In Luke 1–2, we meet a number of devout Jewish people whose piety is described in positive fashion. Zechariah and Elizabeth are described as "righteous before God, living blamelessly according to all the commandments and regulations of the Lord" (1:6). Simeon is said to be "righteous and devout, looking forward to the consolation of Israel, and the Holy Spirit rested on him" (2:25). Anna "never left the temple but worshiped there with fasting and prayer night and day" (2:37). Specific components of the piety of these characters include association with the Temple, obedience to the law, and engagement in prayer and fasting. In addition, both Simeon and Anna express an attachment to Israel. They are awaiting the consolation (*paraklēsis*) of Israel (2:25) or the redemption (*lytrōsis*) of Jerusalem (2:38). Similarly, Zechariah speaks prophetically of the redemption and salvation that God will work in Israel.[17]

Few clues are given about the standard by which these people are to be designated as righteous. It is clear, however, that there is a standard, variously designated as "the law (*nomos*) of Moses"

(2:22), "the law of the Lord" (2:24, 39), "the commandments and
regulations of the Lord" (1:6), and "what was customary under the
law" (2:27). In reference to the rites of purification and presentation described in 2:22–24, quotations from Exodus and Leviticus
are included and provide additional detail to the narrative. But for
the most part the implied reader is not given detailed information
about the contents of the law that serves as a standard for these
pious Jews.

The implied reader would also learn something in these chapters about Jewish concepts of God. The predominant divine at-
tribute would seem to be his love for Israel. The prayers and
prophecies frequently mention this quality, or they embody an expectation that God will save Israel from its enemies. God is seen
here on the side of the poor, the oppressed, the powerless, and, as
we have seen, there are expectations of dramatic reversal. It would
be impossible to overstress the significance of the relationship between God and Israel in these chapters. If it is appropriate to speak
of God as a character in Luke's narrative, then clearly God is the
character with ultimate authority. Whenever the implied reader is
allowed to glimpse something about this character's attitudes, either through scriptural quotations or prophetic utterances, there
is a signal of special importance. Presumably the attitude of God
is also the attitude of the implied author, and the implied reader is
being encouraged to adopt it. This means that God's love for Israel
and his expected championing of its cause against its enemies represents a fundamental concept that is being promoted in this text.

A variety of names is used for the divine being: God (*ho theos*,
numerous references), the Lord (*ho kyrios*, numerous references),
the Most High (*ho hypsistos*, 1:32, 35, 76; 2:14), God my Savior (*ho
theos ho sotēr mou*, 1:47), and the Lord God of Israel (*ho kyrios ho theos
tou Israēl*, 1:68). Although the contexts in all cases suggest that all
of these names refer to only one being, there is also a figure called
the spirit (2:27) or the Holy Spirit (1:15, 35, 41, 67; 2:25, 26), who
fills persons with sanctity and enables them to engage in prophecy. The relationship of Holy Spirit to God is not explained. In addition, there are angels—chiefly Gabriel (1:19, 26), but also a
multitude of the heavenly host (*plēthos stratias ouraniou*, 2:13)—who
act as messengers from God to selected people. A Gentile reader
who has some familiarity with Judaism, someone like a Godfearer,
or a reader who has familiarity with the LXX, would have little difficulty in concluding that only one God is intended in all these

passages. But a reader without this familiarity might be inclined to conclude that a number of related deities inhabit this text. It is notable that Luke never explicitly states that monotheism is a basic Jewish doctrine.

The birth and infancy narratives in Luke thus display a form of Judaism that is Temple-centered, with a priesthood and regular divisions sharing priestly duties. The adherents, faithful to the values of the Hebrew Scriptures, are obedient to a divine law recorded by Moses and containing the commandments that govern their lives. The God of Israel, with whom are associated angels and the Holy Spirit, is seen to be kind and merciful, the mighty savior of the oppressed. With Jewish religious life are also associated marvelous events, prophecy, and visions.

The devout Jew is one who lives in the expectation of release from oppression and deprivation, but there is also a conviction that these hopes are in the process of being fulfilled through the lives of John, the prophet of the Most High (Luke 1:76), and Jesus, the Son of the Most High (1:32) and Christ (2:11). Although the Christian message is not directly presented in Luke 1–2, there are allusions to it in these descriptions of marvelous events that are soon to occur and expressions of hope for relief from oppression. John is expected to "turn many of the people of Israel to the Lord their God" (1:16) and to "make ready a people prepared for the Lord" (1:17). Jesus will "reign over the house of Jacob forever" (1:33). Mary gives voice to the expectation of powerful demonstrations of social reversal (1:52–54); Zechariah expects "a mighty savior" (1:69), the fulfillment of prophetic scripture (1:70), and the rescue of Israel from its enemies (1:71, 73). The birth of Jesus is understood to mean salvation (2:11, 30), peace (2:14), revelation (2:32), glory (2:32), and redemption (2:38).

As an anticipation of the relation of the Christian message to Judaism, the speech of Simeon in Luke 2:29–35 is the key passage in Luke 1–2. Indeed, it serves as a significant anticipation of a number of themes that will find expression later in Luke-Acts. It is best to follow the lead of Raymond Brown and others who have recognized two speeches in these verses.[18] The first, the Nunc Dimittis (Luke 2:29–32), expresses the fulfillment of the promise made to Simeon, that he would live to see the Lord's Messiah. These words constitute a proclamation of Jesus as the Christ and a fulfillment of divine promises. The work of Christ is said to be God's salvation (2:30), which is further defined as "a light for

revelation to the Gentiles and for glory to your people Israel"
(2:32). Already the reader is given an indication that the Messiahship of Jesus fulfills the expectations of more people than just the
Jews. Rather it is full of meaning for both Jews and Gentiles.

If Simeon's first speech may be regarded as a blessing, the second is a prophetic warning: "This child is destined for the falling
and the rising of many in Israel, and to be a sign that will be opposed so that the inner thoughts of many will be revealed—and a
sword will pierce your own soul too" (Luke 2:34b–35). Although
Simeon's grim warning does not include anything about the reception of Jesus by Gentiles, it portends a major division among
the people of Israel: many will fall and many will rise, that is,
many will respond negatively to Jesus' message, and many will respond positively. Some scholars see a chronological relationship
between the falling and rising, in that they understand that the
message of Jesus will first be rejected by Jews and then later it will
be accepted. David Tiede emphasizes this interpretation. He
writes: "The sequence of words is significant. . . . This is a prophetic oracle disclosing the fall which will come before the rising
of many in Israel, and the passive voice alerts the reader once
again that it is God who has set this child for such falling and rising and for being a controverted sign."[19] But Brown is probably
correct when he claims that the oracle intends to designate two
groups that exist side by side.[20] Hence the speech anticipates a division within Israel, a matter that has recently been emphasized by
Jacob Jervell and other scholars who have been influenced by
him.[21]

Luke's Simeon adds that the message of Jesus will constitute a
sign that is contradicted, opposed, or rejected (eis sēmeion antilego-
menon). Although a translator must choose which of these meanings to use, it is likely that the earliest readers of the Greek text of
Luke would have seen multiple connotations here. The verb antilegein would literally signify the act of speaking against someone or
something, and so it means to contradict. But contradiction conveys ideas of opposition and rejection. Fitzmyer states that rejection is the primary connotation of the verb in Luke 2:34, and he
translates the phrase "a symbol that will be rejected."[22] Luke uses
the verb antilegein in only three other passages, all in Acts.[23] He
uses it in connection with the first of three Pauline announcements: "But when the Jews saw the crowds, they were filled with
jealousy; and blaspheming, they contradicted (antelegon) what was
spoken by Paul" (Acts 13:45). Here the verb signifies controversy,

opposition, and rejection. Another use of *antilegein* is found in a speech of Paul to the leaders of the Jewish community in Rome. He is reporting to them on his trial in Judea, and he says: "When they had examined me, the Romans wanted to release me, because there was no reason for the death penalty in my case. But when the Jews objected (*antilegontōn de tōn Ioudaiōn*), I was compelled to appeal to the emperor—even though I had no charge to bring against my nation" (Acts 28:18–19). A few verses later *antilegein* is used by the Jewish leaders, who explain that they had received no letters about Paul, but they say, "With regard to this sect (*haireseōs*) we know that everywhere it is spoken against (*antilegetai*)" (28:22). In these two uses, which lead up to the final announcement of Paul about the Jewish and Gentile missions, *antilegein* connotes controversy, opposition, and rejection. In the three uses of *antilegein* in Acts, the opponents are, in every case, Jews. The passages have the effect of welding a connection between Jews and the images of controversy, opposition, and rejection.

The same meaning is undoubtedly to be found in Luke 2:35: the child Jesus is to be the cause of the fall and rise of many in Israel, and he is to be a sign that brings about controversy and rejection among the Jews. The text requires us to understand that controversy and rejection of Jesus' message will occur within Israel; there is no suggestion that there is such a controversy among Gentiles.

Tiede, who interprets the falling of many in Israel as a preliminary stage to the rising of many, emphasizes the predominantly positive aspects of the oracles of Simeon and stresses the significance of the child Jesus as portending glory for Israel. If this second speech of Simeon spoke only of a division within Israel, chronological or otherwise, one might be led to agree with Tiede, Jervell, and others that Luke does not stress the theme of Jewish rejection. But the problem is that this is not all there is. Simeon's words about the division within Israel are followed immediately by the word that the child Jesus is to be a sign that is contradicted and even rejected. As we have seen, Simeon's first speech conveys nothing but positive expectations of "glory to your people Israel." The second, however, qualifies this hopeful expectation by speaking of division among the people. Although one might think that a division implies both something good and something bad, the second speech of Simeon emphasizes the bad. Rather than rejoicing over the positive response, Luke's Simeon emphasizes the negative.

The negative aspect continues to receive stress in the words
that seem personally addressed to Jesus' mother. Although this
verse in Luke has been variously interpreted and frequently understood to refer to the maternal distress at Jesus' crucifixion,
Fitzmyer, Brown, and others have argued persuasively against
such interpretations. They understand 2:35a as parenthetical but
in continuity with the previous verse. Thus, the sword that pierces
the life of Mary is the sword of discrimination, discrimination between falling and rising. Says Brown, "This interpretation makes
Simeon's prophecy of discriminatory judgment for Israel applica-
ble to Mary as an individual Israelite, and more specially applica-
ble to her as a member of Jesus' family."[24] The interpretation is in
line with other aspects of the Lukan treatment of the mother and
the family of Jesus (see Luke 8:21; 11:27–28), and it is consistent
with the concept that the word of Jesus produces division within
families (see Luke 12:51–53). If 2:35a is parenthetical, 35b must
then continue the thought of the preceding. Omitting the paren-
thesis, Brown summarizes the sequence of thoughts in Simeon's
second oracle as follows, "The child is set for the fall and rise of
many in Israel (34c); but, as the emphasis on 'fall' indicates, for the
majority he is a sign that will be contradicted (34d) since, as they
face him, the hostility of their inmost thoughts toward him will be
revealed (35b)."[25]

Negative tones in Luke 1–2 are confined to the second speech
of Simeon. All the rest is positive in the presentation of Jewish piety and hopeful in terms of the effect of Jesus' message. Only here
do we have a warning that there will be division and contention.
It is remarkable that these points are made immediately after a
prediction in Simeon's first speech that the message of Jesus will
have something for both Gentiles and Jews. Here is only a flicker
of trouble to come, but the reader may store this in memory and
recall it later in the narrative when reading of a situation in which
Jesus' message has exactly the effect that is anticipated here. Perhaps it should also be emphasized that the division and controversy anticipated by Simeon's speech does not involve Gentiles,
although both Gentiles and Jews are objects of the Christian message. The division and rejection about which Simeon speaks is
among Jews, not among Gentiles.

Luke's narrative structure allows the reader a glimpse of Judaism apart from Christianity only in the first two chapters of the
gospel. In all the rest the portrait is, in varying ways, affected by

the confrontation with either Jesus and his message or his succes- sors and the early church. In addition, we have only scattered ref- erences to individual piety in the later sections of Luke and Acts, such as descriptions of Joseph of Arimathea in Luke 23:50–51 and Ananias in Acts 22:12. The latter is already a Christian believer, and perhaps the former should also be perceived in that way.

In conclusion, the infancy narratives in Luke serve not only to introduce themes to be developed in subsequent sections of the two-volume work but also to portray the world into which the Christian message was first introduced. It is altogether a Jewish world, peopled by characters whose lives are governed by the He- brew Scriptures and whose religious center is the Jerusalem Tem- ple. The people, the scriptures, and the Temple are all presented as positive values. The people have experienced oppression from a hostile alien source, but now they expect relief that is somehow as- sociated with the appearances of John the Baptist and Jesus. De- spite the predominantly positive and joyful expressions in the birth and infancy accounts, there is in the second speech of Sim- eon an anticipation of division, controversy, and rejection among Jews in regard to the message of Jesus. But it is important to stress that this negative image of Judaism only emerges in connection with the coming of Jesus. It would be inappropriate to draw on Luke's narrative in order to claim that pre-Christian Judaism was a poverty-stricken religion in need of thorough reformation. Luke's infancy narratives rather dispose the implied reader to think of Ju- daism in fundamentally positive ways and to expect that, for the most part, pious Jews will joyously accept Jesus and embrace his message.

NOTES

1. See, e.g., Henry J. Cadbury, "Commentary on the Preface of Luke"; Loveday Alexander, "Luke's Preface in the Context of Greek Preface-Writing"; Terrance Callan, "The Preface of Luke-Acts and Historiography"; Vernon K. Robbins, "Prefaces in Greco-Roman Biography and Luke-Acts."
2. The use of the first person is found again in the so-called "we sections," Acts 16:10–17; 20:5–15; 21:1–18; 27:1–28:16.
3. See Raymond E. Brown, *The Birth of the Messiah: A Commentary on the Infancy Narratives in Matthew and Luke*, 250–53, for a discussion of the internal organi- zation of Luke 1:5–2:52. Brown states that Luke composed this section in two stages. In the first, there is a perfect diptych, which Brown outlines as follows:

     I. Two annunciations of Conception:
       1. Annunciation about John the Baptist (1:5–23); and Elizabeth's preg-
         nancy and praise of God (1:24–25).
       2. Annunciation about Jesus (1:26–38); and Elizabeth's praise of Mary's
         pregnancy (1:39–45, 56).
    II. Two Narratives of Birth / Circumcision / Naming and Future Greatness:
       1. Narrative about John the Baptist (1:57–66); and a Statement about
         Growth (1:80).
       2. Narrative about Jesus (2:1–27, 34–39); and a Statement about Growth
         (2:40).
    At the second stage, according to Brown, Luke added the Magnificat (1:46–55),
the Benedictus (1:67–79), the Nunc Dimittis (2:28–33), and the incident of Jesus
in the Temple (2:41–52).
4.  See, e.g., Philostratus, *The Life of Apollonius of Tyana*, trans. F. C. Conybeare,
    LCL (Cambridge: Harvard University Press, 1912) 1:4–7; Diogenes Laertius,
    *Lives of Eminent Philosophers*, trans. R. D. Hicks, LCL (Cambridge: Harvard Uni-
    versity Press, 1925) 3:2; Plutarch, *Lives*, trans. Bernadotte Perrin, LCL (Cam-
    bridge: Harvard University Press, 1919), Alexander 1:1–3:5. See also Charles
    H. Talbert, "Prophecies of Future Greatness: The Contribution of Greco-
    Roman Biographies to an Understanding of Luke 1:5–4:15."
5.  The case for taking 3:1 as the original beginning of Luke's gospel was perhaps
    most persuasively argued by proponents of the Proto-Luke hypothesis, a the-
    ory originally associated with the names of B. H. Streeter and Vincent Taylor.
    See Streeter, "Fresh Light on the Synoptic Problem," and his *The Four Gospels:
    A Study of Origins*, 201–22; Taylor, *Behind the Third Gospel: A Study of the Proto-
    Luke Hypothesis*. Although Hans Conzelmann did not discuss the Proto-Luke
    hypothesis, he nevertheless avoided devoting any significant attention to Luke
    1–2. See Conzelmann, *The Theology of St. Luke*. For critiques of Conzelmann's
    position, see H. H. Oliver, "The Lucan Birth Stories and the Purpose of Luke-
    Acts", Paul S. Minear, "Luke's Use of the Birth Stories."
6.  Without subscribing to the Proto-Luke hypothesis, Joseph A. Fitzmyer com-
    mented that Luke "3:1–2 was at one time a formal introduction to the work
    (*The Gospel According to Luke (I–IX)*), 310.
7.  Evidently, Marcion's gospel began at Luke 3:1. See Adolf Harnack, *Marcion:
    Das Evangelium vom Fremden Gott*, esp. 165ff. John Knox states that the birth
    narratives were added to an earlier version of Luke, among other reasons, in
    order to counteract the use Marcion had made of this gospel. About Luke 1–2,
    Knox writes, "Marcion would surely not have tolerated this highly 'Jewish'
    section; but how wonderfully adapted it is to show the nature of Christianity
    as the true Judaism and thus to answer one of the major contentions of the
    Marcionites! And one cannot overlook the difficulty involved in the common
    supposition that Marcion deliberately selected a Gospel which began in so
    false and obnoxious a way" (John Knox, *Marcion and the New Testament: An Es-
    say in the Early History of the Canon*, 87).
8.  See Joseph B. Tyson, *The Death of Jesus in Luke-Acts*, 48–83, and "Conflict as a
    Literary Theme in the Gospel of Luke."
9.  J. K. Elliott, "Does Luke 2:41–52 Anticipate the Resurrection?"
10.  On the significance of the Temple in Luke-Acts, see Michael Bachmann, *Jeru-
    salem und der Tempel: Die geographisch-theologischen Elementen in der lukanischen
    Sicht des jüdischen Kultzentrums*; K. Balzer, "The Meaning of the Temple in the
    Lukan Writings", Francis D. Weinert, "The Meaning of the Temple in
    Luke-Acts."
11.  For a discussion of the infancy narratives as forming a literary frame for the
    Gospel of Luke, see Joseph B. Tyson, "The Birth Narratives and the Beginning
    of Luke's Gospel."

12. Henry J. Cadbury, *The Making of Luke-Acts*, 223.
13. Ibid.
14. On Luke 2:22–24, see especially Brown, *Birth of the Messiah*, 447–51; Fitzmyer, *Luke, I–IX*, 419–26.
15. Note, however, the textual variants.
16. See Reicke, "Jesus, Simeon, and Anna (Luke 2:21–40)."
17. David P. Moessner has questioned the credibility of some characters in Luke 1–2. In particular, he observes that Zecharaiah's credentials are discredited when he is struck dumb for unbelief (Luke 1:20). Moessner claims that the fulfillment of the predictions in Luke 1–2 were not intended by the author to be taken literally but ironically, and he makes this judgment by comparing the predictive statements with fulfillments or nonfulfillments as cited in later parts of Luke-Acts. Moessner's argument is impressive but does not affect the interpretation of the predictive statements as representations of individual Jewish piety. See Moessner, "The Ironic Fulfillment of Israel's Glory."
18. Brown, *Birth of the Messiah*, 454–66.
19. Daid L. Tiede, " 'Glory to Thy People Israel': Luke-Acts and the Jews," 28.
20. See Brown, *Birth of the Messiah*, 460–66.
21. See esp. Jacob Jervell, "The Divided People of God: The Restoration of Israel and Salvation for the Gentiles," in *Luke and the People of God: A New Look at Luke-Acts*, 41–74.
22. Fitzmyer, *Luke I–IX*, 418.
23. In some manuscripts it is found also in Luke 20:27, where Luke reports that Sadducees deny resurrection.
24. Brown, *Birth of the Messiah*, 465. See also Fitzmyer, *Luke I–IX*, 419–32.
25. Brown, *Birth of the Messiah*, 465f.

# 4

# Jesus in Galilee, Samaria, and Judea

(Luke 3:1–19:44)

Luke's description of the ministry of Jesus in Galilee, Samaria, and Judea consumes the great central part of the gospel, specifically Luke 3:1–19:44. Here the figure of Jesus as teacher and healer is presented in a long series of individual narratives and discourses. The section is made up of three subdivisions. Luke 3:1–4:13 is a transition section that connects the infancy narratives with those about the ministry of Jesus and includes narratives about the activity and teaching of John the Baptist and the baptism, genealogy, and temptation of Jesus. In 4:14–9:50, the second subdivision, Jesus is teaching and healing in Galilee,[1] and in 9:51–19:44, a series of loosely connected discourses and narratives set in Samaria and Judea, he is on the way to Jerusalem.[2] But for purposes of studying the ways in which Luke presents Jewish religious life, these subdivisions are unnecessary. In the large body of material in Luke 3:1–19:44, the emphasis is on the activity of Jesus in areas outside Jerusalem that are thought to be predominantly Jewish, and there is a consistency in the ways in which images of Judaism affect the narratives.

There are, however, striking differences between the images of Jewish religious life found here and in Luke 1–2. The generally positive tone that pervades the descriptions of Jewish piety in the Lukan infancy narratives gives way in the present section of the gospel to a more controversial tone that inevitably affects the portrayal of a number of Jewish features in profoundly negative ways.

This phase of the narrative is marked by waves of popular response to Jesus. Although one pericope (Luke 4:16–30, which is discussed below) includes an incident of popular opposition to Jesus, mass support of him is frequently noted and sometimes contrasted with the opposition of Jewish leaders.[3] In Jesus' response to the disciples of John, for example, Jesus and John are supported by "all the people who heard" and by the publicans (Luke 7:29). Opposed to them are the Pharisees and the lawyers (7:30). It is significant that this formidable support for Jesus comes from Jewish people, who form a connection with those pious Jews whose lives are treated so positively in Luke 1–2.

Although the relationship between Jesus and the Jewish people is pictured in predominantly favorable terms at this point, his association with Jewish leaders is, for the most part, marked by controversy. Jesus himself is portrayed as the subject of controversy, perhaps in fulfillment of the prediction of Simeon in Luke 2:34. The controversial aspects of this section help the implied reader to distinguish between the beliefs and practices associated with the Jesus movement and those associated with the Jewish people and their leaders. Thus it is inevitable that images of Judaism will suffer by their being distinguished from those elements associated with Jesus. It is nevertheless imperative for us, in this study, to analyze these images in some depth. So in this chapter we shall take seriously the observation that the ministry of Jesus outside Jerusalem is narrated in terms of controversy, and we will examine the implications of the kind of portrayal we have in this gospel for an understanding of the Lukan images of Judaism and the relationship between Christianity and Judaism.

## THE ROLE OF CONTROVERSY

Although conflict may occur between persons or groups who share few or no areas of agreement, meaningful controversy cannot. In the case of the controversies in Luke between Jesus and his Jewish audiences, there are large areas of agreement. There is a shared heritage in tradition and an acknowledged biblical authority that makes the controversy possible. We cannot pretend to understand either the nature of the controversies in this section of Luke or the images of Judaism conveyed by them until we have recognized those areas of agreement.

The recognition of biblical authority is implicit in many of the controversies. No character or group in the Gospel of Luke contests the authority of the Hebrew Scriptures. Moreover, allusions and quotations from these writings serve in some cases to explain actions of Jesus and his disciples and in others to support points of view embraced by Jesus. The initial sermon of Jesus in the synagogue at Nazareth (Luke 4:16–30), which we will examine below, includes a quotation from Isaiah, specifically Isa 61:1–2; 58:6. In the sermon, Jesus reads from Isaiah and then claims the immediate fulfillment of the scripture. Perhaps the uncontested authority of the scripture is most dramatically asserted in the story of Jesus' temptation, Luke 4:1–13, where both Jesus and the devil quote various passages. Luke claims that the scripture is fulfilled by the appearance of John the Baptist, as he quotes Isa 40:3–5 at Luke 3:4–6 and Mal 3:1 at Luke 7:27. Both Jesus and the questioning lawyer agree on the authority and force of Deut 6:5 and Lev 19:18 (see Luke 10:27). At one point the fulfillment of scripture is claimed by the Lukan Jesus without an express quotation (Luke 18:31).

Many figures of the past, who are known through the Hebrew Scriptures, are familiar both to Jesus and his audiences: Abel and Zechariah (11:51), Jonah (11:29, 30, 32), Lot (17:28, 29, 32), Noah (3:36; 17:26, 27), and Solomon (11:31; 12:27). A number of such figures have special prominence in this section of the gospel. David, for example, is understood to be a special ancestor of Jesus (3:31), in agreement with the birth narratives. Jesus is also addressed as Son of David (18:38, 39), and on one occasion he cites David's action as a precedent for his own permission for the disciples to pick, grind, and eat grain on the Sabbath day.

Abraham is treated with great respect and, in some cases, affection. The image of Abraham as father seems to support the concept of a special relationship between God and the Hebrew people. Although John the Baptist preaches that the fatherhood of Abraham is not enough to save persons from judgment and proclaims that "God is able from these stones to raise up children to Abraham" (3:8), the concept of a special relationship seems implied in some sayings of Jesus. Jesus states that a woman who has been bent over for eighteen years should be healed on the Sabbath day, and he refers to her as a daughter of Abraham (13:16). Similarly, he says that Zacchaeus, the tax collector, has received salvation, in view of the fact that he is a son of Abraham (*kathoti kai autos huios Abraam estin*, 19:9). Abraham, together with Isaac, Jacob, and the prophets, is said to be in the kingdom of God (13:28). We shall examine Abraham's role in the story of the rich man and Lazarus (Luke 16:19–31) below.

Moses also comes in for special treatment in this section of Luke, and he is presented as a figure of great authority. Abraham himself affirms the authority of Moses and the prophets (16:29f.), and at one point Jesus explicitly upholds the commands of Moses about the treatment of cured lepers (5:14; cf. 17:14). We shall examine other references to Moses below.

Elijah is also treated as a significant figure. Jesus cites him as an illustration of the maxim that prophets are not acceptable in their home countries, and he refers to Elijah's and Elisha's actions on behalf of Gentiles (Luke 4:24–26). Elijah's reappearance seems to be taken for granted by Herod Antipas (9:8) and by many Jewish people (9:19). We shall examine other references to Elijah below.

Belief in angels and devils appears to be accepted both by Jesus and by members of his audiences. Angels are mentioned in scriptural quotations (Luke 4:10; 7:27) and in sayings of Jesus (15:10; 16:22). In some important sayings the angels are clearly on the side of Jesus and are associated with the coming of the Son of man and with the glory of the Father (9:26; 12:8–9). Likewise, the devil (*diabolos*, 4:2, 3, 6, 13; 8:12), Satan (10:18; 11:18; 13:16), and Beelzebul (11:15, 18, 19) constitute components of the customary beliefs in Judaism, and their existence is implicitly acknowledged by Jesus.

These and other aspects of agreement between Jesus and the Jewish people and leaders make controversy possible. But of greater importance are the specific issues over which disagreement occurs. The significance of these controversies is laid out in a pericope of signal importance, namely Luke 4:16–30, the inaugural sermon of Jesus at the synagogue in Nazareth. This is an unusual pericope in that it tells of opposition to Jesus that comes from the people rather than leaders. At least there is no explicit reference to a leader. Probably because it serves as Jesus' first speech and, as is frequently observed, functions in programmatic ways to introduce themes to be traced throughout Luke-Acts, this pericope carries special weight in the Lukan gospel and requires serious treatment here.

**Luke 4:16–30.** The episode comes just after the Lukan narrative of Jesus' temptations, which is set in Judea. In Luke 4:14–15, we read that Jesus has returned to Galilee, where news about him has already begun to circulate and that he taught "in their synagogues and was praised by everyone." Then Luke says that at a synagogue service in Nazareth on the Sabbath day, Jesus read from the book of Isaiah and claimed the fulfillment of the reading in the presence of the congregation. The immediate response from the congregation was positive, but when Jesus pointed to the examples of Elijah and Elisha in neglecting Israelites in order to tend

to the needs of a Sidonian widow and a Syrian leper, the members
of the congregation attempted to kill him.

At the beginning of this pericope, Luke comments that Nazareth is the place where Jesus had been brought up, and it is significant that he calls attention to Jesus' customary practice of
attending services at his local synagogue on the Sabbath (4:16).
The reminder is particularly important in establishing Jesus' credentials as an observant Jew and in emphasizing a custom on
which he and his Jewish compatriots would have agreed. The implied reader should not miss the stress on Jesus' Jewishness. Luke
also seems to suggest that Jesus was already highly regarded in the
Nazareth synagogue, since he was invited, or at least permitted,
to read to the congregation on that day. After unrolling the scroll
of the prophet Isaiah, Jesus reads.[4] The reading is from Isa 61:1–2;
58:6, words in which the prophet speaks of being anointed
(echrisen) to minister on behalf of the poor, the prisoners, the blind,
and the downtrodden, and to proclaim the Lord's acceptable year
(eniauton kyriou dekton), probably a reference to the Jubilee year, as
a number of scholars have proposed.[5] After this reading, Jesus begins the exposition of the passages by announcing that this scripture has been fulfilled at the very moment of its being read and
heard. In his act of reading and the congregation's act of listening,
the scripture has found its fulfillment (4:21).. Clearly there is here
an emphasis on the immediacy of fulfillment. Jesus' announcement is met with amazement and apparent approval on the part of
the congregation, and his words are received as words of grace
(4:22). The people ask, "Is not this Joseph's son?" (4:22), a question
expressing amazement. But Jesus then responds to the congregation: You will speak the parable, "Doctor, cure yourself!" and he
says that the people will demand that he do those things in Nazareth that he has already done in Capernaum.[6] Jesus says further
that a prophet is not acceptable in his own country (4:24). There
appears to be intended irony in the juxtaposition of adjectives in
4:19 and 4:24: the prophet who has been anointed to proclaim the
acceptable (dektos) year of the Lord is not acceptable (dektos) in his
own country. Jesus then refers to the stories of Elijah and Elisha
and calls attention to their ministry to Gentiles. Despite the fact
that there were many widows and great need in Israel during Elijah's time, Elijah went only to a widow in Sidon. Similarly, Elisha
neglected Israelite lepers and cured only one from Syria. After

hearing these words, the Nazareth congregation became enraged against Jesus, threw him out of the city, and attempted to execute him.

Almost all scholars agree on the programmatic nature of this pericope.[7] Gerhard Lohfink, for example, sees in it a summary of the entire ministry of Jesus: the time of salvation (4:21), the acceptance of Jesus (4:22), and the rejection of Jesus (4:29).[8] That there is a shift in the disposition of the Nazareth congregation is also generally agreed, although it is possible to argue about the reason for the crowd's hostility and the precise point at which it begins. Some scholars would see the beginning of a hostile tone in the question about Jesus' ancestry in 4:22, while others would see it first in Jesus' response at 4:23.

James A. Sanders has used a method he calls "comparative midrash" to produce a largely convincing argument about the reason for the shift on the part of the Nazareth congregation.[9] Drawing on 11QMelch and other Qumran documents, Sanders shows that two axioms made up the hermeneutic used in Qumran *pesharim*. The first axiom proclaims that the end time has arrived. The second "required that scripture be so interpreted as to show that in the Eschaton God's wrath would be directed against an outgroup while his mercy would be directed toward the in-group."[10] In Luke 4, Jesus made use of the first axiom in a heightened and intensified way in proclaiming that the end time had begun in the hearing and reading of the scripture from Isaiah. But Jesus' second axiom, according to Sanders, is "the contradiction of the Essene second axiom."[11] It is not Jesus' countrymen who will receive the benefits of the end time, but rather outsiders. Sanders calls this a prophetic hermeneutic, and he writes:

> Just as the so-called true prophets of old cited the ancient Mosaic and Davidic Torah traditions of Israel's origins not only as the very authority of Israel's existence, but as a judgment upon and a challenge to the official ideology of their day; so the Lukan account of the Rejection pericope shows Jesus in that same prophetic tradition vis-à-vis *his* contemporaries; by the prophetic-hermeneutic second axiom Jesus turned the very popular Isa 61 passage into a judgment and a challenge to the definitions of Israel of his day. The reason, the whole passage makes clear, that the proverb is true is not only that a hometown figure is overfamiliar and lacks the authority that a measure of strangeness might bring, but it is true principally because of how a true prophet, in a

certain Elijah-type biblical tradition, must cast a light of scrutiny upon
his own people from the very source of authority on which they rely for
their identity, existence and self-understanding.[12]

Sanders concludes that "a true prophet of the prophet-martyr
tradition *cannot* be *dektos* at home precisely because of his
hermeneutics."[13]

Sanders's analysis can be pressed somewhat further to show
that the fundamental issue in this pericope is the divine preference
for Israel, precisely the issue that Jesus' second axiom questions.
The same issue was addressed in Luke 3:8, where John claimed
that God was able to raise up sons of Abraham from stones. Likewise, the sermon of Jesus at Nazareth anticipates not only a divine
preference for those outside Jesus' hometown but also a preference
for those who are not of the people of Israel. Although the ministry of Jesus in Luke continues to be chiefly among Jews, the pericope points forward to issues that will receive a great deal of
attention in Acts, namely those relating to the place and character
of the Christian mission to Gentiles. Justification for such a mission is laid in Luke 4 in the interpretation of Hebrew texts. If Elijah
and Elisha neglected Israelites in order to provide help for Si-
donians and Syrians, then it may be argued that the prophetic
mission initiated by Jesus will also in due course aim itself toward
Gentiles. But in so doing the place of the Jewish people as the people of God is challenged. Thus the implied reader learns at the
very beginning of the ministry of Jesus that Jews assume that they
have a special relationship with God and that Jesus challenges this
assumption and does so on biblical grounds.[14] The priority of Israel is further questioned by Jesus' commendation of the centurion
in 7:9, his parable of the good Samaritan (10:29–37), and the narrative of the ten lepers (17:11–19), even if there is also a story of
Samaritan rejection of Jesus (9:51–56).[15]

Luke 4:16–30 is only the beginning of a series of controversies
between Jesus and his audiences, and the controversial tone in this
section affects the images of Jewish institutions, leaders, and practices. This is the case because the controversies are, for the most
part, set in synagogues, the antagonists are Pharisees, and the issues involve matters of Torah observance.

In the Lukan infancy narratives, the Temple in Jerusalem is
the center of a Jewish piety that is treated in positive ways. But in
Luke 3:1–19:44 the interest in the Temple as the central Jewish in-

stitution gives way to synagogues outside Jerusalem, and the synagogues are for the most part settings for scenes of controversy.[16] Not only is the inaugural sermon of Jesus set in a synagogue, but this narrative serves to introduce a series of controversy pericopes set in synagogues.[17] Synagogues as settings for controversies may be somewhat surprising, in view of the first Lukan reference to these Jewish institutions. In the introduction to the sermon at Nazareth (4:15), Luke reports that Jesus taught in synagogues and received a positive response. Even here, however, there may be a sense of separation between the implied reader and the audiences of Jesus in the expression "their synagogues." In context, "their" may refer to the people of Galilee, but the connotation of synagogues as associated with Jews rather than with the readers of Luke seems also to be present. Even in reporting a positive response on the part of Jesus' Jewish audience, Luke is giving a somewhat confusing signal, by distancing the implied reader from this basic Jewish institution.

In any event, Luke 4:16–30 is the first in a series of controversies set in synagogues. In Luke 6:6–11 Jesus heals a man with a withered right hand, and opposition comes from scribes and Pharisees, who question the legality of this action on the Sabbath day. Jesus answers the objection by asking, "Is it lawful to do good or to do harm on the sabbath, to save life or to destroy it?" (6:9). Again, in Luke 13:10–17, the scene is an unspecified synagogue on the Sabbath day, and Jesus heals a woman of an ailment she has suffered for eighteen years. The ruler of the synagogue objects, and Jesus defends his action.

Synagogues are not in every case associated with conflict and controversy. In Luke 4:31–37, another pericope set in a synagogue on the Sabbath, this one at Capernaum, Jesus performs an exorcism, and the people are astounded at his power and authority. There is no controversy here, and no information about Judaism is included, except that attendance at synagogue on the Sabbath day is a usual practice. But in 12:11, a verse that probably anticipates narratives in Acts, Jesus counsels his disciples about their appearances before synagogues, rulers, and authorities to answer questions about their activities. One would presume that synagogues are places in which religious trials may be held.

The most frequently named Jewish leaders in these pericopes are the Pharisees, with whom are associated scribes, lawyers, and rulers of synagogues.[18] In most narratives members of these groups are pictured in the role of opponents of Jesus.[19] Their opposition to both John the Baptist and Jesus is clearly and frequently noted. In 11:42–12:1 we have a long string of condemnations of Pharisees and lawyers, all put in the mouth of Jesus. According to Luke's Jesus, Pharisees are meticulous about tithing, but they neglect justice and the love of God; they love the best seats in the synagogues and greetings in the market places. Lawyers load people with burdens but do nothing to help them carry them. They consent to their fathers' murder of the prophets, and they have "taken away the key of knowledge." In 12:1 Jesus warns his disciples about the hypocrisy of the Pharisees. In 16:14–15, he accuses them of self-justification and self-exaltation, and in an editorial gloss Luke explains that Pharisees love money. In the well-known parable in 18:9–14, the Pharisee has become the symbol of pride, self-justification, and arrogance.

On three occasions Jesus dines with Pharisees, and the setting itself serves to soften the sense of hostility. But even these meals are occasions for controversy. There is a clear sense of conflict and controversy in Luke 7:36–50, but this pericope is complex. At first we learn that a Pharisee has invited Jesus to dine with him and that Jesus has accepted. The seemingly friendly relationship between the two is surprising in contrast to other narratives in which Jesus and the Pharisees are portrayed as opponents. But, aside from the fact that Jesus addresses his host by name (7:40), the dialogue here is no more friendly than are the controversies between Jesus and Pharisees that are set in synagogues. In any event a woman known to the Pharisee as a sinner intrudes upon the meal in order to anoint Jesus' feet, and when the Pharisee objects, Jesus tells a parable intended to pose a question about the relationship between sin, forgiveness, and gratitude. He concludes that the woman has many sins and therefore is more grateful for forgiveness than is someone who has fewer sins. He then proclaims forgiveness for the woman, and those who are present at the meal ask, "Who is this who even forgives sins?" (7:49). There seem to be two objections within this pericope. The first, that of the host, is directed toward the position of Jesus himself: "If this man were a prophet, he would have known who and what kind of woman this is who is touching him—that she is a sinner" (7:39). The categorization of Jesus as prophet probably connects with the proclamation in 7:16, where, after Jesus has raised the son of the widow of Nain, the people say, "A great prophet has arisen among us!"

(7:16). Thus it is likely that the Pharisee is questioning Jesus' role
as a prophet. But there is also the presumption that someone like
Jesus would not allow himself to be touched by such a sinful
woman. Does this presumption arise because Jesus is regarded by
some as a prophet, or is it generally the case that a holy man is
somehow set apart? Or perhaps the point is that a Pharisee or anyone with whom he dines is under obligation to protect himself
from the pollution of sin. In any event, at the end of the pericope,
the objection expressed by the other diners is not against a form of
uncleanness but against the authority to forgive sins that Jesus
claims to have.

In 11:37–41, we have a second controversy set during a meal
that Jesus takes with a Pharisee. During the meal the Pharisee observes that Jesus has not washed, and Jesus answers the objection
with an accusation that Pharisees clean only the outsides of cups
and dishes. A third incident at a meal hosted by a Pharisee is to be
found in Luke 14:1–6. It is the Sabbath day, and lawyers and Pharisees are anxious to see if Jesus will heal a dropsical man, who apparently presents himself during the meal. Jesus does in fact heal
the man, citing the precedent apparently authorized by Pharisees,
namely that of pulling an ox out of a well on the Sabbath day. The
pericope leaves the impression that the lawyers and Pharisees regard Jesus' action as illegal.

In other pericopes, controversy between Jesus and these Jewish leaders is less explicit. The conversation between Jesus and the
lawyer in 10:25–28 is not described as a controversy but is rather
presented as a test. Even so, there is agreement between the lawyer and Jesus in regard to the requirements in the scripture for one
to inherit eternal life, and the lawyer's reading of the scriptures is
commended by Jesus.

A genuine exception to the controversial relationship between
Jesus and Pharisees is to be found in Luke 13:31–33, where Phar-
isees appear to be supportive of Jesus in warning him about Herod
Antipas.

The controversies between Jesus and the Pharisees concern
matters associated with observance of the Torah. The Pharisees
maintain that God alone can forgive sins (5:17–26); they oppose social intercourse between righteous people and sinners (5:29–32;
7:36–50; 15:1–2); they favor the practice of fasting and the offering
of prayers (as do the followers of John, 5:33–39); they oppose pick-
ing, grinding, and eating grain on the Sabbath (6:2); they oppose

acts of healing on the Sabbath (6:6–11; 13:10–17; 14:1–6). Jesus'
judgment on the Pharisees and lawyers is that, in not accepting
the baptism of John, they "rejected God's purpose for themselves" (7:30).

So it is that the controversies in this section of Luke affect the
images of synagogues, Pharisees, and Torah. In general it may be
concluded that the image of the synagogue is a negative one. Synagogues function in the narratives as social and religious centers,
and attendance at synagogue services on the Sabbath appears to
be an act of piety. But for the most part, synagogues constitute settings for controversy between Jesus and his Jewish audiences.
Only in Luke 4:16–30 do we have anything approaching a description of a synagogue service.[20] We gather from this pericope that a
reading from the Hebrew Scriptures followed by a commentary on
the cited passage was a customary part of a synagogue service.
Apart from this occurrence, there is in Luke's gospel nothing approaching a genuine description of an act of prayer or worship in
a synagogue. Synagogues appear to be places where Jesus offers
himself for the well-being of Jewish people but is rejected.

In general Pharisees, scribes, and lawyers serve in the Lukan
narrative as counterpoints to Jesus. They represent for the reader
an image of Jewish religious life and thought that is distinguished
from that associated with the message of Jesus. These leaders are
dedicated and serious people, devoted to God's law and its interpretation. They are acquainted with the scriptures, and their
interpretations are not at every point opposed to that of Jesus. But
for the most part, the Lukan image of these leaders—Pharisees,
lawyers, scribes—is one of persons who exalt themselves, load
other people with burdens that they themselves do not share, hold
misplaced values, and put too much emphasis on small things
and too little on matters of great significance. In brief, the leaders
are misguided hypocrites. It will be a matter of some surprise that
this image is considerably modified in other parts of Luke-Acts.

The controversies between Jesus and the Pharisees give us an
image of Judaism as a religion that centers its attention on legal
matters. Clearly Torah is understood to include certain specific requirements given by God to his people, and Pharisees are assumed to be the authoritative interpreters of Torah. Jesus himself
affirms the unalterable authority of the law (16:17), and he positively cites commandments against adultery, murder, theft, and
perjury, as well as the command to honor one's parents (Luke
18:20). In 5:14 he requires a cleansed leper to appear before the

priest and make an offering, in observance of a Mosaic commandment, an apparent allusion to regulations affecting priestly control
of leprosy in Leviticus 13 and 14 (cf. also Luke 17:14). Jesus also
agrees with the lawyer who quotes passages from Deut 6:5 and Lev
19:18 as requirements for obtaining eternal life (10:25–28). But
there is sharp disagreement between Jesus and the Jewish leaders
over the meaning of certain commandments, especially those gov-
erning permitted and prohibited activities on the Sabbath. The image of Judaism in this section of Luke is one that strictly forbids
healing on the Sabbath (Luke 6:6–11; 13:10–17; 14:1–6) as well as
grinding and eating grain (6:1–5). In addition to controversies relating to Sabbath observance, Pharisaic Judaism insists on the separation of sinners and others at meals (5:29–32; 15:1–2). Perhaps
dietary regulations lie behind this insistence on segregation, but
the text contains no explicit mention of them. The objections are
usually made in forms that imply the righteousness of Jesus and
his disciples. Even the opponents treat them as basically observant
of Torah, as persons whose righteousness must be protected from
the pollution of sinners. Contact with sinners is also treated as a
violation of God's law (7:36–50).

The controversy pericopes in this section of Luke's gospel provide a rich source of information (accurate or not) about Jewish religious life and thought. Here we learn of the social and religious
importance of synagogues, the dominant role of Pharisees as interpreters of Torah, and the pervasiveness of nomistic considerations in Jewish life. But for the most part these images in Luke are
negative. A great deal of material dealing with this phase of the
ministry of Jesus serves to contrast Judaism with the message of
Jesus, a contrast in which Judaism emerges as a religion of tight
restrictions, meticulous observances, and sharp social distinctions. The Jewish people in Luke put a great deal of weight on
what they believe to be their special relationship with God. As
leaders of the Jewish people, Pharisees may not be malignant, but
they are elitist, conservative, and arrogant. They are not open to
the kind of challenge that John and Jesus intend to bring. They
understand nomistic restrictions in such a way as to prevent the
Lukan Jesus from bringing the healing and saving message of
the gospel.

### THE ROLE OF THE HEBREW SCRIPTURES

In this portion of the gospel, Luke calls attention to certain distinctions between the message of Jesus and the beliefs of the Jewish

people. We have observed that he chose to do so by using a series
of pericopes in which Jesus is shown to be in controversy with various Jewish audiences. These controversies may take place because
there are wide areas of agreement between the protagonists and
significant issues that separate them. We have already observed
the nature of some of these issues. It remains, however, to delve
somewhat more deeply into the implications that emerge from our
examination of one of the areas of agreement, namely the authority of the Hebrew Scriptures.

There are four passages in Luke 3:1–19:44 that have a significant bearing on this question. These are Luke 4:16–30; 9:28–36;
16:16–17; and 16:19–31. All four contain important implications
about the position of the Hebrew Scriptures, and three of them
draw special attention to important figures of the Jewish past, especially Moses and Elijah. These passages need to be considered
carefully and in relationship with each other.

**Luke 4:16–30.**    Sufficient attention has been given to this pericope above. At this point we need observe only that the quotations from Isa 61:1–2; 58:6 assume the authority of this prophetic
book and that the allusions to the activity of Elijah and Elisha serve
to interpret the ministry of Jesus and to provide precedents for his
followers. As we saw above, there is a strong stress here on the
immediate fulfillment of biblical prophecy.

**Luke 9:28–36.**    Although there is a narrative of the transfiguration of Jesus in all three Synoptic Gospels, Luke's version has
some distinctive traces that mark it as of special importance for a
study of images of Judaism. In this narrative, Luke reports that
Jesus' countenance was altered while he was praying in the presence of Peter, John, and James. Then Moses and Elijah appeared
with Jesus and spoke of his *exodus*, which was to occur in Jerusalem. Peter proposed building booths to Moses, Elijah, and Jesus,
but Luke comments that Peter did not know what he was saying.
Then a cloud appeared, and a voice from the cloud spoke, "This is
my Son, my Chosen; listen to him!" (9:35). Afterward, Jesus was
found alone.

On any interpretation, the transfiguration story has a number
of difficulties. It has frequently been understood as a misplaced
resurrection account.[21] Some recent scholars have emphasized the
connections between the Lukan transfiguration story and its immediate context. Joseph A. Fitzmyer, in a study of the composition
of Luke 9, has shown how the entire structure of the chapter aims

"at an identification of him [Jesus] in terms of answers given to the question dramatically posed by Herod (9:9), 'Who is this about whom I hear such things?' "[22] Fitzmyer calls attention to a number of connections between elements in the transfiguration story and other pericopes in Luke 9. In both 9:18 and 9:36, Jesus is said to be alone. In both 9:8 and 9:19, there is speculation that Jesus is Elijah, and in the transfiguration episode Elijah appears with Jesus (9:30). The reference to Jesus' *exodus* in 9:31 reflects the first passion prediction in 9:22 and anticipates the second in 9:44. The heavenly voice that commands the disciples to hear Jesus (9:36) is an explicit confirmation of Jesus' authority. But above all, according to Fitzmyer, the heavenly announcement in 9:35 is an answer to the question of Herod in 9:9. Jesus is the Son of God, the chosen one.[23]

Without denying that one function of the transfiguration narrative is to serve as the definitive answer to the question of Herod in Luke 9:9, I would claim that the story functions in other ways as well. At one level, the transfiguration episode serves as a symbolic narrative that tells the reader about the proper roles and relationships of Moses, Elijah, and Jesus. We have already seen some of the ways in which the figures of Moses and Elijah have been used in this section of Luke. Although in some passages in Acts, Moses is treated as a prophetic figure, most references to him in Luke distinguish him from the prophets and associate him with Torah (see Luke 5:14; 16:29, 31; 20:28; 24:27, 44). Even without specific designations in the passage at hand, it is most likely that Moses stands for the law and Elijah for the prophets. The latter representation was implied in Luke 4:24f., where Jesus claimed that a prophet is not acceptable in his home country and then cited the examples of Elijah and Elisha to support the contention. Further, Elisha is explicitly called a prophet in 4:27. And in 16:29, 31, Moses and Elijah seem to stand for the legal and prophetic components of the Hebrew Scriptures. The appearance of both Moses and Elijah in the story of Jesus' transfiguration likewise suggests that Moses stands for the law and Elijah for the prophets.

Luke's version of the transfiguration account suggests that the proper role of Moses and Elijah is to point forward to Jesus and to what he is to do in Jerusalem. What he is to do is called his *exodus*, a term that reflects the story of Moses.[24] Jesus' *exodus* is to be fulfilled (*tēn exodon autou hēn ēmellen plēroun*, 9:31) in Jerusalem. As in Luke 4:21, we have a claim that Jesus fulfills something. But if it is a fulfillment of something indicated by Moses as law and Elijah as prophet, then it is correct to say that Jesus is the fulfillment of the law and the prophets, or, in brief, of the Hebrew Scriptures. If this is so, a proper reading of the law and the prophets is one that prepares the reader to understand the ministry of Jesus as a fulfillment of these scriptures.

But the reader is not to conclude, as does Peter (9:33), that Moses, Elijah, and Jesus are equal.[25] The Lukan reprimand of Peter is not a way of saying that heavenly figures such as Moses and Elijah do not need physical structures to live in. Rather, Peter's mistake is in placing Moses, Elijah, and Jesus on the same level. Indeed, the nature of Peter's error is made clear in verses 34–36. The voice of God commands the disciples to listen to Jesus, "and when the voice had spoken, Jesus was found alone" (9:36). The implication is that the disciples should listen only to Jesus. So once Moses and Elijah have served their purposes, they disappear (9:36). Law and prophets point forward to Jesus as God's son, and once they have done that, they retreat to leave Jesus himself as sole authority. Although it is tempting to read the disappearance of Moses and Elijah in 9:36 as a sign that the Hebrew Scriptures are no longer necessary in the believing community, such an interpretation cannot be sustained in view of continued reference to them in Acts. Even so, the disappearance signifies that Jesus must not be viewed as an appendix to Jewish belief or an addition to law and prophets. He is their fulfillment and, as such, he stands superior to them.

**Luke 16:16–17.**    Luke 16:16 makes a point similar to that made in 9:28–36. Here Jesus announces that "the law and the prophets were in effect until John came; since then the good news of the kingdom of God is proclaimed, and everyone tries to enter it by force." But the point seems to be taken back in the following verse: "It is easier for heaven and earth to pass away, than for one stroke of a letter in the law to be dropped" (16:17).

The difficulties in these verses are well known. Hans Conzelmann claimed that Luke 16:16 was pivotal for understanding Luke's *heilsgeschichtliche* approach.[26] The verse itself is, according to Conzelmann, a clue to the reader that John the Baptist marked the end of the period of Israel. In Luke, John does not belong to the period of Jesus, since he does not preach the gospel. Conzelmann further claims that, in Luke's view, the period of Israel is marked by law and prophets. But he does not clarify the meaning of 16:17, which seems to assert the permanence of law. Conzelmann writes:

The Law prepares the way for the Gospel just as Israel does for the Church and her mission. It is an element belonging to redemptive history, not something timeless. This is emphatically expressed in Luke xvi, 16, where the connection of the two aspects becomes clear, that of the Law as an epoch, and of the Law as a component part of Scripture (see also Acts xiii, 15). Luke xvi, 17 then goes on to express the 'permanence' of the Law, the fact that its position is one of principle. In other words, the epochs are separate, but there is no break between them, for the elements in the former one persist into the next.[27]

But the distinction between law as an epoch and law as a part of scripture seems to stretch the meaning of the Lukan text. The phrase "law and prophets" in 16:16 almost certainly designates the Hebrew Scriptures, as it does in several Qumran texts.[28] Further, no problem is answered by distinguishing between the epoch of the law and the principle of the law.

I. Howard Marshall has a more coherent discussion about these verses.[29] He rejects the idea that Jesus has pronounced the Mosaic law as having permanent validity. "Rather, the saying is to be understood as Jesus' rhetorical stress on the permanence of the law, but of the law as transformed and fulfilled in his own teaching."[30] Marshall further says that 16:17 "indicates that for Luke the validity of the law and prophets has not ended; it is the activity which produced them which has ended."[31] But Marshall's argument is not finally convincing. It forces us to imagine that Luke thought of Jesus' teaching as law, a concept that is not otherwise suggested in Luke-Acts. And it requires us to provide for the word *nomos* in 16:17 a meaning that is sharply different from its meaning in 16:16, while the Lukan text itself suggests no difference in meaning.

Rather than rushing to find a rational solution to the apparent contradictions in these verses, it may be better simply to let them stand in tension. While Luke 16:16 announces the end of a period of law and prophecy, verse 17 announces the continuing validity of the law. It is precisely in these verses that Lukan ambivalence about the Hebrew Scriptures is most striking. But it is not only here that it is apparent. For while 16:16 announces the end of prophecy with John the Baptist, in 7:26 John himself is said to be a prophet, and more than a prophet. Moreover, several statements imply that Jesus is to be conceived of as a prophet (4:24) and will suffer the fate of the prophets (11:49, 50; 13:33, 34). At the same time there is a suggestion that the popular perception of Jesus as

prophet (9:8, 9:19) is inadequate. And perhaps the statement that
John is more than a prophet is meant to put a damper on such per-
ceptions of him. In any event, Luke displays a profound ambivalence at this point, in announcing the end of prophecy on the one
hand and in using the title for John and Jesus on the other. The
ambivalence in regard to law is even stronger. While law characterizes an era that came to an end with John, it nevertheless has a
permanent validity. The implied author in this section of Luke suggests no way to resolve this ambivalence, and hence no solution is
available to the implied reader.

**Luke 16:19–31.**   We have already observed several places in
this section of Luke where Abraham is treated with respect and affection. Among the references to Abraham, perhaps the most interesting appears in the story of the rich man and Lazarus. In the
story, told by Jesus, both a rich man and a poor man have died.
Lazarus, the poor man, has been taken by the angels to Abraham's
bosom, while the rich man is in torment in Hades. Although there
is an impassable gulf between the two locations, it is possible to
see and to hear across the divide. The rich man pleads with Abraham to send Lazarus to provide mercy and relief from suffering.
But Abraham replies that the rich man has already received good
things, while Lazarus has suffered, and he points out that it is not
possible to cross the chasm between the two locations. Consequently, the rich man pleads that Lazarus be sent to warn his five
brothers, but Abraham rejects this request as well. He first states
that the brothers have Moses and the prophets, and his words suggest that this should be sufficient. But the rich man contends that
it is not enough; rather, "if some one goes to them from the dead,
they will repent" (16:30). But Abraham has the last word, "if they
do not listen to Moses and the prophets, neither will they be convinced even if someone rises from the dead" (16:31).

Abraham is pictured as holding the dead Lazarus in his bosom, an image with nuances of special affection.[32] Lazarus as a
character is important in showing that, for Luke, poor and oppressed Jews will have a special place in the coming judgment.
Throughout Luke's gospel, the poor, the sick, and the excluded are
the special recipients of Jesus' benefits. But in the parable in Luke
16, Abraham is also the one to whom the dead rich man prays from
Hades. Even in Hades, Abraham can be seen and heard. Further,
the rich man addresses Abraham as "father" (16:24, 27, 30), and
Abraham calls the rich man "child" (16:25).[33]

But there would appear to be more here than a condemnation of the wealthy who have not properly read Moses and the prophets.[34] Since the reader already knows that it is in Jesus that the scriptures have been fulfilled (Luke 4:16–30; 9:28–36), he also knows that a proper reading of Moses and the prophets necessarily points in the direction of Jesus. The response of Abraham in these verses is aimed not only at the unheeding wealthy but also at all those who read Moses and the prophets with no understanding of coming judgment. Clearly the allusion in verses 30 and 31 is to the resurrection of Jesus and the failure of many people to accept it as a warning of impending judgment. The reader would be prepared to understand the reference by the prediction in 9:22 and to conclude that not even the resurrection of Jesus could convince those who improperly read Moses and the prophets. Thus the implied reader of this story would be led to conclude that, although the Hebrew Scriptures, when properly interpreted, point to Jesus and although they are sufficient in and of themselves to effect repentance, there are some who do not read the scriptures properly. These people cannot even be convinced by the resurrection of Jesus, the one who fulfills the scriptures.

Who, in Luke's account, are those who read the scriptures improperly? In the context of Luke 16, the parable is ostensibly told for the sake of Pharisees, who in 16:14 are described as lovers of money. Since the parable includes attention to the attitude of the rich toward the poor, that assumption is plausible. Furthermore, the reference to resurrection and the use of the phrase "Moses and the prophets," in a context that assumes the authority of these documents, would be appropriate in anti-Pharisaic polemic. But it is difficult to think that only Pharisees are included among those who fail to interpret the scriptures correctly. It seems more appropriate to think of any wealthy persons who, though they know the scriptures, nevertheless reject Jesus, and it is difficult to say whether it is wealth or misinterpretation of scripture that is the more serious impediment. It seems fair to observe that a Christian reader of Luke in the late first or early second century would probably have no difficulty in determining that it is the unbelieving Jews who have misinterpreted their scriptures and hence have also rejected the risen Jesus. Indeed, it is appropriate to recall that, in Luke 4:25–27, when Jesus gave an illustration of the proper way to read scripture, by his interpretation of the stories of Elijah and Elisha, he was rejected by his Jewish compatriots.

Luke 16:19–31 is significant in amplifying the kind of ambivalence that we saw in 16:16–17. After learning that, although Torah and prophets continue only to John, there is nevertheless a continuing validity to Torah, the reader now discovers that, although Torah and prophets are sufficient to effect repentance, there is nevertheless no hope for those who misinterpret them.

### THE ROLE OF JERUSALEM

As we have already seen, many passages in the central section of Luke point toward the city of Jerusalem. That Jesus' ultimate destination is Jerusalem is repeatedly noted in Luke 9:51–19:44, and the reader is shown that the death of Jesus will occur there. Two pericopes, one near the midpoint of the journey to Jerusalem (13:31–35) and the other at the end of this section of the gospel (19:41–44), reveal little about the role of Jerusalem in Jewish life but nevertheless contain powerful suggestions about the Christian view of the city and its people.

In Luke 13:31–35, certain Pharisees warn Jesus of the menace of Herod, and Jesus responds that he intends to be "casting out demons and performing cures today and tomorrow, and the third day I finish my work" (13:32). He states as a general principle that "it is impossible for a prophet to be killed outside of Jerusalem" (13:33). Then in poignant words, filled with allusions to the Hebrew Scriptures, he speaks of Jerusalem as the special object of his love and as resistant to it.[35] Its citizens kill prophets and messengers and refuse the care and concern that has been offered. In the final verse of this saying, Jesus proclaims that Jerusalem will not see him until the people say, "Blessed is the one who comes in the name of the Lord" (13:35). The implied reader would probably be deeply impressed by the stress here on the persistent divine love directed toward Jerusalem and the equally persistent recalcitrance of its citizens. One should also note that 13:35 anticipates Jesus' entry into Jerusalem, narrated in 19:37–40. In the latter passage, Jesus' disciples greet him with the words, "Blessed is the king who comes in the name of the Lord!" (19:38). The prediction of 13:35 has not, however, been literally fulfilled in 19:38, since it is not the citizens of Jerusalem who so joyously welcome Jesus, but his own disciples. Do the disciples stand for the people of the city, or, what is more likely, is the response of Jerusalem to be contrasted with that of the disciples?

That the second alternative is more likely than the first is seen in Jesus' words at the very end of this section of Luke (19:41–44).

Here, as he approaches the city, he weeps and expresses the wish that "you, even you, had only recognized on this day the things that make for peace! But now they are hidden from your eyes" (19:42). Then he goes on to predict, in some detail, the siege and destruction of the city and to link these events with the city's failure to welcome him: "Because you did not recognize the time of your visitation from God" (19:44). In no uncertain terms the implied reader is prepared for the rejection of Jesus in Jerusalem and led to associate historical disaster with that rejection.[36] In the following chapter, we shall see how this expectation of doom works itself out in the narratives dealing with Jesus in Jerusalem.

## CONCLUSION

The section of Luke that deals with the ministry of Jesus in Galilee, Samaria, and Judea is rich in images of Judaism and pregnant with implications for Jewish-Christian relationships. There are broad areas of agreement between Jesus and his Jewish audiences, but there is little of the positive approach that dominated Luke 1–2. Instead, the character of Luke 3:1–19:44 is one of controversy between Jesus and his various audiences. In the episodes that depict the controversies, images of synagogues and Pharisees suffer. Synagogues are pictured as places in which opposition to Jesus is marshaled. Pharisees are inflexible and hypocritical in their legal interpretations and in their leadership of the people. Jesus and the Pharisees part company especially on issues relating to Sabbath observance and the segregation of the observant and the nonobservant.

The image of the law and prophets has a profound ambiguity in this section of Luke. There is no question about their authority for both Jesus and his Jewish audiences. But for Luke, their function is to point forward to Jesus, and the ministry of Jesus is their fulfillment. Although a proper reading of these scriptures would be sufficient for salvation and, hence, would make even the ministry of Jesus unnecessary, unbelieving Jews do not engage in this kind of reading. Nothing, not even the resurrection of Jesus, convinces them. Further, the disappearance of Moses and Elijah at the transfiguration account suggest that, once the law and prophets have been fulfilled, their authority retreats before that of Jesus. But Jesus nevertheless affirms the continuing validity of *nomos* in Luke 16:17.

Finally, the implied reader is presented with a picture of Jerusalem as the object of God's love and concern and as refusing

God's prophets and messengers. Its destruction is linked with its
rejection of the prophets, Jesus par excellence.

NOTES

1. In Luke 4:14 Jesus comes into Galilee after the temptations in the wilderness of
   Judea and in Jerusalem. He is in Nazareth and Capernaum, the country of the
   Gerasenes, Bethsaida, and several unnamed places ostensibly in Galilee. Jerusalem and Judea seem to lie in the distance, not just geographically but also in
   terms of significance. It should, however, be noted that at least on one occasion
   there are some persons who have come from Judea and Jerusalem to hear Jesus
   (5:17) and in one verse Jesus "continued proclaiming the message in the synagogues of Judea" (4:44). Note, however, the textual variants at this point.
   Since Luke had said in 4:14 that Jesus came into Galilee, the reading "synagogues of Galilee" in 4:44 is probably a correction. See Bruce M. Metzger, *A
   Textual Commentary on the Greek New Testament*, 137f.
2. On the limits and character of this section, see Joseph B. Tyson, *The Death of
   Jesus in Luke-Acts*, 28, note 53. In this subdivision Luke frequently reminds the
   reader that the trip is to end in Jerusalem (9:51, 53; 13:4, 22, 33f.; 17:11; 18:31;
   19:11, 28, 41). Few references to specific locations along the way are contained
   in the travel account. Most are vague, such as, "a village of the Samaritans"
   (9:52), "a village" (10:38; 17:12), "a certain place" (11:1), "through one town
   and village after another" (13:22), "the village ahead of you" (19:30). In 17:11,
   we have the geographically incomprehensible, "region between Samaria and
   Galilee." But specific references begin to occur as Jesus approaches Jerusalem:
   Jericho (18:35; 19:1); Bethphage, Bethany, and the path down from the Mount
   of Olives (19:29); and "the descent of the Mount of Olives" (19:37).
3. See, e.g., Luke 4:15; 5:1, 15; 6:17; 8:19, 40; 9:43; 15:1; 18:43; see also 7:29–30.
4. Although a number of attempts have been made to show that the reading from
   Isaiah was the prescribed reading for that day, Joseph A. Fitzmyer is probably
   correct in saying that "the evidence of a cycle of prophetic readings in first-
   century Palestine is debatable." *The Gospel According to Luke (I–IX)*, 531.
5. See, e.g., Sharon H. Ringe, *Jesus, Liberation, and the Biblical Jubilee: Images for
   Ethics and Christology*.
6. The first Lukan narrative about Jesus in Capernaum follows this incident in
   4:31–37, and so it is quite correct to observe that Jesus has not yet done anything in Capernaum. The apparent problem has sometimes been taken as a
   sign of some clumsiness on Luke's part and has sometimes been explained by
   reference to Luke's sources. Mark 1:21–28 reports the incident at Capernaum
   that Luke has in 4:31–37, and, on the hypothesis that Luke used Mark as a
   source, Luke would have had Mark's report of the Capernaum incident in
   mind as he wrote 4:23. But on this hypothesis Luke 4:23 must probably be
   taken as a Lukan composition, since it was not taken over from either Mark or
   Q. Furthermore, it should be noted that the statement of Jesus in 4:23 is a prediction (*ereite*, you will say). There is in it a note of anticipation: this will be the
   reaction of the Nazareth congregation when it hears of the events yet to be narrated. On any source hypothesis the words of Jesus in Luke 4:23 contain a subtle implication of his omniscience.
7. See, e.g., the essays in Walther Eltester, ed., *Jesus in Nazareth*, by August Stro-
   bel, Robert C. Tannehill, and Walther Eltester.

8. Gerhard Lohfink, *Die Sammlung Israels: Eine Untersuchung zur lukanischen Ekklesiologie*, 46. Jack T. Sanders adds that it is also programmatic in showing "how God's will was carried out in the Jewish rejection of salvation and in the consequent Gentile mission" (*The Jews in Luke-Acts*, 168). See also Sanders, "The Prophetic Use of the Scriptures in Luke-Acts."

9. James A. Sanders, "From Isaiah 61 to Luke 4."

10. Ibid., 95.

11. Ibid., 97.

12. Ibid., 99.

13. Ibid.

14. A number of scholars would reject an interpretation of this sermon that would see in it a challenge of the traditional place of the Jewish people. Robert L. Brawley, e.g., states that the citation of Elijah and Elisha puts Jesus in a line with these venerable prophets but suggests neither the rejection of the Jews nor the mission to the Gentiles. See his *Luke-Acts and the Jews: Conflict, Apology, and Conciliation*, 6–27. Similarly Sharon H. Ringe says, "The Elijah and Elisha traditions are not stories of God's or the prophet's rejection of Israel in favor of the Gentiles. Rather, each story tells of the prophet being given a special responsibility of bringing help or blessing to a Gentile, which has the result that Israelites and Gentiles both benefit. These stories thus would provide a vehicle by which Luke can develop an issue of great importance to his theology, namely, the issue of Jewish-Gentile relations or even reconciliation" (*Jesus*, 107). See also L. C. Crockett, "Luke 4:25–27 and Jewish-Gentile Relations in Luke-Acts." Clearly, one function of the Lukan passage is to present Jesus in the role of a prophet and, specifically, a prophet like Elijah or Elisha. One mark of a prophet is his lack of acceptance in his home country. But the interpretations of Brawley, Ringe, and Crockett ignore the specific references to the activity of the prophets that makes them unacceptable, namely their neglect of needy Israelites and their turning to Gentiles. It is this very activity that calls into question the privileged position of Israel.

15. For other works on Luke 4:16–30 see Bruce Chilton, "Announcement in Nazara: An Analysis of Luke 4:16–21"; David Hill, "The Rejection of Jesus at Nazzareth"; and Waldemar Schmeichel, "Christian Prophecy in Lukan Thought: Luke 4:16–30 as a Point of Departure."

16. The Temple almost totally disappears from view until Jesus enters it in 19:45. It is the setting for one of the three temptations of Jesus (Luke 4:9) and for one of the parables (18:10). But after Jesus comes into Galilee in 4:14, the Temple does not serve as the setting for any narrative of Jesus' early ministry. If the implied reader is not already expected to know that there is only one Jewish Temple and that it is located in Jerusalem, the Lukan text would still convey this concept. When Jesus is in Galilee or between Galilee and Jerusalem, the Temple is not a matter of consideration. It only figures in those narratives that are set in Jerusalem, and in the central sections of Luke, the place of the Temple is assumed by the various synagogues.

17. Although Luke places Jesus in a number of synagogues at unspecified locations, he speaks explicitly of a synagogue in Nazareth (4:16), one in Capernaum (4:31, 33; 7:1, 5), and of synagogues in Judea (4:44). The impression of an indeterminate number of synagogues in Jewish territories is thus quite clear.

18. For an analysis of the Lukan treatment of Pharisees and those associated with them, see Tyson, *Death of Jesus*, 64–72.

19. See, e.g., Luke 5:17–26, 29–32; 6:1–5, 6–11; 11:53–54; 13:10–17; 15:1–7.

20. I. Howard Marshall notes that Luke 4:16-30 is the oldest extant account of a synagogue service. See *The Gospel of Luke: A Commentary on the Greek Text*, 181.

21. See, e.g., Rudolf Bultmann, *The History of the Synoptic Tradition*, 259, and the scholars cited by Bultmann.

78 Images of Judaism in Luke-Acts

22. Joseph A. Fitzmyer, "The Composition of Luke, Chapter 9," in *Perspectives on Luke-Acts*, 149.
23. See also Fitzmyer, *Luke I–IX*, 791–804.
24. The extent to which the figures of Elijah and especially Moses have affected the transfiguration narrative should not be discounted. I. H. Marshall calls attention to a number of resemblances between this narrative and those of Moses: Moses was accompanied by three companions when he approached Yahweh (Exod 24:1, 9), and Jesus is accompanied by three disciples in the transfiguration story. (Marshall fails to note that Moses was also accompanied by seventy elders, see Exod 24:1, 9.) Moses' face shined after talking with Yahweh (Exod 34:29), and Jesus' appearance was altered while he was praying. The cloud is a sign of divine presence at a number of points in Exodus (e.g., 16:10; 19:9; 24:15–18; 33:9–11) and in Luke's transfiguration story. The command of God, "Listen to him," reflects Deut 18:15, "The Lord your God will raise up for you a prophet like me [Moses] from among your own people; you shall heed such a prophet." See Marshall, *Luke: A Commentary*, 380–89. See Acts 3:22 for another reflection of Deut 18:15 in the Lukan writing.
25. Peter's proposal to build three booths is, as Marshall says, "perhaps the most obscure in the whole story" (Marshall, *Luke: A Commentary*, 386). Fitzmyer is probably close to being correct when he relates the proposal to the Festival of Booths (*succot*) and says, "Peter seems to liken his experience on the mountain with Jesus transfigured to the joy of this festival" (Fitzmyer, *Luke I–IX*, 801).
26. See Hans Conzelmann, *The Theology of St. Luke*.
27. Ibid., 160f.
28. For a list of references see Joseph A. Fitzmyer, *The Gospel According to Luke X–XXIV*, 1116.
29. See Marshall, *Luke: A Commentary*, 626–30.
30. Ibid., 627.
31. Ibid., 628.
32. In 4 Macc 13:17, the seven Jewish martyrs are said to be comforted by the thought that Abraham, Isaac, and Jacob will receive them after their deaths. Cf. Luke 13:28, where Jesus states that Abraham, Isaac, and Jacob, together with the prophets, are in the kingdom of God.
33. Although he does not explicitly deal with Luke 16:19–31, Nils A. Dahl cites Luke 16:24, along with 1:73 and Acts 7:2, as supporting his contention that Abraham is considered to be the father of Jews but not Christians in Luke-Acts. See "The Story of Abraham in Luke-Acts."
34. Most modern commentators have followed Bultmann in observing that there are two points in this story. He says, "Whereas vv. 19–26 is meant to console the poor, or alternatively warn the rich by pointing to the equalization in the world to come, vv. 27–31 says that Moses and the prophets have made God's will sufficiently plain, so that there is no need to ask for a miracle of the resurrection of a dead person in order to induce belief" (*Synoptic Traditions* 196). Bultmann states that the two points vie against one another but that Luke received the story in its present form (ibid., 178). J. Duncan M. Derrett has, however, suggested that an ideological unity lies behind the whole of Luke 16 and that the movement of ideas here has parallels in midrashic texts. See "Fresh Light on St. Luke XVI: II. Dives and Lazarus and the Preceding Sayings."
35. See David L. Tiede, *Prophecy and History in Luke-Acts*, pp. 70–78.
36. Jack T. Sanders states that the parable of the pounds (Luke 19:11–27) also contributes to the developing image of Jerusalem. See Sanders, "The Parable of the Pounds and Lucan Anti-Semitism." For a different treatment of this parable, see Luke Timothy Johnson, "The Lukan Kingship Parable (Lk. 19:11–27)."

5

# Jesus in Jerusalem

(Luke 19:45–24:53)

The section of Luke that tells of Jesus in Jerusalem culminates in the passion narrative and emphasizes the part played by the Jewish leaders in bringing about the death of Jesus. In comparison with Matthew and Mark, however, the Gospel of Luke lacks some of the most virulent anti-Jewish statements. The Jewish people do not shout, "His blood be on us and on our children!" as they do in Matt 27:25. Luke does not present Jesus' hearing before the Jewish Sanhedrin (Luke 22:66–71) as a formal trial, with specific charges, witnesses, and conviction. But in the trial before Pilate he takes special pains to list specific charges on which Jesus was tried (23:2) and to make it clear that these were political charges brought in a Roman court, not religious charges appropriate to be heard by a Jewish body. He alone introduces a hearing before Herod as part of the proceedings (23:6–12), and Herod is shown to be a Jewish ruler who judges Jesus to be innocent.

Despite these variations between Luke and the other Synoptic Gospels, Luke does not sufficiently weaken the impression that, although Jesus died as a result of a Roman form of execution, it was the Jewish people and their leaders who brought about the execution. After the hearing before the Sanhedrin, its chief priests, elders, and scribes brought charges against Jesus before Pilate. Luke has carefully shown that the charges brought against Jesus at this point are false, and he stresses the innocent verdict that Pilate himself reaches.[1] But it is the chief priests and their associates, as well as the people, who insist that Jesus is guilty and should be put to death. To be sure, an attentive reader easily gains the impression that the Roman governor, Pilate, is a weak and pliable character. What kind of governor repeatedly asserts the innocence of the accused, resolves to release him, and then consents to his execution? But, as Pilate comes off looking weak, the chief priests appear to be irredeemably unjust and malevolent. Luke emphasizes this image at the end of the Roman trial, where he avoids saying that Pilate gave the order for Jesus' crucifixion and states instead that Pilate turned Jesus over to the will of his accusers (Luke 23:24). At one point, he even counts the Jewish people among those who bring charges against Jesus (23:13), but for the most part the opponents in this section of Luke are the chief priests and their associates, that is, elders and scribes.[2]

### THE PARABLE OF THE VINEYARD AND LUKE'S SECTION ON JESUS IN JERUSALEM

The parable of the vineyard (Luke 20:9–19) brings together a number of major themes that affect Luke's images of Jewish religious life. It also serves as a key to an understanding of the entire section on Jesus in Jerusalem, including Luke's passion narrative. The parable is found also in Matt 21:33–46 and Mark 12:1–12, in the same general context, but Luke has some distinctive features.[3]

The parable occupies a strategic position in Luke. After Jesus has driven away the merchants (Luke 19:45–46), he begins his teaching in the Temple (19:47–48). The first pericope that gives the substance of his teaching is a controversial dialogue between Jesus and the priestly leaders, who ask him about his authority (20:1–8). Jesus answers with a counterquestion about the authority of John the Baptist. The parable of the vineyard follows immediately and in context should serve as an amplified answer to the question of the chief priests and their associates.[4] Ostensibly the parable is addressed to the people (laos, 20:9), but the priestly leaders are also included in the audience and are its chief targets, as 20:19 makes clear. The parable is followed in Luke by a series of controversial dialogues that serve to inform the reader about the teaching of Jesus in the Jerusalem Temple.

The parable is about a vineyard, an owner, and some tenants. The owner allowed tenants to use the vineyard for a long period of time before requiring them to pay rent. But when the time came, he sent a servant, who was beaten by the tenants and sent back with no rent. This happened twice more, and the owner decided to send his son, thinking that he would be respected by the tenants. The tenants, however, regarded the son as heir and thought that they would receive the vineyard upon his death.[5] So they threw him out of the vineyard and killed him. At the end of the parable Jesus asserts that the owner will "come and destroy those tenants and give the vineyard to others" (Luke 20:16). The listeners, presumably including the people, scribes, and chief priests, find the conclusion unacceptable, and Jesus quotes a scripture from Ps 118:22: "The stone that the builders rejected has become the cornerstone" (Luke 20:17). The quotation, which serves to interpret the parable, connects the stone with the son of the vineyard owner. This one, who was rejected by the tenants, has become the cornerstone of the vineyard. Then, Jesus continues with an additional interpretation of the scripture from Psalm 118 and states that the stone will crush anyone who falls on it and anyone on whom it falls.[6] At the conclusion Luke notes that the scribes and chief priests recognized that the parable had been told against them (*pros autous*) and reaffirmed their intention to capture Jesus. They were, however, prevented from doing so at this time because of the people, presumably because of Jesus' popular support.

Commentators generally recognize allegorical elements in the parable of the vineyard.[7] The vineyard is a well-known metaphor for Israel in the Hebrew Scriptures, in passages where God is taken to be the one who planted it and expects to receive its produce.[8] In Luke also we may take the owner to be God and the vineyard to be Israel, in the sense of the people of God. The vineyard may also symbolize Jerusalem as the city of God's people. Although the Lukan Jesus explicitly predicts the destruction of the city (Luke 21:20–24), there is much in the gospel that would evoke the kinds of positive feelings that are appropriate as expressions about the vineyard in the allegory. Although Jerusalem is the city that kills prophets, the Lukan Jesus expresses a special feeling for it (13:34–35). Just as he is about to enter the city, he weeps over its future disaster (19:41–44). On the way to the place of crucifixion he has a special warning for the "daughters of Jerusalem" (23:28–31). Furthermore, in the Lukan context, the vineyard also symbolizes the Temple. The parable is placed by Luke within a large group of teachings that Jesus delivered in the Temple (19:47–21:38), and in its context it is explicitly directed to the scribes and chief priests (20:19), the latter of whom would be most closely associated with the Temple. Thus the best strategy for interpreting the parable is to think of the vineyard as symbolizing a complex of ideas including Israel as God's people, Jerusalem as his city, and the Temple as his shrine. Any one of the three terms that express aspects of Jewish religious life—Israel, Jerusalem, Temple—may be used to express the entire complex of ideas.

The identification in the parable of the rejected one as the owner's beloved son (Luke 20:13) clearly serves to show that it is Jesus himself who is intended here (cf., e.g., Luke 3:22; 9:35, where Jesus is designated by a voice from heaven as the beloved son).[9] Thus the parable anticipates Jesus' rejection, execution, and final domination of Israel. Since the parable is told for the sake of the scribes and chief priests, as Luke 20:19 indicates, it is they who should be thought of as the tenants who are responsible for the vineyard.

Thus, Jesus himself is to become the cornerstone of Israel.[10] As the stone he will be the means of punishing those who have opposed him and God. But who then is intended in 20:16, when Jesus says that the vineyard will be given to others? Other priests? Other Jews? Gentiles? It may be tempting at this point to think that Luke here anticipates the Christian mission to the Gentiles, which will be narrated in Acts.[11] Further, if Luke 20:16 means to suggest that the vineyard as Jerusalem will be turned over to Gentiles, there is a tie-in with 21:24, which speaks about a domination of the city by Gentiles. But whether Gentiles or Jews are intended in 20:16, the implication of the allegory is that Jesus, the beloved but rejected Son of God, will become the cornerstone of Israel, and his followers will replace the deposed tenants, the chief priests.

Thus we may read the allegory in the following way: although God entrusted the chief priests with responsibility for Israel, including Jerusalem and the Temple, they have not fulfilled their responsibilities.[12] God has sent other messengers who have not been successful, but now he has sent Jesus, as his beloved son, who will attempt to reorient Israel. But he too will be rejected by the chief priests and executed.[13] God will, however, destroy the priests and establish Jesus as the cornerstone of Israel. He will become a means of punishment for those who oppose him (20:18), and his followers will take over the responsibilities of the deposed priests.

Understood in this way, the parable of the vineyard serves as the key to an understanding of the entire section of Luke on Jesus in Jerusalem.[14] Indeed, this entire section may be read as Jesus' failed attempt to reorient Israel, in particular the Temple, and the consequences of this failure. The way in which the parable functions to interpret this section of Luke requires some discussion.

### Jesus' Attempt to Reorient Israel

In the parable the vineyard symbolizes Israel, including Jerusalem and the Temple. But in Luke's section on Jesus in Jerusalem, the Temple receives most of the attention. Immediately upon his arrival in Jerusalem, Jesus enters the Temple, drives out the merchants, and begins to teach in the Temple under the watchful and suspicious eyes of the chief priests. In the first pericope in this section (Luke 19:45–46), we see Jesus in conflict over the meaning and use of the Temple, a conflict that is illuminated by his use of scripture. Quoting from Isa 56:7, Jesus claims that the purpose of the Temple is to be a house of prayer, and, in an allusion to Jer 7:11, he says that the sellers have made it a den of robbers. It is notable that Luke omits from the Isaiah quotation a significant phrase. Isa 56:7 has, "for my house shall be called a house of prayer for all peoples" (LXX: *ho gar oikos mou oikos proseuchēs klēthēsetai pasin tois ethnesin*).[15] Fitzmyer suggests that, although the reason for the omission is obscure, Luke (as well as Matthew) was "aware that the Temple no longer existed, and hence for them it could scarcely still be regarded as a house of prayer of all the nations."[16] Marshall writes, "Luke omits reference to the gentiles, probably because he is aware that in fact the temple did not become such, and he did not want to make Jesus the author of false prophecy."[17] Since we cannot be certain about Luke's source material, we probably should not put a great deal of stress on his omission of *pasin tois ethnesin*. Further, it is by no means clear that either implied author or implied reader would have been aware of the omission. But we must say that the quotation as it stands in Luke does not imply that, even in divine intention, the Jerusalem Temple was to be a place of prayer for Gentiles. It will be safe to observe that, for the Gospel of Luke, the Temple is a Jewish institution, a place of prayer for Jews, although no explicit stress should be placed on any exclusivistic claims for it.

The major reason for the quotation of scripture here is to call attention to the contrast between prayer and robbery as two functions of the Temple. Beyond this there is some lack of precision about the way in which the quotation functions in Luke's text. One way of reading it would be to understand the quotation from Isaiah as expressing the will of God for the Temple in Hebrew history: "God intended for the Temple to be a house of prayer, but it has not been one, since you merchants have made it a den of robbers." The emphasis then would be on the failure of the Temple to function in the way in which God intended. In this reading, the image of the Temple would be one of disappointing failure. Nuances of poignancy and regret would accompany the words of Jesus here. But another reading would take *estai* as a future tense from the perspective of Jesus. In this reading, the words of Isaiah would be understood as a statement for a very specific future, that is, for the time of Jesus himself. To bring out this meaning, we may paraphrase Jesus' words in the following way: "Although you merchants have made the Temple a den of robbers, I will make it a house of prayer, as scripture predicted it would become."

The action of Jesus that accompanies the quotations from scripture would seem to favor the second way of understanding his words. First, Jesus, immediately upon his entry into the Temple, drives out the merchants (Luke 19:45), and the quotations are intended to defend his action. Thus by driving out the merchants, Jesus is fulfilling the prediction about the Temple given in Isa 56:7. Second, after this act of cleansing, Jesus begins his practice of teaching daily in the Temple (19:47). The Temple thereafter serves as the locus of his teaching until we reach 21:38. Hans Conzelmann's comments are to the point: "The Entry [of Jesus into the Temple] is not an eschatological event, but the inauguration of the period of the Passion which is now dawning (we are obliged to speak of such a period)."[18] "In Luke it is not a question of the eschatological end of the Temple, but of its cleansing; in other words, Jesus prepares it as somewhere he can stay, and from now on he occupies it as a place belonging to him."[19] Jesus is, therefore, fulfilling the role assigned in the parable to the vineyard owner's beloved son; he goes to the Temple in the attempt to reorient it toward God and to make it a house of prayer.

It is trivial to maintain that, because Jesus subsequently teaches, the Temple has not become a place of prayer but a place of teaching. In any event, the lengthy bit of Lukan material dealing with Jesus in the Temple cannot finally be described as a successful transformation of it, for two reasons. First, the teaching of Jesus in the Temple is set by Luke within a context of controversy and conflict. Second, Jesus himself is rejected by those who have charge of the Temple.

### The Rejection and Execution of Jesus

Although Luke uses the setting of the Jerusalem Temple to exhibit teachings of Jesus, he also employs these occasions to call attention to the opposition of the priestly leaders. Indeed, the entire section of teaching is introduced with a significant statement of opposition (Luke 19:47–48), a statement that, in different ways, is repeated three more times (20:1,19; 22:2). We learn here that, as Jesus teaches daily in the Temple, "the chief priests, the scribes, and the leaders of the people [*hoi prōtoi tou laou*] kept looking for a way to kill him" (19:47). But, adds Luke, they were prevented from achieving their purpose because of the attraction of the people to Jesus. The Temple thus emerges in these scenes as a place where an itinerant teacher, who has previously come into conflict with Pharisees in synagogues, can teach in public, initially with the grudging toleration of malevolent priests. But these priestly leaders are not silently lurking in dark corners. They attempt to find ways to bring public embarrassment to Jesus and to drive a wedge between him and his popular support, and they attempt to entrap him in his teaching. In 20:1–8, they ask directly about his source of authority; and in 20:19–26, they send spies who ask him about paying tribute to Caesar. Likewise, Sadducees attempt to engage him in controversy about resurrection in 20:27–40.

Since the implied reader has already learned to anticipate the opposition of chief priests and their associates (Luke 9:22), the role they play in the passion narrative is no surprise. Though prevented from capturing Jesus as he taught in the Temple, the chief priests and *stratēgoi* contract with Judas and agree to pay him to act as traitor (22:3–6).[20] Thereafter, Jesus' arrest is accomplished by the Temple authorities (chief priests, *stratēgoi* of the Temple, and elders), with the aid of Judas (22:47–53), and Jesus is held overnight at the house of the high priest (22:54).

The following morning he is examined by "their council," which is made up of elders, chief priests, and scribes (Luke 22:66). Although it is ostensibly an examination of his teaching, the members of the Sanhedrin actually are concerned with Jesus' concept of his own identity. There are, in fact, only two questions: Are you the Christ? Are you the Son of God?[21] The second question directly reflects the parable of the vineyard, in which Jesus says that the owner's beloved son comes to collect the proper rents. In this light it is appropriate that the chief priests, who know the parable had been told for their sake, ask if Jesus is the owner's beloved son. Although Jesus' answer, "You say that I am" (22:70), is ambiguous, the response of the members of the Sanhedrin implies that they understood it as affirmative.[22] They conclude that no

witnesses are needed and that Jesus has made a full confession of
his guilt. Although this session of the Sanhedrin cannot be called
a trial in any formal sense, it functions in Luke as the official rejection of Jesus by the Jewish priestly leaders. These leaders then
take him before Pilate, accuse him of violating Roman law, and
take the leading role in pressuring Pilate (and Herod) to convict
Jesus of treason.[23]

The parable of the vineyard is, thus far, a reliable guide to the
passion narrative in Luke. To understand it as a guide to this entire
section of Luke is to understand Luke 22:66–71 as the Jewish
priestly leaders' rejection of Jesus as the Christ and as the son of
God. God's beloved son has come to claim what is rightfully due to
God, but he has been rejected and killed by the tenants. His attempt to reclaim the vineyard for its owner has been unsuccessful.

### The Vengeance of God

The parable of the vineyard ends with a threat against the tenants
of the vineyard: the owner will come and destroy them and give
the vineyard to others. Although Luke does not show this particular threat working itself out in explicit ways, there are predictions
of destruction and renewal that reflect the parable. Outside the
parable the Lukan Jesus does not threaten the destruction of the
priestly leaders, but he proclaims the destruction of the Temple
(Luke 21:5–6) and the capture of Jerusalem by Gentiles (21:20–24).
While the destruction of the Temple is stated simply as a prediction and without comment on its theological significance ("the
days will come when not one stone will be left upon another; all
will be thrown down" 21:6), the capture of Jerusalem is described
as a time of divine vengeance or punishment (21:22).[24] Indeed the
greater detail in Luke's version of the prediction of the capture of
Jerusalem is notable, containing references to such events as the
surrounding of the city by armies, the slaughter of its citizens, and
their exile among the Gentiles (cf. 19:41–44).[25] Most interesting is
the statement that Jerusalem will be "trampled on by the Gentiles,
until the times of the Gentiles are fulfilled" (21:24).[26] Might this be
a subtle reminder of Jesus' words about turning the vineyard over
to others (20:16)? To the extent to which for Luke the holy city is
Israel *in nuce*, it is possible to read Luke 21:24 as a fulfillment of
20:16. In this way, the parable would have prepared the reader to
understand the destruction of Jerusalem as the acting out of Jesus'

threats in the parable and its capture by Gentiles as God's turning the vineyard over to others.

Although plausible, this line of interpretation is not finally satisfactory. In the parable, the turning of the vineyard over to others is connected with Jesus' quotation from Psalm 118, and the implication is that God will turn the vineyard over to the new cornerstone, Jesus, and to his followers. Surely it is not the Gentile followers of Jesus who are intended by Luke 20:16, since Luke does not think of the Temple as intended for Gentiles (see 19:46 and the comments above on this verse). If the parable is to be a guide to Luke's section on Jesus in Jerusalem, there must be some indication that, after the execution of Jesus, God turned the Temple over to Jesus and the disciples.

It is possible to read Luke 23:45 as a symbolic and proleptic victory of Jesus over the Temple. The splitting of the curtain of the Temple, along with a solar eclipse, is given as an omen accompanying the death of Jesus. Although the actual meaning of this omen is unclear, it is plausible to understand it as signifying Jesus' reconquest of the Temple of God.[27] Moreover, the Gospel of Luke ends with a note about the occupation of the Temple by Jesus' disciples, who "returned [from Bethany] to Jerusalem with great joy; and they were continually in the temple blessing God" (Luke 24:52–53). In this concluding word of the gospel, Luke seems to claim that Jesus' disciples are those "others" to whom the care of the Temple has been dedicated. Taking 23:45 and 24:53 together, we gain the picture that the death of Jesus has made possible the renewal of the Temple, including a new orientation and a new group of stewards responsible for its care. A reader could come away from the Gospel of Luke with the understanding that the Jewish Temple has now become a house of prayer as God intended, that the old Jewish tenants have been replaced by Christian stewards. The reader would be led to rejoice with those disciples who are occupying the Temple at the end of the gospel. In addition, in the opening chapters of Acts, the followers of Jesus are still meeting in the Temple (Acts 2:46; cf. 3:1–10).

Although, as we shall see in the book of Acts, the followers of Jesus did not finally gain control of the Temple, to say nothing of Jerusalem or Israel, there are suggestions that their dominance over Jewish institutions forms part of the intention of Jesus. The most important of these indications comes in Luke 22:28–30. In

Jesus' discourse with his disciples at the Last Supper he makes the following promise, "You are those who have stood by me in my trials; and I confer on you, just as my Father has conferred on me, a kingdom, so that you may eat and drink at my table in my kingdom, and you will sit on thrones judging the twelve tribes of Israel" (Luke 22:28–30). There is a partial parallel to this saying in Matt 19:28, but in a different context. Although the saying does not explicitly speak of the followers of Jesus as in some way inheriting the Temple, it nevertheless emphasizes the theme of Christian dominance over Jewish institutions. In other words, the saying confirms the threat in Luke 20:16 that the vineyard will be given to others. Fitzmyer suggests that Luke uses the concept of judging here in the OT sense of ruling, as indicated by the reference to the disciples sitting on thrones.[28] Note should also be taken of Luke 12:32, where Jesus grants the kingdom of the Father to his followers. If Luke means to suggest that Jesus' followers were destined to assume a position of leadership in Israel's religious life, it is a major problem to account for the fact that, according to his own presentation in Acts, they did not do so.[29] But a closer look at Acts is required in order to address this problem.

## THE ROLE OF SCRIPTURE

We have seen in our study of the earlier sections of Luke's Gospel that the Hebrew Scriptures are never far from the center of attention.[30] We have also seen that for Luke the primary function of the scriptures is to point to Jesus. That theme is present in an emphatic and often explicit way in the section on Jesus in Jerusalem.

A quotation from Ps 118:22 plays a major role in Luke's parable of the vineyard (Luke 20:17), as it does in both Matthew and Mark. In the interpretation of the verse, the rejected stone, ostensibly the son of the vineyard owner, is a means of brutal punishment for the opponents, "Everyone who falls on that stone will be broken to pieces; and it will crush anyone on whom it falls" (20:18). In its present context, the opponents are identified as scribes and chief priests (20:19). Thus the Hebrew Scriptures are used here to underscore the force of God's vengeance and to affirm a form of Christian triumphalism that has nuances of militancy.

Throughout the section on Jesus in Jerusalem, the scriptures are quoted to defend or explain a saying or event. Quotations from Isaiah and Jeremiah are used to explain Jesus' driving the merchants from the Temple. A quotation from Isa 53:12 is used in Luke 22:37 to anticipate Jesus' crucifixion, and here the quotation is sandwiched between two explicit statements, "For I tell you, this scripture must be fulfilled in me . . . and indeed what is written about me is being fulfilled." The words anticipate the story in Luke 23:32–43, in which Jesus is executed between two criminals.

In two pericopes in this section there are allusions to controversies about the interpretation of scripture. In Luke 20:27–40, Sadducees raise with Jesus a question about the interpretation of a Mosaic commandment, Deut 25:5 (cf. Gen 38:8). According to the questioners, a man's obligation to father children with the widow of his brother becomes complicated in the case of seven brothers, each of whom took the same widow as his wife. But the question of the Sadducees is not about the complexity of the commandment but about the resurrection. Indeed, as Luke presents this particular controversy, the purpose of the Sadducees is to raise a serious question about the resurrection. By including in 20:27 the editorial comment that the Sadducees do not believe in resurrection, Luke has supplied a key for the implied reader to interpret this passage. Thus the question of the Sadducees is not to be understood as an honest question about the meaning of scripture but an attempt to trip Jesus up, to trap him in something he might say (cf. Luke 20:20, 26). Their contention is that the scripture, properly interpreted, denies the belief in resurrection. In his response to them, Jesus does not challenge the Sadducaic interpretation of Deuteronomy, nor does he offer an alternative interpretation of the command. Rather, he explains that there is no such thing as marriage in the resurrection. Then in 20:37 he goes to the heart of the matter and asserts that, despite the claims of the Sadducees, the scripture, specifically the Mosaic scripture, affirms the concept of resurrection. "And the fact that the dead are raised Moses himself showed, in the story about the bush, where he speaks of the Lord as the God of Abraham, the God of Issac, and the God of Jacob. Now he is God not of the dead, but of the living; for to him all of them are alive" (Luke 20:37–38).[31] The allusion is to Exod 3:6, and the apparent meaning is that since the Lord, who is speaking to Moses, identifies himself as the God of the three patriarchs, who lived and died long before Moses, and since God cannot be God of the dead, the patriarchs must have been raised from the dead. Thus, even the Mosaic scriptures, when properly interpreted, provide a basis for belief in the resurrection. The passage points to the crucial importance of the interpretation of scripture and to Jesus as the dependable interpreter.

In the pericope that follows, Luke 20:41–44, Jesus himself introduces a problem of interpretation, "How can they say that the Messiah is David's son?" (20:41). The personal pronoun ("they") properly represents the Greek here, where there is no expressed subject. Some commentators conclude that the question is directed against the Sadducees, the most recent group to question Jesus (20:27). But it is more likely that the reference is intended as indefinite, and the question may be paraphrased, "How can it be maintained that the Messiah is David's son?" Over against the contention, Jesus quotes Ps 110:1, in which David, as the putative author of the Psalm, uses the phrase "my lord." Without expressly saying so, the Lukan Jesus assumes that "my Lord" in the Psalm is equivalent to the Messiah. Thus, he says, "David thus calls him Lord; so how can he be his son?" (20:44).[32]

In neither of these passages is it proper to talk about controversies in regard to the interpretation of specific scriptures. It is not the case that Jesus gives one interpretation of passage and his opponents give a different one. Rather the key is in the selection of the passage to quote. In the controversy with the Sadducees, Jesus does not tackle the interpretation of Deut 25:5 but rather quotes Exod 3:6 in defense of belief in the resurrection. Likewise, in Luke 20:41–44 he makes no reference to any scriptures underlying the belief that the Messiah is son of David, but rather quotes one verse from one Psalm that, in his interpretation, questions it. Further, in both cases, the interpretation is brief, consisting of one sentence each, but complex and involving unspoken assumptions. Moses' authorship of Exodus and David's authorship of the Psalms are assumed. The words of "the Lord" in the Psalm, "Sit at my right hand, until I make your enemies your footstool," are assumed to be addressed to the Messiah, even if the title does not appear in the passage.

Finally, the Gospel of Luke concludes with a series of claims about the fulfillment of scripture.[33] But what is notable here is that no specific scripture is quoted or alluded to. The risen Christ upbraids Cleopas and the unnamed disciple for being slow to believe all the writings of the prophets. He says, "Was it not necessary that the Messiah should suffer these things and then enter into his glory?" (Luke 24:26).[34] And Luke states that "beginning with

Moses and all the prophets, he interpreted to them the things about himself in all the scriptures" (24:27).[35] In the recognition scene that follows, the disciples recall that Jesus "was opening the scriptures to us" (24:32). Finally, in his appearance to the remaining eleven disciples gathered in Jerusalem, Jesus speaks to them about the scriptures:

> Then he said to them, "These are my words that I spoke to you while I was still with you—that everything written about me in the law of Moses, the prophets, and the psalms must be fulfilled." Then he opened their minds to understand the scriptures, and he said to them, "Thus it is written, that the Messiah is to suffer and to rise from the dead on the third day, and that repentance and forgiveness of sins is to be proclaimed in his name to all nations [or Gentiles], beginning from Jerusalem (Luke 24:44–47).

The intent here is not to indicate specific passages in scripture that point to Jesus, but rather to make the more global claim: all scripture—Torah, prophets, and Psalms—points to Jesus. It is important to keep in mind specifically what is being claimed in Luke 24. It is claimed, firstly, that Jesus is the authentic interpreter of scripture: "Were not our hearts burning within us while he was talking to us on the road, while he was opening the scriptures to us?" (24:32); "Then he opened their minds to understand the scriptures" (24:45). Secondly, it is claimed that, under this authentic interpretation, scripture as a whole and in all its component parts, not just in scattered verses, speaks of Jesus. Third, authentically interpreted scripture speaks of the passion and resurrection of Jesus and of the need to proclaim repentance and forgiveness to all Gentiles (or nations).

What then can we say about the meaning of scripture in the Jerusalem section of Luke's Gospel? First, nothing here leads us to doubt the belief in the authority of scripture. The reference to the components as Moses, the prophets, and the Psalms (Luke 24:44) comes close to reflecting the actual division of Tanach, as the Jewish definition of the scriptures reached explicit formulation. There is a compelling character to scripture that underscores its authority: it *must* be fulfilled.[36] Despite this, Luke feels no obligation to invoke the authority of scripture in rigid ways. For example, in the pericope in which Jesus is being examined by the chief priests and their associates (20:1–8), he is asked about his authority to do the things that he is doing. If Luke here means to signify the thing that

Jesus has most recently done—the driving of money changers out of the Temple (19:45–46)—then it may be said that a scriptural warrant was cited for this action. But the pericope does not directly suggest that this is the nature of the question of the chief priests. It is more natural to read their question as concerning the warrant for Jesus' teaching in the Temple. And for this Jesus does not cite scripture. Instead he asks a counter-question about the authority of John the Baptist, a question that his opponents are unwilling to answer. It is remarkable that, at a point where the question explicitly involves authority, Luke does not invoke scripture. Neither is scripture cited to answer the question about paying tribute to Caesar (20:22). Only the image and inscription on a denarius serve as evidence for Jesus' proclamation (20:24–25). Thus, in order fully to appreciate the role of scripture here we must say that, although the Hebrew Scriptures are authoritative for Luke, they do not constitute the sole source of authority.

Secondly, scripture in its entirety points to Jesus, especially his passion and resurrection, and to the proclamation of the Christian message. It is notable that, in the gospel, Luke rarely cites specific scriptures to bolster the contention that the Christ must suffer (see Luke 20:17; 22:37). That he could have included more explicit references is indicated by the abundant allusions to a variety of OT passages found in the Lukan crucifixion scene (23:32–46). It is likely that Luke felt no need to include specific scriptural references, since his contention was not that one could find one or more references in the scriptures that would give ground for the belief that the Christ must suffer, but that the scripture *as a whole* was fulfilled in the events of Jesus' passion and resurrection. Despite this contention, there is a sense in which the selection of scripture to be interpreted is important, as seen in the controversies of Luke 20:27–40, 41–44.

Third, Jesus is the authentic interpreter of scripture. But Luke implies that, since Jesus has opened the minds of his disciples to the meaning of scripture, they may succeed him in this role. The significance of this point will be seen in Acts.[37]

There is in this section of Luke a sense of a continuing and mutual interplay between the scriptures and Jesus. On the one hand the scriptures are necessary to explain the life, passion, and resurrection of Jesus. On the other, the scriptures need Jesus as their proper interpreter. Our analysis of the Gospel of Luke does not make it possible to say which need is stronger, the need for scripture as interpreter of Jesus, or the need for Jesus as interpreter of scripture.

IMAGES OF JEWISH RELIGIOUS LIFE

The parable of the vineyard implies that the priestly leaders have not fulfilled their responsibilities to care for Jewish religious life, and the Lukan passion narrative shows them to be largely responsible for the rejection and execution of Jesus. The characterization of these priests is determined by the role they play in monitoring Jesus' activities in the Temple and in participating in the judicial actions against him. Even though Luke's trial narrative, in contrast to Matthew and Mark, includes a list of political charges appropriate for a Roman trial, it is nevertheless clear that the chief priests and scribes are the prime movers in bringing Jesus before the Roman governor and insisting on his execution. They convene a meeting of their Sanhedrin and there officially reject him (Luke 22:66–71). They present charges against him before Pilate (23:1–2) and insist on his execution (23:5, 10, 18, 21, 23), despite the repeated declarations of innocence by the Roman governor (23:4,14–15, 22). The religious leadership—chief priests, scribes, elders, and Sadducees—are thus pictured in dark colors in this section of Luke's Gospel. They are malevolent, out of step with the people, and not above using trickery to achieve their ends.

It is notable that we do not see priests here as performing ritualistic duties, as did Zechariah in the infancy narratives. The implied reader would almost certainly come to the judgment that they assumed a responsibility to control any teaching that might be offered in the Temple, since they took pains to monitor Jesus' teaching, to lead him into a trap if possible, and to examine him in semiformal hearings. But it is the political aspect of the priestly leadership that is emphasized in the concluding section of Luke's Gospel.[38]

Similarly, almost no attention is given to the religious function of the Temple beyond the stated ideal that it is to be a house of prayer. If we had only these texts from the Gospel of Luke as descriptions of the Jewish Temple and its priesthood, we would learn almost nothing about the place of these institutions in Jewish religious life. The implied reader could not fail to understand the central importance of the Temple in Jewish life. Its beauty is taken for granted (cf. Luke 21:5). The fact that Jesus makes it his headquarters during his teaching ministry in Jerusalem is sufficient to suggest to the reader that here is the central shrine for the Jewish people. But, aside from the pericope about the widow's coins (21:1–4), where Jesus praises her piety, Luke provides no vignettes that would give the reader insight about what actually went on in the Temple. To depend only on Luke 19:45–24:53 for information on the function of the Temple would leave one with the impression that the Temple was a place intended for prayer and teaching but that in fact it served mainly as a power base for the priestly leaders. Although such an image is not at every point inconsistent with the picture in the Lukan infancy narratives, at least the latter contain allusions to the performance of sacrifices in the Temple (see 1:8–10; 2:22–24).[39]

Other aspects of Jewish religious life are occasionally mentioned in this section of Luke. Synagogues are mentioned twice, but they never serve as settings for narratives or discourses. In one saying of Jesus we have the picture of Jewish leaders competing for the best seats at synagogues (20:46), and in another, synagogues seem to serve as either courts or prisons (21:12).

Sadducees are mentioned only once in the gospel, in Luke 20:27, where it is explained that they do not accept the doctrine of the resurrection. Their inclusion here among those questioning Jesus would tend to associate them with the chief priests, but Luke provides no explicit statement about their relationships. In Acts 23:6–10 we learn that Sadducees and Pharisees are to be distinguished from one another by the teaching about the resurrection, but we have no such explanation here.

Glimpses of individual Jewish piety appear in the pericope of the widow's coins (21:1–4) and the description of the burial of Jesus (23:50–56). In 21:1–4 we learn that it is customary practice for persons to make offerings in the Temple and that rich and poor alike sense an obligation to make contributions. Joseph of Arimathea is described as a good and righteous man who, though a councillor (*bouleutēs*), did not agree with the decision of the Sanhedrin in respect to Jesus (23:50–51).[40] His action in asking for Jesus' body, wrapping it in linen, and placing it in a new tomb is regarded as an expression of deep piety. Likewise, the action of the women in witnessing the burial and preparing aromas and perfumes is seemingly expressive of customary Jewish piety (23:54–56). There are, to be sure, other motifs at work in this pericope, which serves to secure the location of the tomb of Jesus and to provide a motivation for the women to return on the first day of the week (24:1). But Luke has not forgotten to locate the action of the women strictly within the bounds of Jewish piety, and he calls attention to the fact that the anointing of Jesus' body by the women was delayed due to their observance of the Sabbath, "On the sabbath they rested according to the commandment" (23:56).

Finally, mention should be made of the description in Luke 22:7–23 of the observance of Passover. Already in 22:1, Luke had commented that the feast of unleavened bread (*azymos*), called Passover (*pascha*), was drawing near. Then, beginning at 22:7 he describes the observance of this day by Jesus and his disciples. In his description he stresses the fact that the day of unleavened bread was the time when it was necessary to sacrifice a lamb and that Jesus arranged for the preparation and the meal. That Luke intends the Last Supper of Jesus to be understood as his own observance of Passover is clear from the careful preparations that were made (22:7–13), by the solemn note in 22:14 about the hour of the observance, and by Jesus' opening statement to the disciples, "I have eagerly desired to eat this Passover (*touto to pascha*, literally, 'this lamb') with you before I suffer" (22:15).

### CONCLUSION

The nature of Luke's section on Jesus in Jerusalem affects the images of Jewish religious life to be found within it. The Temple, under the stewardship of the chief priests, has not been a house of prayer, as it should have been. The priestly leaders have been irresponsible as stewards of Israel and the Temple; they reject the son whom God has sent, and they arrange to have him executed. Even Jesus has been unsuccessful in providing a proper orientation for Israel. Luke seems intent to stress that, in accordance with scripture as interpreted by Jesus, God will wreak vengeance on these leaders and install Jesus and his followers as the new stewards of Israel and the Temple. Here we find the motif of Christian renewal, which will come more and more to the foreground in Acts. This section of Luke suggests the concept that the followers of Jesus will supplant the Jewish leaders and orient God's people in the direction willed by God and revealed in scripture.

NOTES

1. But see Daryl Schmidt, "Luke's 'Innocent' Jesus: A Scriptural Apologetic." Schmidt argues that, on Luke's terms, the charges brought against Jesus are plausible.

2. On the grouping of scribes and elders with chief priests, see Joseph B. Tyson, *The Death of Jesus in Luke-Acts*, 72–78.
3. Both Matthew and Mark continue the quotation from Psalm 118 to include verse 23, "This was the Lord's doing, and it is amazing in our eyes" (Matt 21:42; Mark 12:11). Matthew only has 21:43, "Therefore I tell you, the kingdom of God will be taken away from you and given to a people that produces the fruits of the kingdom." Mark has no parallel to Luke 20:18, but some texts of Matthew have substantially the same in 21:44. Assuming that Luke derived his parable from Mark 12:1–12, Joseph A. Fitzmyer includes a list of Lukan redactional features but concludes that they are minimal. See *The Gospel According to Luke X–XXIV*, 1277f.
4. Luke and Mark have the parable of the vineyard in exactly the same position, i.e., immediately following the controversy about Jesus' authority. Matthew, however, includes the parable of the two sons (Matt 21:28–32) between these two pericopes.
5. The motivation of the tenants at this point is not completely clear. I. Howard Marshall, *The Gospel of Luke: A Commentary on the Greek Text*, 730, says: "They may have assumed that the original owner had died, so that if they killed the new owner, the vineyard would pass into their hands as the first claimants; it would be regarded as ownerless property, and they would have a good chance of maintaining their claim." Alternatively, Marshall speculates that they may have thought that the owner had deeded the property to his son and had then died. Such speculation is, however, inappropriate to the parable itself, which makes no attempt to explain the motivation of the tenants beyond noting their belief that the death of the supposed heir would be beneficial to them.
6. This saying (Luke 20:18) is not found in Mark, but it is found in some texts of Matt 21:44, in substantially the same form. Fitzmyer, drawing on Strack-Billerbeck, quotes a later Rabbinical parable from *Midr. Esth.* 3:6: "If a stone falls on a pot, woe to the pot! If the pot falls on the stone, woe to the pot. Either way, woe to the pot!" (Fitzmyer, *Luke X–XXIV*, 1286). Fitzmyer rightly comments that this only shows that the saying in Luke 20:18 is proverblike.
7. Fitzmyer, for example, *Luke X–XXIV*, 1281, designates it form-critically as "an expanded and allegorized parable." But the differences between parable and allegory are being minimized in recent scholarship. See, e.g., Madeleine Boucher, *The Mysterious Parable: A Literary Study*. A number of commentators argue that the parable of the vineyard, at least in its present form, could not go back to Jesus, due to its allegorical elements. See, e.g., Rudolf Bultmann, *The History of the Synoptic Tradition*, 177. Referring to the parallel in Mark 12:1–12, Bultmann designates the passage as an allegory, not a parable, and calls it a "community product." Marshall is inclined to accept the passage as authentic to Jesus. He writes, "But the fact that divine sonship would not have been an obvious allegorical key to the parable for the Jews speaks rather in favour of its authenticity, and the suggestion that Jesus did speak in this way to warn the Jews of the consequences of refusing to hear his message is by no means unlikely" (*Luke: A Commentary*, 727). See also Malcolm Lowe, "From the Parable of the Vineyard to a Pre-Synoptic Source." Lowe traces the parable, as well as other pericopes in the Synoptic Gospels, to a Baptist-sequence that lies behind all three gospels.
8. See e.g., Ps 80:8–13; Isa 27:2; Jer 2:21; Hos 10:1; Ezek 19:10–14; and esp. Isa 5:1–7, which may well have influenced the present parable.
9. Moreover, Acts 4:11 also alludes to Ps 118:22, and its reference to Jesus is made explicit.
10. Fitzmyer explains that the cornerstone "designated in antiquity the stone used at a building's corner to bear the weight or stress of the two walls. It would

have functioned somewhat like a 'keystone' or 'capstone' in an arch or other architectural form. It was the stone which was essential or crucial to the whole structure" (*Luke X–XXIV*, 1282).

11. Citing support from the use of Psalm 118:22 in Acts 4:11, Jack T. Sanders claims that Luke 20:16 means that it is the Gentile Christians who will become the new tenants of the vineyard. He writes, "'The Jews' have rejected Christ, who has then become the cornerstone not of a 'renewed Israel,' of 'the redeemed within Israel,' but of the church, which is Gentile." Sanders, "The Prophetic Use of the Scriptures in Luke-Acts," 196.

12. Marshall rightly points out that there is nothing in the parable to indicate that the tenants have been unsuccessful. He writes, "On the contrary, they have presumably been so successful in tending it that they are unwilling to share the profits with anybody else" (*Luke: A Commentary*, 726).

13. Both Matt 21:39 and Mark 12:8 say that the tenants killed the son and threw him out of the vineyard, implying dishonor to the corpse. Luke's order, rejection and execution, encourages the reader to anticipate a narrative about the official Jewish rejection of Jesus prior to this execution. As we shall see, Luke 22:66–71 is this anticipated narrative.

14. Richard J. Cassidy also recognizes the importance of the parable of the vineyard in Luke's narrative. See Cassidy, "Luke's Audience, the Chief Priests, and the Motive for Jesus' Death."

15. Mark 11:17 has the entire phrase, while both Matt 21:13 and Luke 19:46 omit *pasin tois ethnesin*.

16. Fitzmyer, *Luke X–XXIV*, 1261.

17. Marshall, *Luke: A Commentary*, 721.

18. Hans Conzelmann, *The Theology of St. Luke*, 75.

19. Ibid., 77.

20. In view of the verbal cognates of the word, *stratēgoi* should be military figures, but Luke associates them specifically with the Temple (see Luke 22:4, 52; Acts 4:1; 5:24, 26), although he also knows of Gentile officials by this name (Acts 16:20, 22, 35, 36, 38). Josephus also speaks of a *stratēgos*, who seems to be in charge of security at the Jerusalem Temple (*Jewish War* 6.294). But in other places *stratēgoi* have political or military functions in Gentile cities (see *Antiquities* 14.247, 259; 20.131).

21. Conzelmann, *Theology of Luke*, 84, says, "These verses are meant to set out explicitly the fundamental identity of the current Christological titles."

22. Fitzmyer, *Luke X–XXIV*, 1468, calls the response a "half-yes." Marshall, *Luke: A Commentary*, 851, regards it as a grudging admission, "The form of expression is not a direct affirmation; but it is certainly not a denial, and is best regarded as a grudging admission with the suggestion that the speaker would put it otherwise or that the questioners fail to understand exactly what they are saying." There appears to be an intended irony in the contrast between the reaction of the Sanhedrin and the reaction of Pilate (23:4) to what is essentially the same response on Jesus' part. Pilate asks if Jesus is king of the Jews, and Jesus responds, *sy legeis* (23:3). Pilate evidently regards the response as a denial on Jesus' part, and thus he pronounces him innocent. The members of the Sanhedrin, however, take Jesus' response (*hymeis legete hoti egō eimi*, 22:70) as an incriminating confession. Another layer of irony appears if we understand Jesus' response in 22:70 in a literal way: the members of the Sanhedrin have said that Jesus is the Son of God, but they do not really believe it.

23. We need not deal here with the historical problem, i.e., how a confession to be the Son of God might be converted into an accusation of treason, actionable in a Roman court. Suffice it to say at this point that Luke must have been aware that Jesus was in fact tried before Pilate, but he wanted to shift the blame for

Jesus' execution away from him to the Jewish priestly leaders and thus has produced a complex and historically problematic narrative. See my *Death of Jesus*,
114–41. E. Jane Via rightly calls attention to the participation in the execution
of others besides the chief priests. Commenting on Richard J. Cassidy, *Jesus,
Politics, and Society*, she writes: "It was not the chief priests 'and their allies'
who put Jesus to death, however. The trial narrative in the Gospel [of Luke]
and relevant passages in Acts make clear that it was the religious and political
authorities who put Jesus to death, with the support of the multitudes,
crowds, or people (as Luke chooses to say). The chief priests are prominent
among the leaders; but other authorities are included in Luke's account in a
way that merits explicit mention: the scribes, the elders, the Sanhedrin, Roman
Pilate, half-Jewish Herod, who ruled Galilee under Roman authority, and sol-
diers, all of whom Luke refers to as 'rulers' in 23:13 and 23:25" (Via, "According to Luke, Who Put Jesus to Death?" 140). I would agree if she would
describe the chief priests as playing the leading role rather than as "prominent
among the leaders."

24. Fitzmyer, *Luke X–XXIV*, 1345, points out that the phrasing reflects Hos 9:7.
Charles H. Giblin, *The Destruction of Jerusalem According to Luke's Gospel*, claims
that Jesus' words about Jerusalem would be read as a warning about the fate of
other cities that may reject him. See H. J. Klauck, "Die heilige Stadt: Jerusalem
bei Philo und Lukas," who agrees with Giblin. See also Ruthild Geiger, *Die lukanischer Endzeitreden: Studien zur Eschatologie des Lukas-Evangeliums*.

25. The parallels to Luke 21:20–24 in Matt 24:15–22; Mark 13:14–20 are far less detailed and explicit. Indeed, only Luke includes the reference to Jerusalem by
name in 21:20, 24, although all three gospels contain a reference to Judea (Matt
24:16; Mark 13:14; Luke 21:21).

26. Fitzmyer, *Luke X–XXIV*, 1347, is probably correct in reading the phrase to mean
"until the triumph of the Romans over Jerusalem is complete." I understand
him to mean "until the end of Roman domination of Jerusalem." The phrase
thus probably indicates that the time of Gentile domination of Jerusalem is
limited.

27. E. Earle Ellis, *The Gospel of Luke*, 270, lists the three basic ways the tearing of the
Temple veil at Jesus' death has been understood: "It was an omen of the coming destruction of the temple. . . . It signified that through Christ's death the
gates of Paradise, the way to God, were open to all (cf. 23:43). It witnessed that
the temple rites no longer were necessary for the true worship of God." For a
recent expression of the third view, see Klauck, "Die heilige Stadt." See also
Dennis D. Sylva, "The Temple Curtain and Jesus' Death in the Gospel of
Luke." Fitzmyer, *Luke X–XXIV*, 1514, adds a fourth alternative, "The death of
Jesus, attended by such cataclysmic events, is to have an ominous effect on the
'whole land' (v. 44) and on the Temple in Jerusalem (recall 21:5–7)."

28. See Fitzmyer, *Luke X–XXIV*, 1419.

29. Gerhard Lohfink, *Die Sammlung Israels: Eine Untersuchung zur lukanischen Ekklesiologie*, 79–84, entertains the thesis that Luke intends here to designate the
apostolic leadership of the church. But he rejects this interpretation in favor of
one that claims that the apostolic rule of Israel is an eschatological promise. See
also J. Bradley Chance, *Jerusalem, the Temple, and the New Age in Luke-Acts*.

30. On the use of OT quotations in Luke-Acts, see Martin Rese, *Alttestamentliche
Motive in der Christologie des Lukas*; Darrell L. Bock, *Proclamation from Prophecy
and Pattern: Lucan Old Testament Christology*.

31. Fitzmyer, *Luke X–XXIV*, 1307, says that an allusion to 4 Macc 7:19 is contained
here. "Only those who with all their heart make piety their first concern are
able to conquer the passions of the flesh, believing that to God they do not die,
as our patriarchs Abraham, Issac, and Jacob died not, but live to God" (4 Macc

7:18–19, trans. by H. Anderson, in James H. Charlesworth, ed., *The Old Testament Pseudepigrapha*, 2:531–64). Cf. also 4 Macc 16:25: "And they [the seven brothers] knew full well themselves that those who die for the sake of God live unto God, as do Abraham and Issac and Jacob and all the patriarchs" (ibid.). It is not certain, however, that 4 Maccabees is pre-Lukan.

32. For a discussion of the range of possible meanings that may be intended here, see Fitzmyer, *Luke X–XXIV*, 1308–16.

33. On the significance of scriptural interpretation in Luke 24, see Paul Schubert, "The Structure and Significance of Luke 24."

34. Marshall, *Luke: A Commentary*, 896, observes that the form of Jesus' statement here suggests that the disciples should have known already about the suffering of the Christ.

35. Compare the similar phrase in Luke 16:29, 31, "Moses and the prophets."

36. See C. H. Cosgrove, "The Divine *Dei* in Luke-Acts."

37. Conzelmann, *Theology of St. Luke*, 162, puts the point dramatically, when he says that, as a result of the resurrection of Jesus, "Scripture belongs to the Church, for she is in possession of the correct interpretation."

38. So far as he goes, Francis D. Weinert is quite correct in emphasizing the positive assessment of the Temple by Luke. But Weinert has not fully appreciated the more negative images to be found in some of the passages analyzed here. See Weinert, "The Meaning of the Temple in Luke-Acts"; see also his "Luke, the Temple, and Jesus' Saying about Jerusalem's Abandoned House," and "Luke, Stephen, and the Temple in Luke-Acts."

39. See Michael Bachmann, *Jerusalem und der Tempel: Die geographisch-theologischen Elementen in der lukanischen Sicht des jüdischen Kultzentrums*.

40. Matt 27:57 describes Joseph as a disciple of Jesus. Mark 15:43 says that he was a respected member of the council who expected the kingdom of God. Luke 23:50–51 has a much fuller description: "Now there was a good and righteous man named Joseph, who, though a member of the council, had not agreed to their plan and action. He came from the Jewish town of Arimathea [*apo Arimathaias poleōs ton Ioudaiōn*], and he was waiting expectantly for the kingdom of God."

# 6

# The First Christians
# in Jerusalem, Judea, and Samaria

(Acts 1–12)

The geographic and ethnic settings for the first twelve chapters of Acts are primarily Judean and Jewish, and this point has great significance for an understanding of Luke's project as a whole. For the most part the action takes place in Jerusalem, but there are also narratives set in other parts of Judea, and some take place in Samaria. Toward the end of this section of Acts, the horizon broadens, as some of the action occurs in Damascus and Antioch, and there are references to Phoenicia, Cyprus, and Cyrene. These settings have important symbolic significance as they focus the reader's attention first on Jerusalem and then gradually on a larger world. But more than geography is at stake here. Just as the reader follows the movement of the Christians from Jerusalem outward, just so she follows a movement that first locates itself within Judaism but later begins to orient itself toward Gentiles. It will take the entire book of Acts to tell this story, but it begins in the first twelve chapters, which for the most part focus attention on the attempts of the early believers to locate themselves among Jews and within Judaism.

The narrative begins in Jerusalem with the ascension of Jesus, and Jerusalem remains the narrative setting until a persecution produces a scattering of Christian believers (8:1–2). These believers then go into Samaria and Judea (8:4–40). After an introduction of Saul, the story of the church in Judea and Samaria is resumed. Saul's conversion, when he was about to persecute believers in Damascus, is told in 9:1–19, and his early preaching in Damascus and Jerusalem is described in 9:20–30. But instead of following immediately with the story of Saul/Paul, Luke moves us back to Judea and Samaria and focuses attention again on Peter. The centerpiece here is the story of Peter and Cornelius in Acts 10:1–11:18. Most of chapter 12 is given over to the arrest and escape of Peter in Jerusalem, but at the end (12:24–25) we have a transition section, "But the word of God continued to advance and gain adherents," and Barnabas, Saul, and John Mark returned to Jerusalem.[1] The scene is now set for the next section of Acts, the geographic center of which is no longer Jerusalem, but Antioch.

The geographic settings that govern this section of Acts are anticipated in 1:4–8. In his last message to the apostles, Jesus orders them not to leave Jerusalem but to wait there for "the promise of the Father" (1:4). The nature of this promise is not explicitly described, but it is referred to in 1:5 as baptism with the Holy Spirit. Here the resurrected Jesus reminds the apostles of his promise, "For John baptized with water, but you will be baptized with the Holy Spirit not many days from now." These words remind the reader not of a promise of Jesus, but of words of John the Baptist: "I baptize you with the water; but one who is more powerful than I is coming; I am not worthy to untie the thong of his sandals. He will baptize you with the Holy Spirit and fire" (Luke 3:16; cf. Matt 3:11; Mark 1:8). Then in Acts 1:8, Jesus reiterates the promise of the Holy Spirit and outlines something of a missionary itinerary, "You will be my witnesses in Jerusalem, in all Judea and Samaria, and to the ends of the earth."[2]

It seems clear that the promise of Acts 1:5 is fulfilled on the day of Pentecost, when the apostles begin to speak in other tongues (2:1–4). The interval of time that passes between 1:5 and 2:1 would, by implication, be only ten days and would fill the conditions of the promise, "not many days from now." Moreover, in describing the event of Pentecost, Luke says that the apostles were "filled with the Holy Spirit" (2:4), and he associates the gift of tongues with fire (2:3). Further, in the speech that follows, Peter interprets the Pentecost phenomenon as the Father's "promise of the Holy Spirit" (2:33), and he offers the same gift to those of his hearers who repent and are baptized (2:38). This spirit continues with the apostles throughout this section of Acts (4:8, 31; 8:29, 39), and others either receive it (the household of Cornelius: 10:44, 45, 47) or are said to be filled with it (Stephen: 6:5, 10; 7:55; Barnabas: 11:24; Agabus: 11:28). Some receive it through the imposition of hands (Samaritans: 8:17; Saul: 9:17).

The logic of the narrative would suggest that the apostles are free to leave Jerusalem after the day of Pentecost, but Acts 8:1 makes a point of saying that they remained in the city even after a persecution brought about a scattering of the rest of the believers, and they are still headquartered there as late as 11:1–18 (and 15:2). There seems to be some compulsion on the part of the apostles to stay in Jerusalem long after the promise of the spirit has seemingly been fulfilled. Peter and John are the first of the apostles to leave Jerusalem, and they go to Samaria, but only after Philip (apparently the Philip of Acts 6:5, not the apostle of Acts 1:13) has preceded them and introduced the gospel there (8:14). Thereafter Peter is found in parts of Judea and Samaria but returns to Jerusalem in 11:2.

As we have seen, Acts 1:5 quotes a saying in which Jesus orders the apostles to remain in Jerusalem and promises to them the Holy Spirit. The same quotation reappears in 11:16. In the latter passage, Peter is in Jerusalem reporting to the other apostles and the Judean believers on his dealings with Cornelius and his household, and he refers to the promise, "And I remembered the word of the Lord, how he had said, 'John baptized with water, but you will be baptized with the Holy Spirit.'" Recalling that Gentiles experienced the phenomenon of glossolalia as did the apostles on the first Pentecost, Peter reasons that he was justified in going in to them and eating with them. These two references to the same promise, with a quotation of the same saying and a linking of two incidents of glossolalia, form a literary inclusion and suggest that there is a certain integrity to the enclosed material. The unity is provided by the centrality of Jerusalem in Acts 1–12 and by the apostles being firmly situated there and leaving only temporarily. Although the promise of Acts 1:5 is literally fulfilled for the apostles in 2:1–4, the narrative continues to concentrate on Jerusalem well beyond the day of Pentecost, indeed until it becomes abundantly clear, in what might be called a Gentile Pentecost, that the word of the Lord cannot be confined to Jerusalem or Jewish people. The liberating word finally comes in 11:18, when the Judean believers are able to say, "God has given even to the Gentiles repentance that leads to life." After this judgment, Luke begins immediately to focus the reader's attention on Antioch and an incipient mission to Gentiles (11:20–21).

However we may assess these indications of time and place, it is quite clear that the focus of attention in Acts 1–12 is on Jerusalem. This geographic orientation should remind the reader of the setting of the opening and closing narratives in the Gospel of Luke, which are also situated in Jerusalem. The setting is also a powerful suggestion about what is going on in this section of Acts: the Christian message is being offered first to Jews in the traditional territories, later to peripheral people, such as diaspora Jews, and finally to Godfearing Gentiles. This fact inevitably has a profound effect upon the images of Judaism that are found in Acts 1–12 and suggests how we might manage this large mass of material.

As a presentation of the Christian message, Acts 1–12 falls into three subdivisions. In the first, consisting of Acts 1–5, the message is being presented to Jewish people by Peter. In Acts 6–7, the audience is still Jewish but the speaker is Stephen, a representative of a nonapostolic group of believers. In Acts 8–12, the Christian mission is to people who, from the perspective of Jerusalem Jews, may be called peripheral, as well as to Godfearing Gentiles.[3] The chief participants are Saul, Philip, and Peter. Images of Judaism and of the Jewish people differ dramatically in these three segments, and so it will be convenient for us to examine each one separately, although not without an awareness of the whole of Acts 1–12.

### PETER AND THE CHRISTIAN MESSAGE TO JEWS (ACTS 1–5)

The major feature of Acts 1–5 is a series of speeches by Peter, most of them addressed to audiences of Jewish people or leaders.[4] For convenience, the speeches are listed below:

(1) Acts 1:15–22. In a speech to his fellow believers, Peter deals with the problem of replacing Judas among the twelve.

(2) Acts 2:14–40. Peter addresses the residents of Jerusalem on the day of Pentecost.

(3) Acts 3:11–26. After healing a lame man in the Temple, Peter addresses his fellow Israelites.

(4) Acts 4:8–12. Peter addresses Jewish leaders to explain the healing in the Temple.

(5) Acts 5:29–32. Peter and the apostles address the Sanhedrin to answer charges about their teaching.

The speeches that are addressed to the Jewish people or leaders (2–5, above) may be examined together as illustrating the Petrine message to Jews, as it is presented in Acts. As has been frequently noted, there are several common points in these speeches, which are nevertheless adapted to their own unique situations.[5]

A few general remarks about the character of the speeches may be useful at this point. In general they contain a mixture of evangelistic and apologetic motifs. All four of the speeches to Jewish people or leaders are occasioned by situations that would call forth apologies, and all four may be said to function in this way. In the second speech (Acts 2:14–40), Peter must explain the phenomenon of glossolalia on the day of Pentecost. The third and fourth speeches are occasioned by the healing of the lame man in the Temple, and in both Peter addresses this matter. The fifth speech is the most explicitly apologetic, since here Peter and the apostles are called upon by the Sanhedrin to defend their actions. Despite the apologetic motifs, all four speeches contain either evangelistic appeals or declarations about repentance and forgiveness. Peter concludes the second speech with an appeal for repentance and baptism, an assurance that the promise is for those in his audience, and a summons to salvation (2:38–40). Similarly, in the third speech, Peter calls his audience to repentance (3:19–20). No summons or promise is given in the fourth or fifth speech, but there is an announcement that salvation comes only through the name of Jesus (4:12) and a statement that through him repentance and forgiveness have come to Israel (5:31).

Despite the apologetic character of the speeches, there is an impressive lack of contentiousness. Underlying them is a sense that Peter and the apostles share a common heritage with the Jewish audiences, and there is much in the language of the speeches that emphasizes this heritage. For example, Peter addresses his audience as brothers in 2:29 and 3:17, and he and the apostles are similarly addressed in 2:37. Of greater significance is the citation of aspects of a common history and ancestry. The abundant use of quotations from the Hebrew Scriptures in speeches to Jewish audiences requires the assumption that both the speaker and the listeners agree on the status of these writings. In addition, one should note the reference in 3:13, which contains an allusion to Exod 3:6: "The God of Abraham, the God of Isaac, and the God of Jacob, the God of *our* ancestors" (my emphasis).

In the narratives and editorial sections surrounding these speeches, Luke likewise emphasizes a strong sense of harmony between the apostles and their audiences. Those who observed the phenomenon of glossolalia at Pentecost are described as devout, and the response to Peter's speech is positive (2:37) and results in the addition of about three thousand persons, who "devoted themselves to the apostles' teaching and fellowship, to the breaking of bread and the prayers" (2:42). The believers are said to have "the goodwill of all the people" (2:47). All residents of Jerusalem know about the apostles (4:16), everybody praises God because of the events surrounding them (4:21), and the people hold them in high honor (5:12). Although the members of the Sanhedrin vigorously oppose the apostles after their defense (5:29–32), Gamaliel's advice, allowing the possibility that the work of the apostles may be divinely inspired, prevails.

Although each of these speeches may fruitfully be exposed to an exhaustive exegetical analysis, we may for our purposes concentrate on a few common points in order to understand Luke's conception of Peter's message to the Jewish people.[6] In these speeches, the theme of the preaching to Jews may be stated in five major points: (1) Jesus is the Christ appointed for you; (2) you killed him; (3) God raised him; (4) the scripture foretold all of this; (5) repent and be forgiven. Each of these points requires some further attention.

(1) Jesus is the Christ appointed for you.     This theme is either stated or implied in every speech, although the terms vary. In Acts 2:36, Peter announces to Israel that God has made Jesus both Christ and Lord. In 3:13, Jesus is given the status of God's servant; in 3:15, he is the ruler of life, in 3:18 he is the Christ, and in 3:22–23 he is the prophet promised by Moses. The theme is most explicitly stated in 3:20, where Jesus is named "the Messiah appointed for you," but here it is his future coming that is in view. In 4:10 it is Jesus Christ of Nazareth. In 5:31, Jesus is called *archēgos* (leader, prince) and *sōtēr*. Despite the variations in title and implied function, the major point is that Jesus has been appointed for Jews. There is no explicit indication in Peter's speeches that Jesus has a meaning for non-Jews, but Acts 3:25–26 may contain a veiled suggestion of this sort. Here Peter says, "You are the descendants of the prophets and of the covenant that God gave to your ancestors, saying to Abraham, 'And in your descendants all the families of the earth shall be blessed' [Gen 22:18].[7] When God raised up his servant, he sent him first to you (*hymin protōn*), to bless you by turning each of you from your wicked ways." These verses serve as a strong affirmation of the permanence of the relationship between God and the Jewish people, but the language also subtly

suggests that other people are in view and that, although Israel has priority in receiving the blessings of the divine deed in Christ, it does not have a permanent exclusivity.

(2) **You killed Jesus.** In every speech Peter confronts his audience with this accusation. There is no difficulty in determining who the culprits are, since the audiences for these speeches are Jewish people. In Acts 2:23, the words are addressed to "you that are Israelites"; ostensibly the same is the case in 2:36; 3:13, 14. In 4:10, the speech is addressed to the "rulers of the people and elders" (4:8), but the more immediate antecedent is "all the people of Israel" (4:10). In 5:30, the accusation is directed against the members of the Sanhedrin. No significant distinctions are to be pressed in interpreting these accusations. The occasions for the speeches affect the definition of the audiences, and thus the groups to which Peter points his accusing finger vary from one speech to the other. But the accusations in these speeches are general: Jews are responsible for the death of Jesus. To be sure, it is not in these speeches that Luke wants to put a fine point on his assessment of guilt in the case of Jesus' death. That is done more carefully in the narratives in Luke 22–23. There is, however, a possible allusion to the trial scenes in Acts 2:23, where Peter says, "You crucified and killed [Jesus] by the hands of those outside the law (*anomōn*)." As a word used by a Jew in speaking to a Jewish audience, *anomos* would almost certainly signify Gentiles, those without Torah, and hence would serve to remind the reader that the Roman governor Pilate acceded to the wishes of the Jewish priests and others and permitted the crucifixion of Jesus. There is a more certain allusion to the Lukan trial scenes in 3:13–14, where Peter's audience is first accused of betrayal and denial "in the presence of Pilate, though he had decided to release him." The reader is reminded of the narratives in Luke 23, where Pilate repeatedly pronounced Jesus not guilty of the charges brought against him by the chief priests and their associates. Likewise, Acts 3:14 recalls Luke 23:18–19, where the crowd called for the release of Barabbas. But clearly the Lukan Peter is not willing simply to accuse his audience of betrayal and denial of Jesus, for in 3:15 he states, "You killed the Author of life." The accusation is mitigated only by the recognition of ignorance, stated in 3:17. It is difficult to know if this ignorance should be understood as excusable. Since the concession is followed immediately by the proclamation that the suffering of the Messiah was foretold in scripture, one might conclude

that if those in Peter's audience had understood the scriptures, they would not have been ignorant of what they were doing in denying and killing Jesus. But we have already learned that in the Gospel of Luke Jewish people do not understand the scriptures and so are inevitably ignorant. Whether the ignorance is excusable or not, it seems to serve as a ground for repentance and forgiveness, as 3:19 suggests.

(3) **God raised him.**     Peter announces the resurrection of Jesus in every speech, where it serves as a counterpoint to the crucifixion. The structure of these announcements sets the negative action of the Jews over against the positive action of God: Jews killed Jesus, but God raised him up. Observe the following:

> This man, . . . you crucified and killed by the hands of those outside the law. But God raised him up, having freed him from death . . . (2:23–24).
> And you killed the Author of life, whom God raised from the dead . . . (3:15).
> . . . Jesus Christ of Nazareth, whom you crucified, whom God raised from the dead . . . (4:10).
> The God of our ancestors raised up Jesus, whom you had killed by hanging him on a tree (5:30).

The announcement of the resurrection in 2:31–32 is not immediately accompanied by a statement about the crucifixion, but here it functions chiefly as a scriptural interpretation. A similar opposition between the purposes of God and those of Peter's audience appears in 2:36: "God has made him both Lord and Messiah, this Jesus whom you crucified." Finally, the raising of Jesus is probably intended in 3:13, where God's glorification of Jesus is set over against Jewish betrayal and denial.

(4) **The scripture foretold all of this.**     The speeches include extensive quotation, allusion, and interpretation of the Hebrew Scriptures. Only in the last speech of Peter is there no explicit quotation of scripture. In his second speech, Joel 2:28–32 is quoted to show that the phenomenon of glossolalia was foretold (Acts 2:16–21). Later in the same speech, there is a reference to David with a quotation from Ps 16:8–11, the purpose of which is to show that the resurrection of Jesus was anticipated (2:25–28).[8] The key verse in this quotation is Ps 16:10, which receives special attention in Peter's speech. The verse is first quoted in Acts 2:27, "For you will not abandon my soul to Hades, / or let your Holy One experience corruption." Then, after observing that David himself died and

that his burial place is still known, Peter claims that the verse in question could not have applied to David but must apply to a descendant: "Since he was a prophet, he knew that God had sworn with an oath to him that he would put one of his descendants on his throne. Foreseeing this, David spoke of the resurrection of the Messiah" (2:30–31a). Then Peter quotes Ps 16:10 again, but with grammatical changes to show how the verse is to be interpreted: "He [the Messiah] was not abandoned to Hades, / nor did his flesh experience corruption" (2:31b). The logic of the argument is that David's words in the Psalm are true and authoritative but cannot apply to him, since his flesh has experienced corruption. Thus the Psalm must apply to a descendant of David's, namely Jesus, and one may draw the conclusion that Jesus' flesh has not experienced corruption and that he has been raised from the dead.

A similar argument is used to support Peter's claim about the ascension of Jesus. David was not raised to heaven. Rather he spoke of the ascension of Jesus in Ps 110:1: "The Lord said to my Lord, / Sit at my right hand, / until I make your enemies your footstool" (2:34–35). The reader will recall the quotation of this same Psalm in Luke 20:42–43, where the application is quite different from that here.

Two things are worth noting in the third speech of Peter. First, there is the proclamation of Jesus as the prophet like Moses, supported by a quotation from Deut 18:15, with an allusion to Deut 18:19 (Acts 3:22–23). Second, there are two contentions that are not backed up by scriptural quotation or allusion. In 3:18, Peter claims that all the prophets announced beforehand that the Christ would suffer, but no example of such a prophecy is included here. In 3:24, it is said that all the prophets from Samuel on predicted the appearance of Jesus, but again no quotation is included.

In Peter's fourth speech, there is only one scriptural quotation, that of Ps 118:22 (Acts 4:11). The reader will recall the pregnant use of this same quotation in Luke 20:17, the parable of the vineyard. There the quotation was taken to apply to the son of the vineyard owner, who was killed by the tenants. The more explicit identification of the verse with Jesus in Acts 4:11 supports the interpretation of the parable in Luke 20 and the reading of that parable as an allegory of Jesus' own execution.

(5) **Repent and be forgiven.**    In two of the speeches, the offer of repentance and forgiveness is implicit. In 4:12, Peter simply states that salvation is available only in the name of Jesus, and in 5:31 he says that God's purpose in exalting Jesus is "that he might give re-

pentance to Israel and forgiveness of sins." But in the other two speeches the offer of repentance is given directly to Peter's audiences. In 2:38, he responds to a question from the audience by directing them to repent and be baptized, and in 3:19–20 he calls for repentance "so that your sins may be wiped out, so that times of refreshing may come from the presence of the Lord."

The location of these speeches in the narrative scheme of Luke-Acts affects their character and consequently the images of Judaism reflected in them. There is in Acts 1–5 as a whole a dominant tone of good will, qualified by Peter's accusations against Jews and his demand that they repent. For the most part Jews are described as pious, and they make up an attentive and responsive audience for Peter. The common heritage that Peter and his fellow Jews share is exploited abundantly in the speeches. At one point Peter calls them "descendants of the prophets" (Acts 3:25). In view of the role that the Hebrew prophets play in all of Luke-Acts, this metaphor is remarkably positive. In the speeches in Acts 1–5, Peter is looking at his fellow Jews as potential converts, and he stresses the point that his message is for them. Indeed, the language is strong: the gift of Christ has been intended by God for the Jews. Jesus is the Christ appointed for you (3:20). Peter's expectation is high, and, for the most part, the response is positive. Even those Jerusalemites who did not become believers respected the apostles and revered their healing abilities (5:12–16).

The response of the Jewish leaders, however, contrasts markedly with that of the people. Priests, chief priests, *stratēgoi* of the Temple, Sadducees, rulers, elders, and scribes are all listed among the groups of leaders who attempted to restrict the apostles (Acts 4:1, 5, 8, 23; 5:17, 21, 24, 26). Personal opponents—Annas, Caiaphas, John, Alexander (4:6)—are also named. The apostles were brought to appear formally before the Sanhedrin (5:27), and the members were prepared to execute them (5:33).

But even in the hearing before the Sanhedrin, the apostles gain support from Gamaliel, who is described as a Pharisee, a member of the Sanhedrin, and a teacher of the law (Acts 5:34). Gamaliel argues that the apostles should be left alone, and so they are released with only a beating and a warning. The appearance of Gamaliel at this point would alert the implied reader to the absence of Pharisaic opposition to the apostles. Although Jesus and Pharisees had a number of controversies, Luke has neither included them in the group that brought about Jesus' death nor in the group that opposed the apostles in Jerusalem. If Gamaliel is to be understood as speaking for Pharisees generally, we should now include them among those who, though not converts, are at least tolerant of the new preaching.

There are a few references to Jewish practices and observances in Acts 1–5 that should be noted.The day of Pentecost (2:1) is probably the most significant, although we are not told what Jews observe on that day. Although the language of the inhabitants of Jerusalem is noted in 1:19, the description in 2:5–13 evokes an image of a polyglot community of ex-diaspora Jews and proselytes.

Synagogues are not mentioned in Acts 1–5, but the Temple may be more significant than it might at first sight appear. The first meeting place of the new believers is the "room upstairs" (1:13), presumably the location of the Passover meal with Jesus (Luke 22:12). But after the events of Pentecost, Luke observes that they attended the Temple daily and broke bread in their homes (2:46). The participation of the apostles in the Temple ritual is assumed. Peter and John go there "at the hour of prayer, at three o'clock in the afternoon" (3:1), where they heal the man who has been lame from birth. Peter's third speech is delivered in Solomon's portico (3:11). Presumably Peter and John are arrested in this portion of the Temple (4:1), which subsequently becomes a regular meeting place (5:12). But the Temple also becomes a point of contention. After the apostles are rearrested, an angel appears, releases them, and commands them to speak to the people in the Temple (5:20). At daybreak they do so and are again captured in the Temple (5:21–26). But, due to the influence of Gamaliel, they are again released, and Acts 5 concludes with the words, "And every day in the temple and at home they did not cease to teach and proclaim Jesus as the Messiah" (5:42).

When we recall the major section of the Gospel of Luke that deals with the teaching of Jesus in the Temple, the apostolic preaching in the Temple takes on a new light. Just as Jesus attempted to restore the Temple to its God-intended purpose, just so must his apostles attempt to occupy the Temple and use it as a place of teaching. But just as Jesus was opposed by the Temple priests, so are the apostles. At the end of Acts 5, the apostles seem to have won the day, for they are free to teach in the Temple daily. But Luke has not yet finished with the Temple, as we shall readily see in Acts 6–7.

Despite the generally positive images of Judaism in Acts 1–5, we must not forget that Peter repeatedly charges the Jewish people and their leaders with killing Jesus, an act in which they are said to oppose the purposes of God. Although Peter at one point concedes that this act was done in ignorance, he also makes it clear that Jews must repent of it. Despite the fact that the suffering and death of Jesus was a divine necessity and was foretold in scripture, the Jewish people and their leaders are pronounced guilty of betraying, denying, and killing Jesus. The members of the Sanhedrin perceive correctly that the apostles intend to bring the blood of Jesus on them (5:28).

We conclude then that the images of Jews and Judaism in Acts 1–5 are ambivalent. For the most part the people exercise good will toward the apostles, whom they respect. Multitudes of Jews accept the preaching of Peter and become believers. But most of the leaders are opponents, the Temple is shown to be a point of contention, and Jews are pictured as killers of Jesus.

### STEPHEN AND THE CHRISTIAN MESSAGE TO JEWS (ACTS 6–7)

In Acts 6:1–7 we are faced with the difficult exegetical problem of a controversy between Hebrews and Hellenists. Ostensibly these names designate groups of believers in Jerusalem, but Luke provides the implied reader no additional information about either group. The Hebrews are not mentioned again, but Hellenists reappear in 9:29 as disputants of Saul, and in 11:20 as objects of a mission of preachers from Cyprus and Cyrene.[9]

Most commentators think that Hebrews and Hellenists in Acts 6:1 designate language groups.[10] Since it is clear that both are believers and that only Jews have been offered the gospel up to this point, we should think of the two groups as Jewish Christians who speak different languages. But Henry J. Cadbury argued that "Hellenists," as referred to in Acts 6:1, must mean Greeks. He observed that, etymologically, *Hellēnistēs* designates "anyone who practices Greek ways—whether a Greek himself or a foreigner."[11] He also claimed that *Hebraioi* refers to the Jewish people, and not to language. Thus, he argued that, not only here in Acts 6:1 but also in 9:29 and 11:20, Hellenists are Greeks. In regard to the narrative structure of Acts, Cadbury did not see a straight-line movement from a Jewish to a Gentile setting. Rather he saw "successive and, one might almost say, repeated beginnings of Gentile Christianity."[12] Acts 6:1–7 is one such beginning; Philip's baptism of the Ethiopian eunuch (Acts 8:26–40) is another; the story of Cornelius is a third.

Cadbury was correct in insisting that we cannot interpret
*Hellēnistēs* in Acts 6:1 without examining Luke's other uses of this
word, in 9:29 and 11:20. And, although his etymological argument
is sound, he neither allows for contextual variation nor gives sufficient weight to the narrative structure of Acts. Bruce M. Metzger
is probably closer to the mark when he interprets *Hellēnistēs* simply
as "Greek-speaking people" and allows the context to determine
their more precise characteristics.[13] Under this interpretation Hellenists in 6:1 are Greek-speaking Jewish Christians. In 9:29, those
Hellenists who oppose and intend to kill Saul are Greek-speaking
Jews. In 11:20, the word designates "the mixed population of Antioch," in contrast to the Jewish population.[14] The narrative structure of Acts also tends to work against Cadbury's identification of
Hellenists in Acts 6:1 as Gentiles. As we shall see below, there are
a number of indications of the fact that, for Luke, Cornelius is the
first Gentile to whom the Christian message is offered. Thus, although it must be admitted that the word is unusual and its uses
in Acts unclear, it probably means Greek-speaking Jewish Christians in Acts 6:1.[15]

I have elsewhere argued that the conflict between the two
groups is one that involves dietary regulations.[16] The pericope reflects the practice of the common meal shared by the Christians in
Jerusalem and referred to in Acts 2:42, 46. The practice of the common meal is regarded by Luke as fundamental to the unity of the
Christian movement, but the problem in Acts 6:1 threatens to dis-
rupt this unity. It must be agreed that no clear explanation of the
neglect of widows is given here, but the problem, which concerns
"daily distribution" and "serving tables," seems most naturally to
involve food. If the problem is one involving the distribution of
food at a daily common meal, it is reasonable to suspect that some
aspect of dietary regulations lies at the bottom of it. But it would be
inadvisable to go any further than this, since Luke makes no explicit reference to the issue of dietary regulations. Rather we
should simply note at this point a vague and imprecise acknowl-
edgment on the part of the implied author that food practices were
at one time problematic. This point takes on further significance
when we get to the story of Peter's vision in Acts 10:9–16.

Whoever the Hebrews and Hellenists may be and whatever
the issue between them was, a major function of the story in Acts
6:1–7 is to introduce Stephen. He is introduced as a member of the
council of seven, the group that is charged to resolve the problem
between the Hellenists and the Hebrews. Luke does not explicitly

state that the council of seven consisted only of Hellenists, although most commentators assume this, since all members of the group have Greek names.[17] But on any interpretation, we encounter here a major rift in the early Christian church. Up to this point the apostles, with Peter as chief spokesperson, have been the leaders of the movement. It is important that the group consist of twelve, and it is clear that it has the authority to determine who are and who are not authentic Christians. For example, in Acts 5, Ananias and Sapphira were required to explain their actions to Peter. But in Acts 6, we meet a new group of church leaders, the seven. And, although the appointment of the seven is made here to cohere with the authority of the twelve, the story of Stephen that follows suggests that we have to do with a body of believers that functions independently of the apostles.[18]

The independence is seen not only in the charges brought against Stephen but even more clearly in his speech. The charges arose out of disputes that Stephen had with members of a synagogue (or perhaps a group of synagogues) in Jerusalem. Whether one or more synagogues are involved, the members are to be thought of as ex-diaspora Jews, from Cyrene, Alexandria, Cilicia, and Asia (6:9). These Jews charge Stephen with blasphemy (6:11), specifically with speaking against Temple and Torah (6:13) and with claiming that Jesus will destroy the Temple and change the customs of Moses (6:14). Luke states that these are false charges supported by the testimony of false witnesses (6:13). But he then goes on to include Stephen's speech in 7:2–53, which provides evidence to support the charge about the Temple, if not the one about Torah.[19]

The speech of Stephen (7:2–53) is by far the longest in Acts. The context would lead us to expect an apology at this point, since Stephen is facing a hearing before the Sanhedrin. But it differs significantly from the more apologetic speeches of Peter in Acts 4 and 5. There, although evangelistic notes are also found, Peter responded directly to the issues that had been raised. But there is no explicit mention of the charges in Stephen's speech. Neither is this an evangelistic speech. After the speech proper, Stephen prays for the forgiveness of his executioners (7:60) as did Jesus (Luke 23:34), but there is nothing of an appeal to the audience to repent, as there is in the speeches of Peter.[20]

Stephen's speech begins with a recital of some moments in Hebrew history. For much of the speech there is a sense that Stephen and his audience share a common heritage, and we have

a number of expressions such as "our race" (7:19), and "our ancestors" (7:19, 38, 39, 44). The speech is packed with quotations of
and allusions to scripture, most of them from the Pentateuch, and
references to ancient Hebrew figures—Abraham, Isaac, Jacob, Joseph, Moses, Aaron, Joshua, David, and Solomon. But the speech
is more than a simple recital of Hebrew history.[21] There are at least
two themes running through the speech that should be considered
in any study of the images of Judaism in Acts.

One theme is the rebelliousness of the Hebrew people, a
theme that is illustrated by two stories about Moses. In the first
(Acts 7:23–29), Stephen maintains that Moses' fellow Hebrews rejected him as judge even when he defended a man who was being
oppressed by an Egyptian. In the second (7:39–41), Stephen says
that after the exodus the people rejected Moses, intended to return
to Egypt, and worshiped images. Later, without citing specific incidents, Stephen charges that the ancient Hebrews murdered all
the prophets (7:52). And he concludes by identifying his present
audience with the rebellious Hebrews of the past. He describes
them as "stiff-necked people, uncircumcised in heart and ears"
(7:51), and he says, "You are forever opposing the Holy Spirit"
(7:51). He charges them with the betrayal and murder of Jesus
(7:52) and with not observing Torah (7:53). It is not unimportant
that the expressions of a common heritage (our fathers, etc.) that
we find near the beginning of the speech have given way to expressions of separation (your ancestors, 7:51, 52). The theme of rebelliousness, culminating in the charge that Jews did not keep
Torah (7:53), is an ironic answer to the accusation against Stephen,
"This man never stops saying things against . . . the law" (6:13).

A second theme, more subtly developed in Stephen's speech,
relates to holy places and acts of worship. Stephen first refers to a
place of worship in connection with the story of Abraham (7:7) and
again in his recital of the theophany to Moses at Mount Sinai
(7:30–34, with quotations from Exod 3:2–10). He calls attention to
the divine word that the place where Moses stood was "holy
ground" (gē hagia, 7:33). Next he refers to a meeting between
Moses and an angel that took place in the "congregation in the wilderness" (en tē ekklēsia en tē erēmō, 7:38). In 7:44–45, Stephen speaks
of the "tent of testimony" (hē skēnē tou martyriou). This tent is described as being made by Moses in accordance with a divine
plan.[22] It was brought into the promised land with Joshua and remained until the time of David. David wished to find a habitation

(*skēnōma*, 7:46) for God.[23] Finally, Stephen refers to the house that Solomon built.[24] He states that "the Most High does not dwell in houses made with human hands" (*all'ouch ho hypsistos en cheiropoētois katoikei*, 7:48), and he quotes from Isa 66:1–2 to back up his contention. The force of the argument is that Solomon's act of building the Temple was an act of disobedience, akin to the idolatry of those who, in 7:41, "reveled in the works of their hands." This God, according to Stephen, must not have a permanent dwelling, a house built with hands, and so the present Temple in Jerusalem cannot be called the house of God.[25]

A common element that ties Stephen's speech with the speeches of Peter is the charge of the Jewish audience with the murder of Jesus. But Stephen speaks of this act in the context of general Jewish rebelliousness. It is one more illustration, perhaps the culmination, of Jewish resistance against the purposes of God. It means that Jews in the time of Stephen are just like their ancestors, who persecuted all the prophets. In Peter's speeches, the killing of Jesus is an act of ignorance rather than a typical illustration of general rebelliousness. It is significant that Peter can still refer to this audience as "descendants of the prophets and of the covenant" (3:25), while Stephen charges, "Which of the prophets did your ancestors not persecute?" (7:52).

Stephen's words against Solomon's Temple find no echo in Peter's speeches, but they fit with a developing theme in Luke-Acts. As we saw in chapter 5 above, Jesus was portrayed in the Gospel of Luke as attempting to transform the Temple from a den of robbers into a house of prayer. His own act of teaching in the Temple was seen as his failed attempt to accomplish this transformation. But at the end of Luke and in the first five chapters of Acts, the apostles are frequently in the Temple, making Solomon's portico a kind of Christian meeting place. Their right to speak in the Temple is challenged by the Sanhedrin, and although there is no clear conclusion to the conflict between the apostles and the Jewish leaders in Acts 1–5, Stephen's speech serves as a Christian protest of the Temple. In terms of narrative development, the speech is a strong signal that the Jewish Temple will not finally be transformed, as Jesus had intended. And although Luke denies that Stephen had said that Jesus would destroy the Temple, the reader recalls that, in Luke 21:6, Jesus did predict its destruction.[26]

What images of Judaism are given in these chapters, and how is the implied reader led to think about the Jewish people? Here there is less ambivalence and greater clarity than in the gospel and in the earlier chapters of Acts. The images are fundamentally negative. The opposition to the Christian movement seems to be mounting in Acts 6, precipitated by conflicts between Stephen and members of Jerusalem synagogues. Jewish leaders—elders and scribes (6:12) and the high priest (7:1)—prosecute Stephen, but they seem now to be joined by the people (6:12). Stephen's death marks the beginning of a major persecution in Jerusalem (8:1).[27]

Although divine promises to Abraham and the covenant of circumcision are affirmed, Stephen's speech conveys almost totally negative images of the Jewish people. He charges that they have always rebelled against God, his purposes, and his appointed leaders. As they rejected Moses and Torah, so they rejected the one Moses foretold. As they killed all the prophets, so they killed Jesus. Solomon's building of the Temple is an example of rebelliousness akin to idolatry. Although Luke states that Stephen was unjustly charged, his speech is a prime illustration of Christian protest of the Jerusalem Temple and condemnation of the Jewish people.[28]

### THE CHRISTIAN MESSAGE TO PERIPHERAL PEOPLE AND GENTILES (ACTS 8–12)

After the death of Stephen there is a scattering of the Christian believers, although the apostles remain in Jerusalem.[29] This scattering results in an enlargement not only of the geographical setting in Acts 8–12 but also of the ethnic diversity among believers. In these chapters Christian missionaries go out to Judea and Samaria; a convert comes from Ethiopia; we learn that there are Christians in Damascus; a centurion from the Italian regiment at Caesarea is converted; and Hellenists at Antioch accept the gospel.

Although, as has been indicated above, Cornelius is to be regarded as the first Gentile believer, the narratives that lead up to this incident prepare for it. Acts 8–12 is to a large extent a transitional section that stands between those parts of Acts that locate the Christian movement in Jerusalem and among Jews to those that focus attention on the spread of Christianity to diverse people in distant lands. The question of how a movement made this kind of major change is answered by Luke in an anecdotal fashion that shows how the change was prepared for by missionary enterprises among Samaritans and diaspora Jews, people who, from the perspective of Jerusalemite Jews, were regarded as peripheral.[30]

The main actors in Acts 8–12 are Philip, Peter, and Saul. Philip, a member with Stephen of the council of the seven, conducts missionary work in Samaria (8:4–13) and Judea (8:26–40). Peter, with John, follows up on the work of Philip in Samaria (8:14–25). Peter then travels to Lydda (9:32–35) and Joppa (9:36–43). In Joppa he has the vision that leads to his meeting with Cornelius at Caesarea (10:1–48). After his return to Jerusalem and his meeting with the other apostles (11:1–18), Peter is arrested by Herod, but he escapes with the help of an angel (12:1–17). Saul is first introduced in connection with the execution of Stephen. It is said that he witnessed the execution (7:58), approved of it (8:1), and engaged in a vigorous persecution of the church (8:3). With the permission of the high priest, he goes to investigate the situation in Damascus, intending to arrest Christians and bring them back to Jerusalem (9:1–2). But on the way he is converted (9:3–19), and he begins to preach in the synagogues of Damascus (9:20–25) and in Jerusalem (9:26–29). Because of the opposition of Hellenists, Saul is dispatched to Tarsus (9:30), where he remains until Barnabas picks him up and takes him to Antioch (11:25–26). At the onset of a famine, he goes with Barnabas on a trip to Jerusalem with relief for the believers there (11:27–30). At the end of this section Barnabas and Saul return, apparently to Antioch (12:24–25).[31]

These narratives are interwoven in Acts 8–12 in such a way that it is difficult to see a particular sense of order. But it is impressive that the major target for Christian preachers is no longer the Jews of Jerusalem but Samaritans, diaspora Jews, and Godfearing Gentiles. Still, images of Judaism and Jewish people are not lacking here. We can best uncover these images by concentrating our attention on three narratives within Acts 8–12.

The first narrative of interest is that of Philip and the Ethiopian eunuch (Acts 8:26–40). The eunuch is carefully identified as "a court official of the Candace, queen of the Ethiopians, in charge of her entire treasury" (8:27). Unfortunately, we are not explicitly told if he is Jewish or Gentile.[32] But he has come to worship in Jerusalem and is reading from the Hebrew Scriptures; that is, he engages in activities that the narrative so far associates with Jewish people. In addition, the narrative structure of Acts demands that no Gentile precede Cornelius into Christian faith. Not only does the story of Cornelius form the most extensive continuous narrative in this section of Acts, but his conversion is later cited (15:7–9) as proof that God selected Peter to present the gospel to Gentiles.

So we should regard the Ethiopian official as Jewish. But, from the perspective of Judean Jews, he is peripheral. As a eunuch he probably would come under the restriction of Deut 23:1, which prohibits castrated males from entering religious assemblies (but see Isa 56:3–5). And as an Ethiopian, he is a diaspora Jew, the first such convert about whom we have a specific narrative. He is peripheral in the same way the Samaritans are peripheral; he is not a Semitic-speaking Jew from Jerusalem or Judea and thus not among those who first embraced the Christian gospel.

The narrative of the Ethiopian eunuch is also interesting in providing us with an instance of the understanding of scripture in Luke-Acts. When Philip meets him, the eunuch is reading from Isa 53:7–8, which is quoted in Acts 8:32–33. When Philip asks him if he understands what he is reading, the eunuch replies that he is unable to understand the scripture without an interpreter. This comment reaffirms a theme that we encountered in the Gospel of Luke, namely the scripture is authoritative but requires interpretation. Philip's explanation shows that the required interpretation is Christological, as he explains that Isaiah pointed to Jesus. It is also notable that this is one of the few instances where a specific passage is quoted to support the frequently encountered contention that the suffering of the Christ was foretold in scripture.

The second story that calls for comment is that of Saul and his preaching in Damascus (9:20–25) and Jerusalem (9:26–30). Although there are two narratives that report Saul's preaching, there is a common literary pattern in them. Saul preaches but is met with surprise and skepticism on the part of the believers. He continues to speak boldly, his opponents attempt to kill him, and his supporters enable him to escape. Saul's audiences, who become his opponents, though different in the two stories, are to be understood as peripheral people. In Damascus he preaches to Jews, by definition diaspora Jews. In Jerusalem he speaks to Hellenists. As we saw above, these cannot be the same as those believing Hellenists who in Acts 6:1 grumbled against the Hebrews, since the narrative structure virtually demands that Saul's opponents be unbelievers. These Hellenists must be a group of Greek-speaking Jews, who from the perspective of Semitic-speaking Jews would be considered peripheral or marginal people.

Images of Jewish people underlie these accounts, particularly the former (Acts 9:20–25). Here as in the gospel, synagogues are places of controversy. In his proclamation of Jesus as the Christ,

Saul stirred up the Damascus Jews. The verb *sygcheō* means to confound or to confuse, and the connotation is one of conflict. For the first time in Luke-Acts we encounter the use of the general term "the Jews" (9:22) to designate opponents of Jesus and his followers. Prior to this occurrence, the opponents have been either individuals or specific groups of Jews, such as Pharisees, Sadducees, chief priests, elders, or scribes. In 9:22, the specific denotation is the Jews of Damascus, but this passage marks the beginning of a tendency to designate opponents not by any specific name but rather as "the Jews." A little later in Acts 12:3 we read that Herod's action in putting the apostle James to death pleased the Jews. After Peter's escape from prison, he explains that God's angel rescued him "from the hands of Herod and from all that the Jewish people were expecting" (12:11). This usage inevitably leads the reader not to think of specific subgroups of Jews or even of certain local Jewish groups but of Jews in general as opponents of Christians. The immediate reaction of the Jews in Damascus is to plot to kill Saul, and Luke calls special attention to their vigilance, "They were watching the gates day and night so that they might kill him" (9:24). But Saul's disciples enabled him to escape from Damascus in a basket.

The twin account in Acts 9:26–30 changes the scene to Jerusalem and substitutes Hellenists for Jews. Here Barnabas acts as Saul's sponsor, and he arranges a meeting with the apostles, who grant their approval. In Jerusalem Saul speaks and debates with (*elalei te kai sunezētei*, 9:29) Hellenists. Again the connotations are those of controversy and threatened murder. These two narratives about Saul show how the Christian message was offered to peripheral groups, diaspora Jews in Damascus, and Greek-speaking Jews in Jerusalem, and they show how the message was rejected and the messenger threatened.

The third narrative in this section of Acts is the most important. It is the story of Peter and Cornelius (Acts 10:1–11:18), a narrative that finally tells of the conversion of a Gentile and his admission into the Christian movement. The size and complexity of the narrative indicate its importance for Luke, and the inclusion of visions, angelophanies, divine commands, and apostolic judgments shows that something momentous is being described here. The character of this long narrative, with its explicit characterization of Cornelius as a Godfearing Gentile and its focus on certain impediments to Jewish-Gentile social intercourse, demands that it be understood as Luke's story of the first Gentile Christian. At the end of it (Acts 11:18), we have the solemn apostolic judgment affirming the general admission of Gentiles. The narrative is made up of seven subsections that may be listed here for convenience.

(1) Cornelius' vision (10:1–8): An angel appears to Cornelius in Caesarea and tells him to summon Simon Peter to come from Joppa.

(2) Peter's vision (10:9–16): A large sheet, with all kinds of animals, appears to Peter, who is told to kill and eat.

(3) Peter and Cornelius' Servants (10:17–23a): The servants report to Peter at Joppa and arrange a meeting with Cornelius in Caesarea.

(4) Peter and Cornelius (10:23b–33): Each tells the other about his vision.

(5) Peter's speech (10:34–43): Peter preaches to Cornelius and his household about Jesus.

(6) The Baptism of Cornelius (10:44–48): The Holy Spirit falls on all those in Peter's audience, and they are baptized.

(7) Peter at Jerusalem (11:1–18): Peter is required to explain his actions to the other apostles in Jerusalem.

The story of Peter and Cornelius is not only important for Luke's effort to explain the early Christian Gentile mission, it is also significant in what it implies about Christian views of Judaism. But the interpreter of the story is met with a number of difficult exegetical problems that have a bearing on both the Gentile mission and images of Judaism.

The major problem is that, although Peter's vision in Acts 10:9–16 is ostensibly about the abolition of the distinction between clean and unclean foods, Peter's own interpretation of it is that the distinction between clean and unclean people has been abolished (10:28). With this the judgment of the other apostles and the Judean Christians, recorded in 11:18, agrees. Later, Peter again speaks of the cleansing of the hearts of the Gentiles in Acts 15:9. These and other problems led Martin Dibelius to conclude that Luke drew on a rather simple story about the conversion of Cornelius, a story similar to that of the conversion of the Ethiopian, and that he added to it several materials that obscured its meaning.[33] Although Dibelius' conclusions have recently been questioned, the problems remain.[34]

If we had only the vision of Peter, we would be forced to conclude that the subject is the Jewish dietary regulations, at least those that distinguish between edible and inedible animals. The sheet that Peter sees descending from the sky has on it all kinds of animals. Clearly, both kosher and nonkosher animals are to be thought of as included.[35] This is implied not only by the inclusion of reptiles but also by the emphatic *panta*, literally, "all quadrupeds, reptiles of the earth, and birds of the sky" (Acts 10:12, my translation). Thus, when Peter is told to kill and eat, it seems clear that the dietary regulations of Leviticus 11 and other places are being annulled. The voice that Peter hears is that either of the ascended Jesus or of God, since he uses the address *kyrios*. His response is perfectly appropriate to this situation. Even while recognizing the voice as that of ultimate authority, he expresses horror and initially refuses to obey. It is inconceivable to him to kill and eat those animals that were declared unclean in Torah. But then the voice speaks again, "What God has made clean, you must not call profane" (10:15). The meaning would appear to be that all meats have become cleansed; there are no unclean meats and hence no prohibitions against eating them. The threefold repetition of the heavenly command appears necessary in order to overcome Peter's reluctance and to emphasize the significance of what has occurred.

The plain meaning of this ecstatic experience is not, however, drawn out by Peter. He remains uncertain about its meaning as the delegation from Cornelius arrives (10:17), and when he explains it to the household of Cornelius in Caesarea, he says, "But God has shown me that I should not call anyone profane or unclean" (10:28). The focus has shifted from the annulment of dietary regulations to the abolition of distinctions between Jews and Gentiles. This concern is also affirmed in 10:34, where Peter says, "I truly understand that God shows no partiality," and by the conclusion drawn by the apostles in 11:18: "Then God has given even to the Gentiles the repentance that leads to life."

Ernst Haenchen claims that the vision of Peter, in its present setting, has nothing to do with dietary regulations.[36] He maintains that the point of the whole story is expressed in 10:28 and 11:18. He says further, "Expositors would not have thought of interpreting the vision in terms of food (the actual text sees it only in terms of men!) if 11.3 had not emboldened them to do so."[37] But Haenchen has not only overlooked the significance of Acts 11:3 in its present setting, he has also refused to consider the plain meaning of Peter's vision and the connections that hold this narrative together.

The need for legitimating the Gentile mission is recognized in Acts 11:3, which notes the objection of the circumcision party to Peter's actions. But the objection is not to his baptizing Cornelius and his household, but rather to his visiting and eating with them. Although Luke has no explicit statement about Peter's eating with Gentiles, such is implied in 10:48, which says that he accepted the invitation to remain for some days with Cornelius in Caesarea. Moreover, in Acts 10:28, Peter himself recognized that an objection could be raised against his conduct. He began his address to the people at Caesarea by reminding them that it was unlawful for a Jew to visit a foreigner (*allophylos*).

If we read Acts 11:3 in connection with Peter's vision in 10:9–16 and his statement in 10:28, we are able to perceive a sense of the connection between the general considerations affecting Jewish social intercourse with Gentiles and the specific considerations affecting dietary regulations. J. N. Sevenster and others have shown that, in the Hellenistic period, Gentile hostility toward Jews frequently involved suspicions that rooted in what appeared to them to be social isolation and that the isolation was almost altogether a result of Jewish adherence to dietary regulations and laws of impurity.[38] Similarly, Strack and Billerbeck explain that the barriers to social intercourse between Jews and Gentiles included the fear, on the part of Jews, of contacting something or someone unclean and the necessity to adhere to the food laws.[39] The connection is explained in Leviticus 11, which distinguishes between clean and unclean animals and declares that anyone who comes in contact with unclean carcasses is likewise unclean. Thus, anyone who does not observe the dietary regulations is unclean and to be avoided; unclean diet means unclean person.[40]

If it is legitimate to assume that the connection between unclean diet and unclean person is a close one in Luke's world and hence in the narrative world of implied author and implied reader, then the entire passage can be coherently interpreted. In order to prepare the way for the baptism of Cornelius and his household, it was necessary for a great social barrier between Jews and Gentiles to be broken down, namely the restrictions against eating certain meats.[41] That was done in Peter's vision. As a result of the annulment of these dietary restrictions, Peter was able to visit with Gentiles and eat with them. If God has annulled the distinction between clean and unclean foods, it follows that he has also annulled the distinction between clean and unclean persons. It then becomes clear that God shows no partiality (10:34) and that he has granted repentance to Gentiles (11:18).

Thus, not only does the story of Peter and Cornelius signal the new openness of the Christian movement to Gentiles, it also shows a new departure in which certain restrictions are being jettisoned. It is significant that Luke calls attention to a Christian group that resists the relaxation of these restrictions and that he names them the circumcision party. It is clear from the name that this group has other issues to air, but those issues will not be faced until Acts 15.

What images of Judaism do we have in the story of Peter and Cornelius? We should note first the way in which Cornelius is described. He is "a devout man who feared God with all his household; he gave alms generously to the people and prayed constantly to God" (10:2). The delegation that he sends to Peter describes him as "an upright and God-fearing man, who is well spoken of by the whole Jewish nation" (10:22). Cornelius himself states that he was keeping the ninth hour of prayer (10:30). The Godfearing Cornelius worships the Jewish God and observes the Jewish times of prayer. The reader is reminded of another centurion in Luke 7:1–10, who had built the synagogue at Capernaum. Both are Gentiles who are positively disposed toward the Jewish religion; in Luke's language they are Godfearers.[42] In addition, there is an incidental reminder that Jewish believers were in Peter's entourage (10:45). Here the reader's attention is drawn to Jews who are believers and to Godfearers who are about to join them. These are certainly positive images of Judaism.

The speech of Peter in Acts 10:34–43 may be compared with his speeches in Acts 1–5.[43] Although it is addressed to a Gentile rather than to a Jewish audience, the same major points are still present. Peter makes a reference to the word that God sent to Israel (10:36),[44] he charges that the Jews put Jesus to death (10:39), he proclaims the resurrection of Jesus (10:40), he says that scripture foretold these events (10:43), and he announces the forgiveness of sins (10:43). In terms of Christian views of Judaism, however, there are subtle but important differences in this speech. It begins with

Peter's observation that questions the fundamental concept of the unique relationship between God and the Jewish people: "I truly understand that God shows no partiality, but in every nation anyone who fears him and does what is right is acceptable to him" (10:34).[45] The lack of distinction between Jews and Gentiles is repeated by Peter in 11:12. Although he retains the older concept that Jesus was appointed for Jews, Peter also speaks of him as Lord of all (10:36), and he makes a point of the fact that after his resurrection Jesus did not appear to all the people (10:41). Peter judges that the prophets taught that "everyone who believes in him [Jesus] receives forgiveness of sins through his name" (10:43).[46]

The narrative as a whole shows that there are certain restrictions in the Jewish religion that limit social intercourse with Gentiles and that classify Gentiles as unclean people. Reference to a Christian group known as the circumcision party (11:2) also calls attention to Jewish restrictions that Christians must overcome. In addition, Jews are shown to be people who think of themselves as enjoying a special relationship with God, and hence as unable to treat a truly righteous Gentile, such as Cornelius, as an equal.

It is important to observe that scripture plays almost no role whatsoever in the story of Peter and Cornelius. The only explicit reference is in the general statement with which Peter's speech concludes, Acts 10:43. Here the claim is made that the prophets bore witness to the possibility of repentance for all who believe. One might be led to compare the usage here with that in the story of the eunuch, for in both there is a sense in which the prophetic testimony to the Christ plays a role in conversion. But in the story of the eunuch, the reading of a particular prophetic scripture, together with the attempt to understand it, provides the occasion for Philip to give his Christological interpretation. Acts 10:43, however, makes no reference to a particular scripture, answers no specific questions about interpretation, and serves only as one of several items leading to the conversion of Cornelius. We shall see that there is in Acts 15 a retrospective justification for Peter's mission, together with a quotation from Amos (Acts 15:16–18). But within the story of Peter and Cornelius itself, prophetic scripture plays a very minor role. The justification for social intercourse between Jews and Gentiles, which permits the Gentile mission, is supplied by the vision of Peter and the actions of the spirit in leading him to Cornelius. The justification for baptizing Gentiles is given in their experience of glossolalia. Although the story of Cornelius is Luke's centerpiece in describing the initiation of the Gentile mission, there is no attempt to provide a scriptural justification for the dramatic changes required by this mission. On the contrary, the Hebrew Scriptures, which include the dietary regulations, seem to stand in the way of the Gentile mission at this point. It is difficult to avoid the conclusion that the implied author provides a signal of a problem precisely by omitting quotations and allusions to scripture in this story. What is required is the annulment of dietary regulations, and scripture provides no basis for it. Thus it becomes necessary to call upon an authority higher than scripture—the heavenly voice and the Holy Spirit—which means that for the implied author there are significant qualifications to the authority of scripture. It is authoritative where it is useful and when it is correctly interpreted. It is irrelevant at those points where God has provided subsequent alteration.

## CONCLUSION

In Acts 1–12 there appears to be a progressive movement toward negative images of Judaism and Jews. In the first five chapters, which focus attention on the speeches of Peter to Jewish people, there is a dominant tone of good will. The response to Peter's speeches is primarily positive, and multitudes of pious Jews become believers. There is an emphasis on the common heritage shared by Peter and his audience. At one point Peter refers to his hearers as "descendants of the prophets and of the covenant" (Acts 3:25). In his speeches, Peter shows that the event of Jesus was meant for Jews and that the Hebrew Scriptures predicted these latter days. Peter accuses the Jews of murdering Jesus and shows that his resurrection was God's response to their action. But at one point he attributes the execution of Jesus to Jewish ignorance, and he offers them repentance and promises forgiveness. The Temple is shown to be a point of contention between the Jewish leaders and the apostles, but even some leaders are friendly, and the people as a whole respect and revere the apostles. In an appropriate and striking phrase, Gerhard Lohfink referred to this period as the "Jerusalem springtime."[47]

But things begin to take a different turn in Acts 6–7, the centerpiece of which is the speech of Stephen. Like Peter, Stephen accuses the Jews of killing Jesus, but unlike Peter, he classifies it as one in a long series of disobedient acts. Here Jews are presented as perennially resistant to the will of God and disobedient to Torah.

Solomon's building of the Temple is said to be an act contrary to the will of God, and Stephen announces that God does not inhabit such a building. He identifies his audience as descendants of those who killed all the prophets.

In Acts 8–12, where the focus of attention is on the Christian mission to peripheral people and finally Godfearing Gentiles, Jews are shown to be persecutors of the Christian believers. They are vicious opponents of Saul, and they are pleased at the execution of James. Jewish religious life is pictured as being supported by claims of divine partiality and marked by restrictions that limit relations with Gentiles. Although Luke makes it clear in the story of the Ethiopian eunuch that the scriptures foretold the coming of Jesus, he makes no use of these texts in the story of Cornelius. Clearly the Gentile mission is divinely ordained, but the annulment of those impediments that hinder it—the concept of divine partiality and the imposition of dietary restrictions—are not here supported by scripture but by divine command.[48]

## NOTES

1. Although the context would seem to demand *apo* or *ex* in Acts 12:25, the earliest and best witnesses have the reading *eis Ierousalēm*. See Bruce M. Metzger, *A Textual Commentary on the Greek New Testament*, 398–400, for a discussion of this problem.

2. Ernst Haenchen observes correctly that Acts 1:8 already implies a mission that is not restricted to Jews. See Haenchen, *The Acts of the Apostles: A Commentary*, 143f. See also Luke 24:47.

3. Jack T. Sanders, *The Jews in Luke-Acts*, 132 and elsewhere, uses the term *periphery* to designate "Outcasts, Samaritans, Proselytes, Godfearers." Although the term is apt, it should also, from the perspective of the implied author, include diaspora Jews.

4. On the importance of speeches in Acts, Haenchen says, "Without them Acts would be like a gospel consisting only of miracle-stories, without any sayings of Jesus" (Haenchen, *Acts*, 212).

5. See, e.g., Henry J. Cadbury, "The Speeches in Acts"; Cadbury, *The Making of Luke-Acts*, 184–93; Martin Dibelius, *Studies in the Acts of the Apostles*, 138–85; Eduard Schweizer, "Concerning the Speeches in Acts"; Ulrich Wilckens, *Die Missionsreden der Apostelgeschichte: Form-und traditions geschichtliche Untersuchen*; Max Wilcox, "A Foreword to the Study of the Speeches in Acts."

6. On the speeches in Acts 2 and 3, see Richard F. Zehnle, *Peter's Pentecost Discourse: Tradition and Lukan Reinterpretation in Peter's Speeches of Acts 2 and 3*. Zehnle concludes that, while Acts 2 represents Lukan theology, Acts 3 is closer to pre-Lukan conceptions.

7. The quotation in Acts differs from Gen 22:18 at a significant point. Gen 22:18 has, "And by your offspring shall all the nations of the earth (*ta ethnē tēs gēs*) gain blessing for themselves." In place of *ethnē*, Luke has *patriai*.

8. On the use of Psalm 16 here, see Martin Rese, "Die Funktion der alttesta-mentlichen Zitate und Anspielungen in den Reden der Apostelgeschichte."

9. Although UBSGNT 3 accepts the reading *Hellēnistas* in 11:20, there is ancient support for *Hellēnas*. For a discussion of the textual problems here, see Metzger, *Textual Commentary*, 386–89. Hans Conzelmann, *Acts of the Apostles*, 87, says that the sense of the passage demands the reading *Hellēnas*.

10. See, e.g., Conzelmann, *Acts*, 45; C. H. Dodd, "The History and Doctrine of the Apostolic Age"; Joseph A. Fitzmyer, "Jewish Christianity in Acts in Light of the Qumran Scrolls"; Haenchen, *Acts*, 260; Martin Hengel, *Between Jesus and Paul: Studies in the Earliest History of Christianity*, 1–29; Gerhard Schneider, "Stephanus, die Hellenisten und Samaria." For a discussion of the various options see Everett Ferguson, "The Hellenists in the Book of Acts."

11. Cadbury, "The Hellenists," 60.

12. Ibid., 66.

13. Metzger, *Textual Commentary*, 386–89.

14. Ibid., 389.

15. For a discussion of the literary and historical aspects of Acts 6:1–7, see Haenchen, *Acts*, 264–69.

16. See Joseph B. Tyson, "Acts 6:1–7 and Dietary Regulations in Early Christian-ity." Although I continue to think that problems of dietary regulations are re-flected in the passage, I am less certain about the identification of the Hellenists. In this article, I cited a number of reasons to support Cadbury's identification, but I now find these reasons less compelling. For a helpful dis-cussion of the problems of dietary regulations, from a "socio-redactional" per-spective, see Philip F. Esler, *Community and Gospel in Luke-Acts: The Social and Political Motivations of Lucan Theology*, 71–109.

17. Cadbury, however, observes that Palestinian Jews must often have been bilin-gual and have borne Greek names. See Cadbury, "Hellenists," 62.

18. See, e.g., Haenchen, *Acts*, 264–69; Hengel, *Between Jesus and Paul*, 1–29.

19. On the literary function of Acts 6:14, see Sasagu Arai, "Zum 'Tempelwort' Jesu in Apostelgeschichte 6.14." Jacob Jervell asked "why Luke labels these charges [in Acts 6:13] as false in spite of their being partly confirmed in Acts 7, espe-cially the criticism of the temple." Jervell, "The History of Early Christianity and the Acts of the Apostles," in *The Unknown Paul: Essays on Luke-Acts and Early Christian History*, 14. Jervell concludes that Luke's intention is to portray a conservative, law-abiding church that results at the end of Acts. He writes: "From the account in Acts 21 and from the idea of a dominating Jewish-Christian part of the church based upon the Pharisee Paul, the accusations are evidently false. The loyalty of the church to the law is beyond doubt, and this loyalty is that of Jewish Christians and the circumcised" (24).

20. On the parallels with the death of Jesus, see David P. Moessner, " 'The Christ Must Suffer':New Light on the Jesus—Peter, Stephen, Paul Parallels in Luke-Acts." Moessner also shows that Stephen's speech is modeled on a Deutero-nomic pattern. His work would suggest that we should think of the polemic in Stephen's speech as a version of what Douglas R. A. Hare called "prophetic anti-Judaism." See Hare, "The Rejection of the Jews in the Synoptic Gospels and Acts."

21. On the traditional aspects of summaries of Hebrew history, see Helmer Ring-gren, "Luke's Use of the Old Testament."

22. Conzelmann, *Acts*, 56, notes that Philo spoke of the tent as *cheiropoiēton*, "but without any deprecatory sense."

23. UBSGNT 3 accepts the reading *skēnōma tō oikō Iakōb*, "a habitation for the house of Jacob."

24. For a discussion of the various terms used here for holy places, see John Kilgallen, *The Stephen Speech: A Literary and Redactional Study of Acts 7:2–53*, 87–95.

25. But see Dennis D. Sylva, "The Meaning and Function of Acts 7:46–50." See also Francis D. Weinert, "Luke, Stephen, and the Temple in Luke-Acts."
26. It should be noted that the accusation brought against Stephen in Acts 6:14 is essentially the same as that brought against Jesus in Mark 14:58 (cf. Matt 26:61). Neither the Markan nor the Matthean form of the saying appears in Luke's trial narratives.
27. The sympathetic character of the reference to "a great many of the priests" (6:7) should, however, be noted as a positive image.
28. Gerhard Lohfink, Die Sammlung Israels: Eine Untersuchung zur lukanischen Ekklesiologie, 47–62, also called attention to the dramatic change from positive to negative images of the Jewish people that begins with the introduction of Stephen.
29. Haenchen, Acts, 297, maintains that historically it was the Hellenists, and probably only the leaders of this group, who were persecuted. But Luke had no intention of portraying a divided Christian community. "As he could not conceive that it fell into two distinct groups, he was obliged to think of a dispersion of the whole community. On the other hand, tradition said nothing about a persecution of the Apostles—so they must have held out and thereby assured the continuity of the primitive Church!" (297). In agreement is Esler, Community and Gospel, 139–40.
30. Peripheral people appear, however, in earlier chapters of Acts. For example, diaspora Jews and proselytes are among those addressed by Peter at Pentecost (2:5, 10). Barnabas is described as a Levite from Cyprus (4:36), and Nicolaus as a proselyte from Antioch (6:5).
31. See note 1, above.
32. Haenchen, Acts, 315, regards Acts 8:26–40 as originally an account from the Hellenists of "the first conversion of a Gentile." But Luke cannot present the eunuch as a Gentile. "Otherwise Philip would have forestalled Peter, the legitimate founder of the Gentile mission! For that reason Luke leaves the eunuch's status in a doubtful light. . . . And so it remains uncertain what the eunuch really is; but it is precisely this screen of secrecy about his person which is best suited to the stage now reached in the history of the mission. Without permitting the emergence of all the problems which an explicit baptism of a Gentile must bring in its wake, Luke here leaves the reader with the feeling that with this new convert the mission has taken a step beyond the conversion of Jews and Samaritans" (314). Conzelmann agrees about the original setting and meaning of the story, and he says, "Luke has placed the story here so that it now functions as a prelude to Cornelius's conversion" (Acts, 67). Robert C. Tannehill argues that in its context in Acts the eunuch is a Gentile, but he must then deal with the fact that the episode has no consequences in the narratives that follow. He thus refers to it as a private event. See Tannehill, The Narrative Unity of Luke-Acts: A Literary Interpretation, 2:102–12. See also Beverly R. Gaventa, From Darkness to Light: Aspects of Conversion in the New Testament, 96–129.
33. See Dibelius, Studies, 109–22.
34. Cf. Klaus Haacker, "Dibelius und Cornelius: Ein Beispiel formgeschichtlicher Überlieferungskritik." See also Gerhard Schneider, Die Apostelgeschichte, in loc. See also Wilckens, Die Missionsreden.
35. Haenchen, however, argues that only unclean animals are included on the sheet. He says that Peter's reaction does not make sense if clean animals are present, that he simply would not have objected to killing and eating permitted animals. See Haenchen, Acts, 362.
36. See ibid., 343–63.
37. Ibid., 362. Haenchen also said: "Luke shrinks from having the Church protest in so many words against the baptism just effected, though that is what is re-

ally meant. Instead he represents the accusation as leveled against table-fellowship with the uncircumcised" (359).

38. See J. N. Sevenster, *The Roots of Pagan Anti-Semitism in the Ancient World*. See also John G. Gager, *The Origins of Anti-Semitism: Attitudes Toward Judaism in Pagan and Christian Antiquity*.

39. See Str-B 4,1:374–78.

40. J. Duncan M. Derrett, "Clean and Unclean Animals (Acts 10:15, 11:9): Peter's Pronouncing Power Observed," claims that Peter's vision required the use of the Noachide diet for Christians.

41. F. F. Bruce saw this connection clearly and assumed that Peter did also, "Actually, the terms of his vision on the housetop at Joppa taught him to call no *food* common or unclean if God pronounced it clean; but he was quick to grasp the analogy between ceremonial food-laws and the regulations affecting intercourse with non-Jews" (*The Book of Acts*, 222).

42. On Godfearers, see Folker Siegert, "Gottesfürchtige und Sympathisanten"; A. Thomas Kraabel, "The Disappearance of the 'God-fearers'"; idem., "Greeks, Jews, and Lutherans in the Middle Half of Acts"; Jacob Jervell, "The Church of Jews and Godfearers"; P. W. Van der Horst, "Jews and Christians in Aphrodisias in the Light of Their Relations in Other Cities of Asia Minor."

43. For a discussion of various studies of Peter's speech in Acts 10, see Frans Neirynck, "Le Livre des Actes: 6. Ac. 10,36–43 et l'Évangile."

44. Note also that in 10:42, Peter says that God commanded the apostles to preach to the people (*kēryxai tō laō*), i.e., to preach to Jews.

45. Haenchen calls attention to the revolutionary character of Peter's words in Acts 10:34f. He points out that these verses challenge the entire concept of Israel as God's elect people. See Haenchen, "Judentum und Christentum in der Apostelgeschichte," especially p. 168.

46. For a discussion of the concept of divine impartiality, see Jouette M. Bassler, "Luke and Paul on Impartiality." Bassler comments that Luke's view is similar to Greco-Roman expressions of universality. In Acts, Cornelius, though a Gentile, is thought of as having achieved sufficient virtue to be regarded among God's elect.

47. See Lohfink, *Sammlung*, 55. The phrase is also applied to Acts 1–5 by Robert Maddox, *The Purpose of Luke-Acts*, 52, and by Jack T. Sanders, *Jews in Luke-Acts*, *passim*.

48. See, however, Luke 3:6; Acts 13:47; 15:16–18, where scripture is used to support the concept that the Gentiles have a place in God's plan.

7

# The Pauline Mission

(Acts 13:1–21:14)

After the narratives about the Christian mission among Jerusalem Jews and peripheral people, Luke begins in Acts 13 the story of the Christian mission among diaspora Jews and Gentiles in the eastern Mediterranean world. The geographic horizon expands well beyond Judea and Samaria, as Christian missionaries move into Cyprus, Pisidia, Asia, and Achaia. There is even a prospect of a mission in Rome. The narrative function of this and the following section of Acts is governed by the divine announcement in 9:15–16. After the experience of Saul on the road to Damascus, Ananias received a vision in which he was told to find Saul and cure him of his blindness. Ananias was hesitant since he had heard of Saul's role in persecuting Christians in Jerusalem. But the divine voice commanded, "Go, for he is an instrument whom I have chosen to bring my name before Gentiles and kings and before the people of Israel; I myself will show him how much he must suffer for the sake of my name" (Acts 9:15–16).[1] Although the divine command is not carried out in this precise sequence, it serves to signal the reader about the function of Paul. Paul will carry out the mission to the people of Israel and the Gentiles in Acts 13:1–21:14, and in 21:15–26:32 he will speak to a king.[2] Thus the narrative function of Acts 13:1–21:14 is to present the ways in which the Christian message was presented to and received by Jews and Gentiles in the eastern Mediterranean, and this section of Acts is a rich resource for us in searching for images of Judaism.

Although he is accompanied by a number of fellow missionaries and travelers, Paul is clearly the hero from Acts 13 to the end of the book, as is Peter in the earlier section. It is striking to mark the parallels between Paul in Acts 13:1–21:14 and Peter in Acts 1–

12. Both Peter and Paul deliver speeches, perform healings and resurrections, defeat workers of magic, correct inadequate teaching, are miraculously released from prison, and witness the giving of the spirit and the phenomenon of glossolalia among converts. Paul delivers a speech to Jews in Pisidian Antioch (Acts 13:16–41, 46–47), a speech to Gentiles in Lystra (14:15–17), one to Gentiles in Athens (17:22–31), and a farewell speech to the Christian elders at Miletus (20:18–35). The healing in the Temple by Peter and John of the man born lame (2:1–10), has a close parallel in Paul's healing in Lystra of the man born lame (14:8–10). Indeed, both narratives are followed by overreactions on the part of the crowd. After the healing in the Temple, the people run together in astonishment, and Peter is forced to disclaim that the miracle occurred by his own power (3:12). After the healing at Lystra, the crowd worships Barnabas as Zeus and Paul as Hermes, and the priest of Zeus begins preparations for a sacrifice. So Paul and Barnabas attempt to quiet the crowd by asserting that they are only humans (14:15). In Acts 5:14–16, it is reported that Peter's shadow had miraculous curative powers. In 19:11–12 it is said that people were healed by handkerchiefs or aprons that had contacted Paul's body. Peter raises Tabitha from the dead in 9:36–43, and Paul raises Eutychus in 20:7–12. Paul's meeting with the seven sons of Sceva (19:13–20) is reminiscent of Peter's (and Philip's) meeting with Simon of Samaria (8:9–24), although with different outcomes. Simon becomes a believer, but the sons of Sceva, a Jewish high priest, become the victims of demonic power. The defeat of magic is, nevertheless, a major component in both stories. The defeat of Elymas the magician by Paul (Acts 13:6–12) also reminds one of the earlier Petrine story, and the narrative in which Paul corrects the inadequate teaching received by the disciples of Apollos (19:1–7) is similar to the story in which Peter and John correct the abuses of Simon (8:14–24).[3] Both Peter (12:1–19) and Paul (16:19–40) suffer imprisonment but are miraculously freed. Finally, both have the opportunity to observe the giving of the spirit and the phenomenon of glossolalia among converts, Peter with the household of Cornelius (10:44–48) and Paul with the disciples of Apollos (19:1–7).

The literary effect of these parallels between Peter and Paul is to lead the reader to think of Paul as a legitimate bearer of the Christian message, fully equipped, miraculously chosen and empowered.[4] Although Luke has not granted the title apostle to

Paul, except in 14:14 and implicitly in 14:4 (in both cases with Barnabas), and has strictly removed him from this status by the criteria for apostleship listed in Acts 1:21–22, he nevertheless clothes him with all apostolic power and authority.[5]

## THE JEWISH RESPONSE TO PAUL

Although the movement of the narrative forces the reader increasingly to focus attention on the ways in which Gentiles are offered opportunities to come to Christian belief, there is still a remarkable component here that does not allow one to forget the Jewish people. Indeed, for many of the narratives that describe Paul's missionary efforts, Luke employs a literary pattern that calls special attention to the Jewish component of early Christianity. The general pattern is familiar to readers of Acts. When Paul arrives in a city, he goes immediately to the synagogue, where he speaks to Jewish people and Godfearers, interpreting the scriptures to show that the Christ is Jesus. He meets with some success in the synagogue, but the overwhelming response is Jewish rejection. Paul then presents his message to the general public, apparently consisting entirely of Gentile people, and meets with a great deal of success. The success breeds increased Jewish opposition, which, sometimes coupled with official repression, forces Paul's departure. Although there are variations, the general pattern establishes itself clearly and forcefully.

The mission of Barnabas, Paul, and John Mark on Cyprus (Acts 13:4–12) adheres to the basic literary pattern but does so with an interesting variation. The missionaries begin their visit by speaking in "the synagogues of the Jews" (13:5) at Salamis, and then they move on to Paphos. At Paphos they meet a Jewish false prophet and magician, Bar-Jesus/Elymas, and a proconsul, Sergius Paulus. The Jewish magician opposes the efforts of the missionaries, but Paul commits him to a temporary case of blindness and converts the proconsul. The incident is an illustration of conflict between the divine and the demonic, as Susan R. Garrett has shown.[6] In contrast with many later narratives, this particular one features individual persons rather than groups. Notably absent is any mention of a positive Jewish response. But the negative is certainly present in Elymas, who is not only a magician but a Jew, and the positive Gentile response is shown in Sergius Paulus. Thus, in this pericope, the reader understands that the Christians speak in a synagogue, are opposed by a Jewish magician, with whom they successfully deal, and that their message is positively received by a Gentile. Perhaps we should regard this first narrative as an expression in miniature or in tight focus of the general literary pattern.

The next (Acts 13:13–52), however, expresses the general literary pattern in all its fullness. Paul and Barnabas, now without John Mark (see 13:13), arrive in Pisidian Antioch and enter the synagogue on the Sabbath day. Paul speaks to the assembled people, many of whom respond positively, and he is invited to speak again on the next Sabbath. But on this occasion, the Jews oppose Paul and Barnabas, who vow to turn to the Gentiles. Finally, increased Jewish opposition leads to a persecution, and Paul and Barnabas are forced to leave. Because of its significance and depth of detail, a fuller discussion of this passage appears below.

A similar pattern is found in the narratives about Iconium (14:1–7) and Thessalonica (17:1–9). At Beroea (17:10–15) Jewish opposition is supplied by Thessalonian rather than native Jews, but the outcome is the same. The narrative about Corinth (18:1–17) is fuller, but the same basic pattern controls it. Paul speaks every Sabbath at the local synagogue, where many Jews and Greeks respond positively. But after Jews resist his message, he vows, "From now on I will go to the Gentiles" (18:6). Paul then leaves the synagogue and headquarters in the house of a Godfearer, Titius Justus. Luke notes in 18:8 that Crispus, the synagogue leader, had accepted Paul's message. But after some eighteen months, "the Jews" accuse Paul before the proconsul of Achaia, Gallio. Gallio dismisses the case and permits the beating of one of Paul's accusers.

Although Paul and his associates initially address audiences in synagogues, they never receive a positive response from Jews alone in any of these incidents. At Pisidian Antioch, Paul's synagogue speech is directed to both Jews and Gentiles. In 13:16, the address is to "You Israelites, and others who fear God (*hoi phoboumenoi ton theon*)." Similarly, in 13:26 we have, "My brothers, you descendants of Abraham's family, and others who fear God (*hoi en hymin phoboumenoi ton theon*)." In both cases, the address distinguishes between those who are Jewish and those who fear God. If, as it seems we are compelled to do, we must think of the latter as Gentiles who are attracted to the synagogue but who have not yet made a total commitment to Judaism, it is evident that Luke here presents Paul as speaking to a mixed audience.[7] In a similar

way our attention is called to the fact that the initially positive response to Paul is one that issues both from "Jews and devout converts to Judaism (*polloi tōn Ioudaiōn kai tōn sebomenōn prosēlytōn*,"
13:43). To be sure, the proselytes should probably be considered to
be on a different footing from the Godfearers addressed in 13:16,
26, but the important point is that the positive response came from
the combination of Jews and some other group, not from Jews
alone. At Iconium, likewise, Paul and Barnabas received an initially positive response from Jews and Greeks (14:1), and at Thessalonica Paul and Silas were joined by Jews and "a great many of
the devout Greeks and not a few of the leading women" (17:4). At
Beroea it is many Jews and "not a few Greek women and men of
high standing" (17:12). And in Corinth Paul "would argue in the
synagogue and would try to convince Jews and Greeks" (18:4). It
seems clear that the synagogue, although sometimes referred to as
the synagogue of the Jews, is thought of as open to non-Jews and
that the Christian preachers are able to find a mixed audience
whenever they enter one. But it is notable that, in his use of a basic
literary pattern to describe Paul's mission to Jews and Gentiles,
Luke never speaks simply of a positive response on the part of any
group made up exclusively of Jews. This emphasis tends to qualify
the positive Jewish response to Paul, and it serves as a counterpoint to the theme of Jewish opposition, in which Jews either act
alone or instigate Gentile involvement.

Some narratives contain elements of the literary pattern outlined above even if they do not, as a whole, conform to it. The mission in Lystra (Acts 14:8–20) has nothing about initial preaching in
a synagogue but rather focuses on the healing of a lame man and
the crowd's reaction to it. Even so, after the attempt to worship
Barnabas and Paul has been quelled, Jews from Pisidian Antioch
and Iconium arrive and foment a persecution that leads to the departure of the missionaries. The narrative about Philippi (Acts
16:11–40) has nothing about Paul's speaking to Jews nor about Jewish opposition. But the narrator, who at this point includes himself
in the Pauline party, states that they looked for a place of prayer on
the Sabbath (16:13) and made contact with Lydia, who is described
as a worshiper of God (*sebomenē ton theon*, 16:14). The narrative of
Paul in Athens (17:16–34) is designed to show how Paul's message
was presented to Greek philosophers, but it nevertheless contains
a note about his speaking in the local synagogue "with the Jews
and the devout persons" (*tois sebomenois*, 17:17). On his first visit to

Ephesus, Paul speaks in the synagogue but departs with a promise to return (18:19–21). On his second visit (19:1–40), he deals with the disciples of Apollos and then speaks in the synagogue for three months before withdrawing to "the lecture hall of Tyrannus" when a negative reaction sets in. The seven sons of Sceva, a Jewish high priest (19:13–20), may be conside.ed Paul's opponents at Ephesus, but the real opposition there comes from the Gentile Demetrius, a maker of silver shrines of Artemis (19:23–40).

The narratives of Paul at Troas (20:7–12), where he raises Eutychus, and at Miletus (20:17–38), where he bids farewell to the Ephesian elders, do not conform to the basic pattern. It is notable, however, that in the farewell speech, Paul explains that he witnessed about Jesus to both Jews and Greeks (20:21) and that his work was hampered by "the plots of the Jews" (20:19).[8]

As was observed above, the narrative about Paul in Pisidian Antioch (Acts 13:13–52) expresses in fullest fashion the literary pattern that is found in a number of other narratives. Because of its length and strategic location, as well as its use of the basic literary pattern outlined above, this narrative requires special attention. The narrative, which includes the only recorded speech of Paul to Jews (and Godfearers), has been widely recognized as paradigmatic for the last half of Acts, in much the way that the story of Jesus in Luke 4 is paradigmatic for the gospel.[9]

John Mark deserted before the trip to Pisidian Antioch, and so it is only Paul and Barnabas who are involved in this narrative. The two missionaries enter the local synagogue on the Sabbath day, sit down, and, after the reading from Torah and prophets, are invited by the leaders of the synagogue to address the congregation. It is Paul who does so, and he delivers a speech that has affinities with the sermon of Jesus in Luke 4, the speech of Stephen in Acts 7, and the speeches of Peter to Jewish people in Acts 1–5.

Paul's speech in Acts 13:13–52 may be compared with the sermon of Jesus in Luke 4:16–30, in terms of its setting and reception. The reader will recall that the sermon of Jesus was delivered in the synagogue of Nazareth on the Sabbath day and that it began with a reading and interpretation of scripture as part of the usual Sabbath day service. In a similar way Paul is invited to speak during the usual service. Furthermore, Jesus' words were initially greeted with surprise and favor. But when he began to talk about the deeds of Elijah and Elisha performed for Gentiles, he was almost stoned to death. At Pisidian Antioch, as the story is told in Acts 13, Paul spoke on two Sabbaths. After the first, many Jews and proselytes joined up with Paul and Barnabas, and Paul was invited to speak again. But on the second Sabbath there was nothing but opposition, "But when the Jews saw the crowds, they were filled with jealousy; and blaspheming, they contradicted what was spoken by Paul" (13:45). In both narratives, initial acceptance is followed by rejection, in a pattern that is familiar to the readers of Luke-Acts.[10]

At its beginning, the speech of Paul in Pisidian Antioch most resembles the speech of Stephen in Acts 7. Both begin with recitals of ancient Hebrew history, although different phases of the history are emphasized. While Stephen's speech starts with Abraham, Paul's begins with the exodus. Stephen ends with Solomon and with the objection to his building the Temple. Paul concludes his history with David, mentioning neither Solomon nor the building of the Temple.

But parallels between the two speeches are limited to the historical reviews, the evident purposes of which are not the same. With the speech of Stephen, as we have seen, the two themes embedded within the history are the recurring disobedience of Israel and the condemnation of Solomon's temple. Although there are some nuances in Paul's speech that echo the first theme (see, e.g., 13:18),[11] this theme is not dominant, and the second is absent altogether.

The apparent function of the historical summary in Paul's speech is to support the theme of promise and fulfillment. This is indicated by the repeated use of verbs expressing the idea of God's giving or granting: "he gave them their land as an inheritance (*kateklēronomēsen tēn gēn autōn*)," 13:19; "he gave (*edōken*) them judges," 13:20; "God gave (*edōken*) them Saul," 13:21. The theme is expressed primarily in the stress on David as the chief character in the historical summary. The summary culminates with him, and the reason is that Paul intends to link David to Jesus as promise to fulfillment. In 13:23 he announces that Jesus, a descendant of David, is God's promised savior for Israel. Then, after telling of John's baptism and Jesus' death and resurrection, Paul returns to the connection between David and Jesus. He quotes from Ps 2:7 in 13:33, identifying it explicitly as the second Psalm[12] and implicitly as a writing of David. In the following verse he quotes Isa 55:3, "I will give you the holy promises made to David," a scriptural verse that no doubt is intended to support the link between David and Jesus. Following this is a quotation from Ps 16:10, with an interpretation similar to that in Acts 2:29–31. Thus we learn that in Psalm 16 David affirmed that God would not allow his holy one to see corruption. Since we know that David himself saw corruption, it is evident that he was not speaking of himself but of his descendant Jesus.[13]

The employment of the theme of promise and fulfillment provides a basis of comparison between Paul's address in Pisidian Antioch and the speeches of Peter to the Jewish people in Acts 1–5. This theme relates specifically to promises and fulfillments for the Jewish people, and Paul stresses the special place of Jews no less than does Peter. Indeed, the speech in Acts 13 begins with Paul's affirmation of the election of Israel (Acts 13:17). In chapter 6, we noted five major points in the Petrine speeches: Jesus is the Christ appointed for Jews; you killed him; God raised him up; the scripture foretold all of this; and forgiveness is available through Christ. All five points are found in Paul's speech in Acts 13. In 13:23, Paul says, "Of this man's [David's] posterity God has brought to Israel a Savior, Jesus, as he promised." Again in 13:26 he asserts that "to us the message of this salvation has been sent"; and in 13:32f. Paul speaks of the promises to the fathers being "fulfilled for us, their children." As Peter had announced the coming of Jesus for Jews in Jerusalem, so Paul announces the same for Jews in Pisidian Antioch. The point about Jesus' crucifixion is adapted for a diaspora audience when Paul states that Jesus was put to death by the Jews in Jerusalem and their leaders (13:27). The charge is made more specific in 13:28, where Paul explains that the Jerusalem Jews and their leaders asked Pilate to have him put to death. In Acts 13:30 Paul announces the resurrection of Jesus in the same way that Peter did. It holds a position as God's answer to the act of the Jewish people and their leaders in putting Jesus to death. The scriptural support for all that has happened comes in Paul's quotations from Psalm 2:7 (Acts 13:33); Isa 55:3 (Acts 13:34); Ps 16:10 (Acts 13:35); together with the quotation from Hab 1:5 (Acts 13:41), which Paul uses as a warning. At the end, Paul announces the forgiveness of sins through Jesus (13:38).

Despite the parallels between Paul's speech in Acts 13 and those of Jesus, Stephen, and Peter, a quite different point is made near the end, in 13:38–39. The NRSV has "Let it be known to you therefore, my brothers, that through this man forgiveness of sins is proclaimed to you; by this Jesus everyone who believes is set free (*dikaioutai*) from all those sins from which you could not be freed

(*dikaiōthēnai*) by the law of Moses." The appearance at this point of
the verb *dikaoō*, a notorious Pauline term, is striking. No less striking is the NRSV translation, which obscures the resemblance to
those passages in Paul's letters in which the verb is usually translated by "justified," or some variant. One may say that Luke has
used some of Paul's own language at this point, but he has done
more: he has also used one of Paul's concepts, namely that of the
ineffectiveness of the Mosaic Torah (see Rom 3:20; 8:3). This concept may be compared with the remark of Stephen in 7:53, "You
are the ones that received the law as ordained by angels, and yet
you have not kept it." But in fact nothing in Acts 1–12 has prepared
us for this, aside from the charge that Stephen spoke against the
law (6:14), a charge that Luke regards as false.

Acts 13:39 also contains a note about divine impartiality that
may be compared with Peter's statement in 10:34–35. In his address to Cornelius and his household Peter observed that there are
worthy Gentiles who are acceptable to God; more specifically,
there are among the Gentiles those who fear God and do what is
right. Peter makes the point again in his reprise of the Cornelius
incident, in Acts 15:9, and in his sermon to Jews at Pisidian Antioch, Paul also talks about divine impartiality. In 13:39, he announces that anyone who believes will be justified (*en toutō pas ho
pisteuōn dikaioutai*). Furthermore, the *en toutō* means that this justification occurs in the one who has been raised from the dead. We
can see that in these few words the Lukan Paul has not only challenged the effectiveness of Torah but has also put the risen Christ
in its place and proclaimed that through him justification is available for all who believe. Although it is not here stated precisely
what it means to believe, the whole tenor of the sermon suggests
that it means to accept the crucified and risen Jesus as the fulfillment of God's promise to send a descendant of David.

Paul's audience at Pisidian Antioch is not offended by his reference to the ineffectiveness of Torah or his affirmation of divine
impartiality. Rather, Luke, in 13:42–43, only reports a positive response. Many Jews and proselytes joined Paul and Barnabas, and
the missionaries are invited to return on the following Sabbath.
But, although great crowds assemble to hear Paul on the next Sabbath, there is no second speech. Instead we read that "the Jews"
become jealous of the large crowd and contradict what Paul said.
As a result, Paul and Barnabas announce their intention to turn to
the Gentiles: "It was necessary that the word of God should be
spoken first to you. Since you reject it and judge yourselves to be

unworthy of eternal life, we are now turning to the Gentiles" (13:46). This, the first of three such announcements in Acts, is supported by a quotation from Isa 49:6 (Acts 13:47), which is used as a kind of commission for Paul and Barnabas to bring salvation to the Gentiles. Luke concludes the narrative about Pisidian Antioch with a note about positive Gentile responses to the Christian missionaries, renewed Jewish opposition, persecution of the missionaries, and the departure of Paul and Barnabas (13:48–52).

The narrative of Paul and Barnabas in Pisidian Antioch, together with its paradigmatic speech and programmatic announcement, conveys a number of features that are important to our study of images of Judaism. It is essential to emphasize that the first full-scale speech of Paul in Acts is addressed to diaspora Jews and Godfearers and that Paul speaks to this audience in friendly terms. He addresses them as brothers in 13:26 and 13:38. He emphasizes his and his audience's connection to a common history in such phrases as "our ancestors" (13:17) and "us their children" (13:33). He emphasizes his contention that God sent Jesus for Israel (13:23, 26, 32f.). His treatment of the theme of Jesus' death removes Paul's audience from any sense of direct responsibility. It is the people who live in Jerusalem and their leaders who should suffer the blame for Jesus' death, not Jews of the Diaspora.

Despite these friendly approaches in Paul's speech, the dominant tone conveys negative images of the Jewish people. Although the speech says that it is the citizens of Jerusalem and their leaders who bear the responsibility for Jesus' death and not those being addressed, there is no mistaking the fact that Paul is talking about Jewish people. For he goes on to say that they did not understand the scriptures, which they heard read every Sabbath (13:27). Since they did not understand, they could not have known what they were doing. So again we have the assertion of ignorance, as we had in one of Peter's speeches (3:17). Paul makes it clear that there is no excuse for the ignorance, since God had made these things known through the prophets and since the people of Jerusalem and their leaders heard the prophets every week. The theme of Jewish misunderstanding of the scriptures, an important one in most sections of Luke-Acts, is prominent here as well.

It is the controlling literary pattern that finally suggests to the reader the ways to think of the Jewish people: initial acceptance by some Jews has given way to rejection by most. Moreover, a significant clue is given in the solemn announcement in 13:46–47. This saying serves not only as a summary of the events at Pisidian

Antioch but also as a programmatic statement of first importance. The missionaries say, "It was necessary that the word of God should be spoken first to you" (13:46). The compulsion to present the Christian message to the Jewish people first doubtless rests on the assumption that the Christ was intended for the Jewish people, an assumption held both by the Lukan Peter and the Lukan Paul and thus almost certainly an assumption of the implied author as well. If Christ is intended for the Jewish people, the Jewish people should be the first to hear the message about him. Further, the Hebrew Scriptures, when properly interpreted, contain the promise of the Christ, and the Jewish people have heard these scriptures on a weekly basis. It seems, therefore, that the connection between the Hebrew Scriptures, the meaning of the Christ, and the Jewish people provides the compulsion that is announced in 13:46: it is necessary for the news about the Christ to be presented first to the Jewish people.

But the missionaries continue, "Since you reject it and judge yourselves to be unworthy of eternal life" (13:46). In one sense this assessment is inappropriate and unfair on the part of Paul and Barnabas. Not all of the Jewish people who have heard the message of the missionaries have rejected it. Luke has just called attention to the many Jews and proselytes who followed Paul and Barnabas after the sermon on the previous Sabbath (13:43). And the reader will surely recall the large numbers of Palestinian Jews who in Acts 1–12 became believers. But these observations miss the point, for what is being emphasized here is Jewish rejection, and the implied reader is required to de-emphasize Jewish acceptance. The movement of the narrative has been from an initial acceptance of Paul's message by some Jews and Godfearers to a final rejection by "the Jews." The solemn proclamation of Paul and Barnabas serves to underline what Luke notes in 13:45, where he calls attention to the jealousy of "the Jews" and their practice of contradicting what Paul said. We should also note that before the missionaries leave Pisidian Antioch there is more Jewish opposition, "But the Jews incited the devout women of high standing and the leading men of the city, and stirred up persecution against Paul and Barnabas" (13:50). The positive response of many Jews from Pisidian Antioch is valued by the implied author as less significant than the opposition of "the Jews" (13:45, 50). This opposition is sufficient for the missionaries to conclude that Jews have rejected the word of God.

The missionaries conclude, "We are now turning to the Gentiles" (Acts 13:46). To support this decision a passage from Isa 49:6 is quoted in Acts 13:47. The decision is met with rejoicing among the Gentiles and a wide broadcast of the missionary message (13:48–49). The decision is problematic for several reasons. In Acts 9:15 it was announced that God had set aside Saul/Paul "to bring my name before Gentiles and kings and before the people of Israel." Unless the speech at Pisidian Antioch is intended to constitute the fulfillment of the charge to "bring my name before . . . the people of Israel," the announcement in 13:46–47 may be regarded as an act of disobedience on Paul's part. In fact, however, Paul does not cease to speak to Jewish people. Even after the solemn announcement, he frequently begins a missionary endeavor in a synagogue and meets with some success. Thus, Acts 13:46 is not the end of the Pauline missionary effort among Jews. But the question remains, what does it mean for Paul and Barnabas to turn to Gentiles?

In this connection we must also give some attention to the repetition of this solemn announcement in 18:6 and 28:28. The announcement in 18:6 is made in Corinth after Jews there reject Paul's message. He says: "Your blood be on your own heads! I am innocent. From now on I will go to the Gentiles." Despite this decision, Paul meets again with Jews in Ephesus (18:19; 19:8, 10) and will meet with Roman Jews in Acts 28:17–29. Finally, during this meeting with Roman Jews, Paul issues his third announcement and supports it with a quotation from Isaiah 6.

On one level, each of the three announcements is meant for the locality in which it is proclaimed.[14] Acts 13:46 means that Paul and Barnabas ceased their efforts among Jews in Pisidian Antioch and turned to the Gentiles in that area. Acts 18:6 means the same for Corinth, and 28:28 for Rome. It is likely, however, that the announcements are not aimed only at these specific localities. As Ernst Haenchen has written, "The Jews who in Pisidian Antioch grow envious of the Christians are at the same time the Jews in general."[15]

Two considerations may help us to understand the function of these three solemn announcements. First, we have already observed that Acts 9:15–16 controls the narrative movement in the latter half of Acts. The divine command in these verses requires Paul to present the Christian message to Gentiles, kings, and Jews, and to suffer for God's sake. The order in 9:15–16 is unusual and certainly does not represent either a kind of theological priority of Gentiles or the chronological sequence in which Paul's mission moved. Clearly, the mission to the Jews has a theological and chronological priority in Acts. So in 13:46 Paul and Barnabas speak of the necessity to present their message first to Jews, and in 13:47 they cite a biblical passage to support the claim that they must turn to Gentiles. In other words, the missionaries are here claiming that they have been obedient to the word of God and have discharged the responsibility to present the gospel to the people of Israel.

Second, we should observe the function of these three announcements in conjunction with the literary pattern that is to be found throughout this section of Acts. As we have seen, the pattern that Luke uses for many of the individual episodes has Paul begin his activity in a local synagogue. The use of this pattern in individual episodes reflects the main course of Paul's ministry as shown in the three announcements. The use of this pattern in descriptions of Paul's activity in Thessalonica, Iconium, Beroea, and Corinth repeats in sharp focus what the announcements proclaim for the ministry as a whole. Thus we have the anomaly of Paul visiting synagogues even after he has disavowed a mission to Jews. Within the individual narratives, the announcements function as announcements intended for Pisidian Antioch, Corinth, and Rome. But taken together they function as general summaries: *Jews have heard but rejected the message, which is accepted by Gentiles.* Luke's decision to put these announcements in Paul's mouth and at the same time to employ a literary pattern that requires repeated action may confuse the reader, since Paul speaks to Jews after resolving to go to Gentiles. But the announcements, together with the repeated use of the basic literary pattern, have a cumulative effect. The reader learns from them that no effort has been spared to present the Christian message to the Jews and that, despite some success, the message has been rejected by them.[16] In view of this the missionaries are free, indeed obligated, to go to the Gentiles. We shall re-examine the function of the announcements when we look at Acts 28:28 in chapter 8 below.

However we understand the function of Acts 13:46 and the other announcements, the image of Jews in Pisidian Antioch is clear. They have heard and rejected the message. No emphasis is placed upon the fact that some accepted it. The dominant idea here is a negative one that places "the Jews" in the role of jealous and obstinate opponents of Paul, who are not above forming plots and intrigues with influential people and authorities in order to drive Paul and Barnabas away.

The image of the Jews as opponents carries through the entire section of Acts 13:1–21:14. Despite the fact that a large number of both Jews and Greeks accepted the message of Paul and Barnabas in Iconium (14:1), the reader is presented with the strongly negative figure of unbelieving Jews who stir up and poison the minds of the Gentiles (14:2). As a result of their activities, the populace of Iconium was divided, "some sided with the Jews, and some with the apostles" (14:4), and Gentiles, Jews, and rulers attempted to molest and stone the missionaries. Although Paul and Barnabas were first hailed as Gods in Lystra, Jews from Pisidian Antioch and Iconium turned the crowds against them and stoned them (14:19). Again in Thessalonica, although some of the Jews joined Paul and Silas, "the Jews became jealous" (17:5) and stirred up the crowd against the Christian missionaries. Members of the synagogue in Beroea, "more receptive" than those in Thessalonica (17:11), accepted the preaching of Paul and Silas, but Jews from Thessalonica arrived to incite the crowds. In Corinth, Paul convinced both Jews and Greeks, but "the Jews" resisted and blasphemed (18:4–6). Later "the Jews" in Corinth took Paul before Gallio and accused him of "persuading people to worship God in ways that are contrary to the law" (18:13). On his first visit to Ephesus, Paul debated with Jews in the synagogue and then left for Syria, although he was invited to remain longer. But on his second visit, "some stubbornly refused to believe and spoke evil of the Way before the congregation" (19:9). A plot of "the Jews" in Greece leads to a change in Paul's travel plans (20:3), and in his speech to the Ephesian elders Paul recalls "the plots of the Jews" (20:19). He is warned about a pending Jewish plot in Jerusalem by the prophet Agabus in Caesarea (21:11).

The Christian preachers meet opposition from others than Jews. They are imprisoned at Philippi (16:11–40), there is a demonstration against them at Ephesus, led by Demetrius the silversmith (19:23–40), and a controversy with Pharisaic Christians about circumcision (15:1–5). There are anticipations of post-Pauline opponents and heretics (20:29–30). But the opposition of non-Jewish groups cannot be compared with that of Jews in terms of covert intrigue, repeated occurrence, and sustained hostility. Several incidents of Gentile repression were fomented by Jewish incitement.

What is remarkable here is the juxtaposition of Jewish acceptance and rejection. Over and over we read that, although some
Jews accepted Paul's message, "the Jews" opposed him. Such juxtaposition cannot fail to influence the implied reader to regard the
Jews in the narrative in ambivalent ways. Of course, those Jews
who accepted the hero Paul are to be praised, and those who rejected him are to be condemned. But the stronger emphasis in
these episodes is always placed on the condemnation of Paul's
Jewish opponents. The terminology underlines this emphasis,
since the opponents are almost always referred to simply as "the
Jews" (13:45, 50; 14:4; 17:5; 18:5, 12, 14, 28; 20:3, 19). In a few cases
Luke adds a local designation (14:19; 16:3; 17:13), but he never
speaks of the opponents as if they were only a part of a larger
group that also included believing Jews. The usual terminology is
simply not equipped to recognize the distinction between the accepting and the rejecting groups. Instead the reader is subtly led to
de-emphasize the accepting group and to emphasize "the Jews" in
their role as opponents of Paul.[17]

Individual Jews play some role in the narratives in this section
of Acts, but for the most part they are objects of ridicule and contempt. Bar-Jesus/Elymas is described as a Jewish false prophet and
magician, who is temporarily blinded by Paul and who finds it
necessary to look around for someone to lead him by the hand
(13:4–12). Paul calls him a "son of the devil" and an "enemy of all
righteousness," and he describes him as "full of all deceit and villainy" (13:10). Sosthenes, the synagogue ruler at Corinth, is as-
saulted in view of Gallio, who pays no attention to the incident
(18:17). The seven sons of the Jewish high priest, Sceva, who attempt to practice exorcism, are forced to flee naked and wounded
(19:13–20). Hans Conzelmann appropriately refers to the incidents
involving Sosthenes and the sons of Sceva as burlesque
episodes.[18] Exceptions to the pattern of Jews as objects of ridicule
and contempt are, of course, found in the portrayals of Paul and
his Jewish-Christian fellow-travelers. In addition there are Aquila
and Priscilla (18:2), Crispus (18:8), and Apollos (18:24–28). The
role of Alexander in 19:33–34 is unclear. Amidst the confusion
caused by the demonstration instigated by Demetrius, "the Jews"
put Alexander forward, but when he tried to speak and was recognized as a Jew, the crowd drowned him out. At one level the
Alexander episode simply adds to the confusion that Luke had al-

ready described ("some were shouting one thing, some another," 19:32). At another level Alexander is yet another individual Jew who, at best, is ineffective.[19]

### JEWISH PRACTICES AND OBSERVANCES

Some Jewish practices and observances are mentioned, generally without comment, in this section of Acts. Observance of the Sabbath by both Jews and Christians is assumed (Acts 13:14, 27, 42, 44; 15:21; 16:13; 18:4), although 20:7 seems to refer to a Christian observance of Sunday. We learn that Moses and the prophets are read in synagogues every Sabbath (13:27; 15:21) and that there is an association between Sabbath and prayer in 16:13. There are references to the "days of Unleavened Bread" (20:6) and Pentecost (20:16) and implications that the Christian leaders observe these festivals. Fundamental Jewish concepts are affirmed in Paul's speech at Athens (17:16–34), where he proclaims the one creator-God as the only proper object of worship and condemns idols. We should also note here a repetition of Stephen's statement that God "does not live in shrines made by human hands" (17:24; cf. 7:48).

The most significant references to Jewish practices deal with the Torah generally and with circumcision in particular. We have already noted the claim of the Lukan Paul that the law of Moses does not bring the freedom enjoyed by Christian believers (13:39). In the hearing before Gallio in Corinth, Jewish law is contrasted with Roman law (18:14–15). Gallio addresses the Jewish opponents of Paul to say, "If it were a matter of crime or serious villainy, I would be justified in accepting the complaint of you Jews" (18:14). But he throws the Jewish charges out of court since they raise "questions about words and names and your own law" (18:15). Even if Gallio is not a reliable spokesperson in Acts, the contrast that he draws would leave the implied reader with an impression that Roman law deals with important matters that are necessary in the promotion of the social good but that Jewish law deals with minor matters, such as the meaning of names and words.[20]

The most important expressions about Torah and circumcision are to be found in Acts 15, Luke's story of the so-called apostolic conference. Ernst Haenchen is representative of a number of scholars who point to the significance of Acts 15. He calls it the turning point in Acts, and he notes that Jerusalem is central before this chapter but not after, and that Petrine leadership of the Jerusalem community gives way to that of James and the elders after Acts 15. Further, Paul is no longer of secondary importance among Christian missionaries; he becomes the dominant figure after Acts 15.[21]

The conference was convened because some believers insisted on the necessity to circumcise Gentile Christians and to require their observance of Torah (15:1, 5). These believers are said to be from Judea and from the Pharisaic party. There was no specific mention of the practice of circumcision prior to Acts 15:1, and so the reader would probably be led to infer that male Jewish converts had already been circumcised and that Paul and his party did not require it of their Gentile converts. In order to settle the controversy, Paul and Barnabas were sent from Antioch to meet with the apostles and elders. Peter first addressed the group, reminding them about his role in the conversion of Cornelius and his household. He recalled that they received the spirit and that God did not discriminate between Gentiles and Jews, and he urged that no additional burden be laid on Gentile believers (15:7–11). After hearing from Paul and Barnabas, James quoted a passage from Amos 9:11–12 and decided that no requirements should be laid upon Gentiles other than "to abstain only from things polluted by idols and from fornication and from whatever has been strangled and from blood" (15:20).

There are a number of problems in Acts 15, among them the relationships with Galatians 2, that need not detain us in our analysis of images of Judaism. There are, however, certain significant and perhaps surprising elements in Luke's report of this conference. We should not neglect to note the presence, reported without comment, of Pharisaic Christians among the believers in Judea. Although we had read of some priests who had accepted the faith (Acts 6:7), nothing had previously been said of the conversion of any Pharisees.[22] There seems to be a gradual reappraisal of the Pharisees going on in Luke-Acts. They appear first as antagonists of Jesus, but then, in the person of Gamaliel, as quasi-sympathizers of the Christian movement. Now, we find that some have accepted the faith. In the closing section of Acts we will find another report of sympathetic Pharisees, and in his trial Paul will claim to be a Pharisee.

Circumcision is admitted to be a requirement of the Mosaic Torah, although Luke is by no means as open as Paul is about the biblical basis of this requirement. Nor are the characters in Acts occupied with deeply involved argumentation or interpretation of its meaning. For Peter, it is a simple matter: Cornelius received the spirit with no previous requirements, so none should be imposed on other Gentile believers. Peter says, "Why are you putting God to the test by placing on the neck of the disciples a yoke (*zygon*) that neither our ancestors nor we have been able to bear (*bastasai*)?" (15:10). Although the Lukan Peter uses a term (*zygon*) that is customarily used to express the idea of obedience, frequently used in Hellenistic Jewish writings in a positive sense, it does not seem to have that sense here.[23] When used in association with the verb *bastazō*, it points to something that is regarded as a burden, and here it is said to be an intolerable burden.[24] James likewise implies that the imposition of circumcision would constitute trouble for the Gentiles (15:19; cf. 15:28). Scholars who are familiar with concepts expressed in Hellenistic Jewish writings and later Rabbinic writings find these attitudes surprising, for in these documents Torah is predominantly understood as a blessing and not a burden.[25] But if we take a literary rather than a historical approach to this passage and interpret it within the context of a series of Lukan images of Jewish observances and practices, it loses its significance as a possible description of an early Jewish-Christian viewpoint. The implied reader of this text, who it will be recalled is something like a Godfearer, is presented with an image of Torah that has no power to save either Jews or Gentiles. Within the narrative world of Acts, Torah is therefore a theologically ineffective burden that includes commands that have not been and cannot be obeyed, and thus it is inappropriate to expect Gentile Christians to attempt to carry it.

At the same time we must recognize that the so-called apostolic decree (Acts 15:20, 29; cf. 21:25) functions in the narrative as something of a substitute for Torah observance. The decree is reported first in 15:20, within the context of Luke's report of the controversy itself and then again in a letter prepared by the apostles for delivery to believers in Antioch, Syria, and Cilicia (15:29). A third report appears in the last section of Acts in the context of a meeting between James, the elders at Jerusalem, and Paul (21:25). There are variations among the three reports and textual problems within each of them, and thus it is probably impossible to determine precisely in what form these verses left the hand of the author. The editors of UBSGNT3 settle on the following phrases: (1) Acts 15:20: *tou apechesthai tōn alisgēmatōn tōn eidōlōn kai tēs porneias kai tou pniktou kai tou haimatos* ("to abstain only from the things polluted by idols and from fornication and from whatever has been strangled and from blood"). (2) Acts 15:29: *apechesthai eidōlothytōn kai haimatos kai pniktōn kai porneias* ("abstain from what has been sacrificed to idols and from blood and from what is strangled and from fornication"). (3) Acts 21:25: *phylassesthai autous to te eidōlothyton kai haima kai pnikton kai porneian* ("abstain from what has been sacrificed to idols and from blood and from what is strangled and from fornication").[26] In this edition, as translated by NRSV, there is a certain consistency in the three reports. The only significant differences are between the order of the four requirements and in the wording of the first. The order need not concern us. In 15:20, *alisgēma*, a hapax legommenon in the NT, refers to a ceremonial impurity, i.e., a pollution. *Eidōlothytos* in 15:29; 21:25 refers more specifically to meat offered to an idol, and the term is also used with this meaning by Paul in 1 Cor 8:1, 4, 7, 10; 10:19 as well as in Rev 2:14, 20 (cf. 1 Cor 10:28, where the term *hierothytos* is used in what is intended to be a quotation from a pagan).

Determining the meaning of these reports is as difficult as establishing the text. Despite the differences in wording, it seems probable that the phrases about contact with idols are to be taken as equivalent in meaning in all three reports. The requirement assumes that consuming meat that has been offered to idols renders the eater ceremonially impure, that is, the meat is polluted because of its contact with the idol, so it is to be avoided. The requirement to avoid something strangled (*pniktos*) is almost certainly to be taken as a dietary regulation. The requirement to refrain from blood has sometimes been taken as a prohibition of murder, but, when grouped with the prohibition of meat offered to idols and things strangled, reads more naturally as a dietary prohibition, based on Gen 9:4; Lev 3:17; 17:10–14, that is, a prohibition against eating meat without first draining the blood from it. If this is correct, the avoidance of *porneia* probably should also be taken as a ritualistic, not an ethical, requirement. It may be understood as a prohibition against ritual prostitution, or it may designate laws prohibiting marriage within consanguineous relationships (cf. Lev 18:6–18). Under this interpretation, the so-called apostolic decree means that four ritual requirements are laid upon Gentile believers: they must avoid food offered to idols; they must avoid meat from a strangled animal; they must avoid meat containing blood; and they must avoid either consanguineous marriages or ritual prostitution.[27]

That these requirements come out of the Jewish tradition would probably be clear to any Greek reader of Acts, but it would be perfectly clear to one whom Luke regards as a Godfearer, our probable implied reader. The use of the term *eidōlon*, in whatever combination, is a signal of the Jewish background of the apostolic decree. But the narrator wants to assure that the implied reader not miss the point, and he adds in 15:21 the explanatory phrase, "For in every city, for generations past, Moses has had those who proclaim him, for he has been read aloud every Sabbath in the synagogues." The function of this verse in this context, immediately following the first report of the apostolic decree, is to affirm that the requirements, which are understood to be Mosaic, are familiar to those Gentiles in the Diaspora who have attached themselves to synagogues.

In its narrative setting, Acts 15 is significant as an illustration of the kinds of compromises accepted by early Christians that permitted Jews and Gentiles to associate with one another in a harmonious society. But in terms of the ways in which Jewish practices and observances are pictured in this narrative, Acts 15 is a dramatic illustration of Lukan ambivalence. Here where the issue of requirements for Gentile believers is formally established and communicated, the only matters that are contemplated relate to the Jewish tradition. Although some Christian Pharisees insist that the new converts must become subject to the entire Torah and must undergo circumcision, the leaders determine that such would be unnecessarily burdensome. At the same time, however, they agree that certain minimal ritualistic requirements, drawn from the Mosaic legislation, should be imposed on Gentiles. If we should imagine a spectrum of opinions ranging from those on the right that would advocate the retention of the entire Torah to those on the left that would totally dispense with it, Luke-Acts occupies a centrist position. It teaches that while observance of the entire Torah is burdensome, it cannot be totally jettisoned. It is good to observe certain parts of it (15:29).[28]

The ambivalence becomes even more striking in Acts 16:1–5, where Luke reports on Paul's visit to Derbe and Lystra. There he meets Timothy, a believer and the son of a Jewish woman who is a believer, and a Greek man, whose religious orientation is unspecified. Luke states that Paul wanted Timothy to accompany him and that he circumcised him "because of the Jews who were in those places, for they all knew that his father was a Greek" (16:3).[29] Due

to previous uses of the term *the Jews*, we should take the explanation here as one denoting opposition. Paul thus circumcised Timothy in order to neutralize Jewish opposition. Their knowledge
about his father must include an awareness that he had not fulfilled the duties that a Jewish father would normally perform for
his son. It is usually assumed that Timothy would have been regarded as Jewish because of his mother, but questions about the
origin of this view have recently been raised.[30] Whether or not the
matriarchal principle applied in the first century, the text of Acts,
although by no means clear, suggests something of this sort. It
suggests that Jews expected Timothy to have been circumcised but
knew that a non-Jewish father would not observe this practice. So
Paul acts for Timothy as a Jewish father and does for him what his
real father had not done.

In this pericope, Luke makes a point of observing that in
Derbe and Lystra, Paul and Silas delivered to the believers the
rules that were recently drawn up in Jerusalem. The implied
reader could not be unmindful that circumcision was intentionally
omitted from these requirements, and the narrative about Paul
and Timothy constitutes a surprise, perhaps an anomaly. The
reader must, however, keep in mind the fact that the apostolic decree was intended as a concession to Gentile believers. Nothing
had been said either about the abandonment or the retention of
circumcision for Jewish believers. It is true that Peter had observed
that "neither our ancestors nor we" have been able to keep Torah
(15:10), but this objection could hardly have been raised in regard
to the discussion of the narrower issue of circumcision. Thus Paul's
circumcision of Timothy, the son of a Jewish believer, reminds the
reader that Jews and Gentiles come into the Christian movement
on different footings. For Gentiles, the apostolic decree with its
four ritualistic requirements is sufficient. For sons of Jewish believers, circumcision continues to be practiced.

In addition, Paul's circumcision of Timothy conforms to an important thesis that Luke will propound in the last section of Acts.
In 21:22 it is said that Paul has been suspected of counseling diaspora Jews not to circumcise their sons, but in his defensive
speeches Paul insists that he is a loyal Pharisee who has not de-
parted from any aspect of the Jewish tradition. It is likely then that
we should regard Acts 16:1–5 as providing a basis for denying the
charge that will be made later.[31] Luke used this device in the gospel to anticipate and deny certain charges against Jesus.[32]

The city of Jerusalem plays an important role in this section of Acts. It continues to be the focal point of the church, as it had been in Acts 1–12.[33] The significance of Jerusalem is made abundantly clear in Acts 15, where it is the setting for the apostolic conference, despite the fact that the issues that precipitated the conference were first raised in Antioch. Jerusalem also acts as a kind of magnet for Paul and his associates at a number of points. In 19:21, Paul, in Ephesus, makes a solemn decision to go to Jerusalem (and Rome) by way of Macedonia and Achaia. From this point on, the city takes on a menacing character, reminiscent of the references to Jesus' approach to Jerusalem in the Gospel of Luke.[34] In travelling from Troas to Miletus, Paul bypasses Ephesus in order to hasten on to Jerusalem, where he hopes to arrive in time for Pentecost (20:16). In his farewell speech to the elders at Miletus, the menacing character of Jerusalem becomes clearer. Paul tells the elders that he does not know what to expect in Jerusalem, "except that the Holy Spirit testifies to me in every city that imprisonment and persecutions are waiting for me" (20:23). While in Tyre he receives a message from the spirit, delivered by local believers, that he should not go to Jerusalem (21:4). In Caesarea the prophet Agabus performs a dramatic sign to warn Paul about his fate in Jerusalem, but Paul asserts his readiness even to die there (21:10–14). Thus, although in Acts 13:1–21:14 Jerusalem continues in its role as the city where authoritative decisions for the entire church are made, it increasingly becomes the city in which the Pauline mission is to have its supreme test.[35] The reader must await the resolution of these images in the next section of Acts.

The scripture and the history of Israel play a role here similar to that in previous sections of Luke-Acts. The chief function of scripture is to point forward to Jesus as the Christ and to certain events and practices of the early Christian movement. We have previously observed that Paul in his speech at Pisidian Antioch made abundant use of scripture to support his contention about the relationship of the Christ to David and to confirm the Lukan theme of promise and fulfillment. It is in this speech that most of the quotations and allusions to scripture in this section of Acts are to be found. But the importance of scripture is affirmed in other places as well. In 15:21, James comments that the words of Moses have been read every Sabbath in every Gentile city. In 17:11 it is said that the Jews of Beroea studied the scriptures daily to test the preaching of Paul and Silas. Apollos is described as "well-versed in the scriptures" (18:24). After correction by Priscilla and Aquila he preaches to Jews in Achaia, "showing by the scriptures that the Messiah is Jesus" (18:28).

A quotation from Amos 9:11–12 is used by James in Acts 15:16–18. Here James comments on Peter's remarks about the admission of Gentile believers, and he states that the words of the prophets anticipated these events (15:15). The quotation from Amos is intended to show the agreement between the prophets and the experience of Peter. It seems to suggest a two-stage event, the first involving the rebuilding of David's tent and the second the call of the Gentiles.[36] Although James provides no exegesis of the passage, we are apparently urged to think of the fulfillment in terms of the very history that is being narrated in Acts, which tells first of the formation of a group of Jewish believers and second of a group of Gentile believers. Actually, James uses the quotation from Amos not only to provide scriptural support for the Gentile mission but also to conclude that only minimal requirements should be imposed on Gentile believers.

It is notable in this section of Acts that references to scripture are confined to narratives involving Jews and to speeches in which Jews are being addressed. This is the case when the speech is given in full, as in Paul's speech at Pisidian Antioch, and when it is simply noted, as in Apollos' debates with Jews (18:28). Outside of these occasions, scripture is used only to support a particular resolution of the problem of Gentile believers in Acts 15, where James calls on the prophet Amos and then draws the apostolic decree from passages in Torah.

It is remarkable to note that scripture is employed only allusively in speeches to Gentiles. The speech at Lystra (Acts 14:15–17) contains the proclamation of the living creator-God, with allusions to Exod 20:11; Ps 146:6, but there are no quotations, and there is nothing to call attention to the predictive role of the Hebrew Scriptures. Similarly, Paul's speech at Athens (17:22–31) has a number of allusions to the scriptures but no specific mention of them or of any incident reported in them.[37] A quotation from an unnamed Greek poet (17:28), probably Aratus, functions in a way similar to that in which quotations from the Hebrew Scriptures function in Paul's speech at Pisidian Antioch and Peter's speeches in Acts 1–5.[38] The ethnic character of the Christian elders addressed by Paul in Acts 20:18–35 is not specified, but the narrative movement would lead the reader to assume that most if not all are Gentiles.

In any event, this farewell speech of Paul has only allusions to the Hebrew Scriptures. In view of the importance of the scriptures in speeches to Jewish audiences, the absence of explicit reference to them in speeches to Gentiles is striking. Not only are quotations nonexistent in these speeches, but there is also no summary statement in which Paul debates with Gentiles about the meaning of scripture and nothing to indicate a sense of its authority. What are we to make of this fact? One may observe that the Hebrew Scriptures were not familiar to Gentiles. But Luke, through James, has already told the reader that Moses is known by Gentiles (15:21), and he has repeatedly called attention to the presence of Gentiles at synagogue services. The implied reader does not gain a picture of Gentiles who are unfamiliar with the Hebrew Scriptures, but he nevertheless is drawn to associate these scriptures more closely with the Jewish people. Acts would simply confirm what the implied reader would presume, namely that the Hebrew Scriptures, not unknown in the Gentile world, do not function among Gentiles as they do among Jews. Thus Paul and his associates may assume the authority of the scriptures in speaking to an audience composed of Jews, at least in part, but they do not make this assumption when addressing a Gentile audience.

### CONCLUSION

The ambivalence in Acts 13:1–21:14 in regard to images of Judaism and Jewish people must be stressed. It is clear from the narrative that Jesus was sent by God for Israel and that there was a divine compulsion to present the message about him first to Jewish people. It is also clear that some Jewish people, always accompanied by some Gentiles, accepted the Christian message. Moreover, Christians continued to observe certain Jewish practices and continued to preach the God who was thought to have revealed himself in the Hebrew Scriptures. But the Jews as a whole not only rejected the message of Paul and his associates, they opposed them and incited crowds to join in the opposition. For the most part, Jewish people in these narratives take on the role of hostile unbelievers, and sometimes they are objects of ridicule and contempt. The Torah at best is ineffective and at worst a burden.

From the solemn announcements in 13:46; 18:6 (cf. 28:28), the reader is prepared to acknowledge that, at the end of this section of Acts, Paul has completed two stages of his divinely given task (cf. 9:15–16). While undergoing punishment, he has presented

God's message to Israel, where it was rejected, and he is presenting it to Gentiles, who are accepting it. In the concluding section of
Acts, Paul will complete the third stage of his divinely imposed
task by speaking to kings, and the required suffering will come to
its climax.

NOTES

1. For an analysis of the function of Acts 9:15–16 in the narrative of Luke-Acts, see
Walter Radl, *Paulus und Jesus im lukanischen Doppelwerk: Untersuchungen zu Parallelmotiven im Lukasevangelium und in der Apostelgeschichte*, 68–81. Radl finds a
parallel between the word of Simeon about the infant Jesus in Luke 2:32, 34
and the divine word to Ananias in Acts 9:15–16. He calls attention to the fact
that both function to control the subsequent narratives about Jesus and Paul.
2. See Robert L. Brawley, *Luke-Acts and the Jews: Conflict, Apology, and Conciliation*.
Brawley recognizes the force of Acts 9:15–16 in the narrative of Paul, but, following Jacob Jervell, insists that the latter half of Acts is not the story of the
progress of Christianity in the Gentile world. For Brawley the latter half of Acts
is only the biography of Paul. See Jervell, "Paul: The Teacher of Israel: The
Apologetic Speeches of Paul in Acts," in *Luke and the People of God: A New Look
at Luke-Acts*, 153–83. In this essay, Jervell focuses attention on the speeches of
Paul that will be examined in chapter 8 of this book. Jervell does not claim that
the entire second half of Acts is concerned only with the life of Paul as an
individual.
3. See also Acts 18:24–28, where Priscilla and Aquila, disciples of Paul, correct
Apollos himself.
4. See Charles H. Talbert, *Literary Patterns, Theological Themes and the Genre of Luke-
Acts*. Talbert treats these and other parallels in Luke-Acts and claims that Acts
is a succession narrative, the purpose of which is to indicate who are the legitimate successors of Jesus.
5. See Jacob Jervell, "Paulus in der Apostelgeschichte und die Geschichte der Urchristentums."
6. See Susan R. Garrett, *The Demise of the Devil: Magic and the Demonic in Luke's
Writings*, 79–87.
7. On Godfearers, see Folker Siegert, "Gottesfürchtige und Sympathisanten"; A.
Thomas Kraabel, "The Disappearance of the 'God-fearers' "; idem., "Greeks,
Jews, and Lutherans in the Middle Half of Acts"; Jacob Jervell, "The Church of
Jews and Godfearers"; P. W. Van der Horst, "Jews and Christians in Aphrodisias in the Light of Their Relations in Other Cities of Asia Minor."
8. Note also the reference to a Jewish plot in Acts 20:3, in a pericope dealing with
Paul's travel plans.
9. In reference to the narrative of Paul at Pisidian Antioch, Ernst Haenchen says,
"The whole Pauline mission—as Luke and his age saw it—is compressed and
epitomized in this scene" (*The Acts of the Apostles: A Commentary*, 417). See also
Radl, *Paulus und Jesus*, 82–100. Radl provides a detailed analysis of the paral-
lelism between Acts 13:14–52 and Luke 4:16–30.
10. For a treatment of this theme, see Joseph B. Tyson, "The Jewish Public in Luke-
Acts"; idem., *The Death of Jesus in Luke-Acts*, 29–47.
11. But note textual variants.

12. But note textual variants in Acts 13:33.
13. On the theme of promise and fulfillment, or "proof from prophecy," see Paul Schubert, "The Structure and Significance of Luke 24." In this essay Schubert deals almost exclusively with the Gospel of Luke.
14. See Martin Dibelius, *Studies in the Acts of the Apostles*. Dibelius understands the three announcements as a "sign of the active part taken by the author" (149). He also calls attention to the fact that they are carefully spaced so that there is an announcement in each of the provinces in which Paul's missionary work was carried on, namely, Asia Minor, Greece, and Italy. Haenchen, *Acts*, takes Acts 13:46 as holding good only for Pisidian Antioch, but he notes that "the reader senses that these happenings bear a significance which surpasses the immediate occasion" (p. 417). Jervell, *Luke and the People*, emphasizes the applicability of each announcement to its own locality. The judgment of Paul must, he says, be pronounced at each place in order to purge Israel of unbelievers. He writes, "The events in the synagogues stand out not only as typical incidents; they also represent events that are necessary to clarify who belongs to Israel. According to Luke, one cannot be purged from the people vicariously" (62).
15. Haenchen, *Acts*, 417.
16. Commenting on Acts 18:6, Haenchen, *Acts*, 539f., writes: "The repetition of these scenes is intended to impress upon the reader that it is not the fault of Christians or of Christianity that it has become a religion distinct from Judaism and standing hostile alongside it. So far as Paul was concerned (and he represents for Luke here Christianity in general!), the Christians had always remained within Judaism. It is exclusively the fault of the Jews if Christianity now appears as a separate community."
17. *Pace* Jervell, *Luke and the People*, 41–74, who finds the emphasis to be on the division within Israel that issues from the apostolic preaching. Jervell is technically correct in insisting that Luke has called attention to the large number of believing Jews. Jervell has not, however, given sufficient attention to the rhetorical effect of the narrative and to the way in which Luke has used the theme of initial acceptance and final rejection. Neither has he dealt with the effect of Luke's tendency to use the term "the Jews" when speaking of their opposition to Paul and their rejection of his message.
18. Hans Conzelmann, *Acts of the Apostles*, 154, 163.
19. Haenchen, *Acts*, points out that the "Jewish intermezzo . . . shows besides how unpopular are the enemies of the Christians, the Jews . . . " (578). Conzelmann, *Acts*, says, "The verse [19:34] provides some feel for ancient 'anti-Semitism' " (166). For an investigation of the social background of Acts 19:23–41, see Robert F. Stoops, Jr., "Riot and Assembly: The Social Context of Acts 19:23–41."
20. For an alternative view, see Haenchen, *Acts*, who says that Luke presents the Gallio scene as the ideal way in which Romans should deal with Christians. They should judge "that Christianity is an inner-Jewish affair in which Rome does not meddle" (541). Likewise, Conzelmann, *Acts*, 153, writes, "Here the legal situation from the standpoint of the Roman state is defined in a way that Luke would like to suggest as the ideal for Roman practice: the state should not become involved in controversies within the Jewish community involving Christians—the disputes lie outside the jurisdiction of Roman law."
21. See Haenchen, *Acts*, 461f.
22. On the treatment of Pharisees in Luke-Acts, see Jack T. Sanders, *The Jews in Luke-Acts*, 84–131; Brawley, *Luke-Acts and the Jews*, 84–106; Tyson, *Death of Jesus*, 48–83.
23. See, e.g., PsSol 7:8; 17:32; and citations in Str-B 1.608–10.

24. But see J. L. Nolland, "A Fresh Look at Acts 15.10." Nolland argues that Acts 15:10, read within the context of 15:7–11, reflects a Rabbinic view that Israel has failed to carry the yoke of the law but does not characterize the burden of the law as intolerable. Nolland argues that Luke has already pictured the Jerusalem apostles as observing Torah, so he cannot here be saying that its fulfillment is impossible. Peter is, therefore, speaking for the nation as a whole and not for the apostles when he characterizes Torah as a yoke "which neither our fathers nor we have been able to bear" (15:10). Despite Nolland's argument, it seems difficult to avoid the impression that the historic inability of Israel to carry the yoke of Torah finally means that the burden is intolerable.

25. Commenting on Acts 15:10, Haenchen, *Acts*, 459, says that the viewpoint is not that of the historical Peter. "Luke is rather portraying the image which Hellenistic Gentile Christians had of the law: a mass of commandments and prohibitions which no man can satisfy." Conzelmann, *Acts*, 117, agrees: "It expresses the view of a Christian at a time when the separation from Judaism already lies in the past. On this basis we can also understand why Luke does not draw the conclusion which logic demands, that this yoke should also be removed from Jewish Christians."

26. For a discussion of the textual problems in Acts 15:20, 29; 21:25, see Bruce M. Metzger, *A Textual Commentary on the Greek New Testament*, 429–34.

27. But for an excellent attempt to interpret the apostolic decree as embodying ethical requirements, see Stephen G. Wilson, *Luke and the Law*, 68–102. Wilson finds it necessary to make use of those manuscripts that omit the prohibition of *pniktos*, and he understands the remaining requirements to prohibit idolatry, murder, and sexual licentiousness. Drawing on Str-B, Wilson asserts, "There is the rabbinic tradition which considers the three primary sins of the Gentiles to be precisely idolatry, shedding of blood and immorality" (80). Wilson's argument has the virtue of making a careful distinction between historical and literary interpretations, but the omission of *pniktos* from the decree is a problem he readily admits. For a defense of the ritualistic interpretation of the decree, see Haenchen, *Acts*, 468–72. Haenchen says that the decree reflects Leviticus 17–18 and that the order of the decree in 15:29; 21:25 is exactly the same as that in Leviticus. Lev 17:8 condemns heathen offerings and thus things offered to idols. Lev 17:10ff. prohibits consuming blood, 17:13 *pnikton* and 18:6ff. marriage to near relatives. He writes: "What links these four prohibitions together, and at the same time distinguishes them from all other 'ritual' requirements of 'Moses', is that they—and they only—are given not only to Israel but also to strangers dwelling among the Jews. Whereas in other respects the law applies solely to the Jews, it imposes these four prohibitions on *Gentiles also!*" Haenchen, *Acts*, 469. Wilson, however, correctly points out that these are not the only rules for resident aliens given in the Pentateuch and that the connection between Lev 17:13 and *pniktos* is obscure. See Wilson, *Luke and the Law*, 84–94. For our purposes it should be observed that the decree, understood either as ritualistic or ethical, draws on the Jewish tradition, as Acts 15:21 makes clear.

28. Agreeing at this point with Haenchen, that the apostolic decree reflects the Levitical rules for resident aliens, Jervell concludes that the Jewish law remains valid both for Jewish and for Gentile Christians. He claims that the apostolic decree required of Gentiles no more than the Mosaic Torah required. "No matter how the complicated passage Acts 15:21 is to be interpreted in detail, the function of the verse is to validate the decree, to call upon Moses as witness. Everyone who truly hears Moses knows that the decree expresses what Moses demands from Gentiles in order that they may live among Israelites (15:15–17). The four prescriptions are what the law demands of Gentiles; perhaps Luke

consciously refers to what Lev 17–18 demands from the 'stangers' that sojourn among Israelites" (*Luke and the People*, 144). See also Earl Richard, "The Divine Purpose: The Jews and the Gentile Mission (Acts 15)." Richard provides a structural analysis of Acts 15 and concludes that the law is still valid for both Jewish and Gentile Christians.

29. Conzelmann, *Acts*, 125, writes: "For Luke, Timothy's circumcision is required because of the schematic portrayal of Paul's mission in Acts which requires that Paul always go first to the synagogue. For that reason he must be accompanied by Jewish associates (therefore, for example, not Titus)." Conzelmann evidently had in mind the Titus of Paul's letters and the Pastorals, who is not mentioned in Acts.

30. See Shaye J. D. Cohen, "Was Timothy Jewish (Acts 16:1–3)? Patristic Exegesis, Rabbinic Law, and Matrilineal Descent."

31. Haenchen, *Acts*, 482, explains that Luke used an unreliable tradition about Paul's circumcision of Timothy because "it seemed to speak in favour of his pet theory that the Pharisee Paul strictly observed the law, and came into conflict with Judaism only through his proclamation of the resurrection."

32. See Tyson, *The Death of Jesus*, 129–33.

33. Although he says that the focus has shifted away from Jerusalem after Acts 15, Haenchen maintains that it remains the spiritual center of the Christian movement. See Haenchen, *Acts*, 461f.

34. See Luke 9:51, 53; 13:22, 33–34; 17:11, 18:31–34; 19:11, 28, 41–44.

35. Haenchen points out the parallels between Paul's approach to Jerusalem and that of Jesus, and he writes, "Everything once again has happened as in the passion story of Jesus. The Jews have taken prisoner not only the Lord, but also his greatest missionary, and they have delivered both into the hands of the Gentiles" (*Acts*, 605). See also Talbert, *Literary Patterns*, 15–23; Radl, *Paulus und Jesus*, 103–26.

36. The quotation is from the LXX of Amos 9:11–12. The Hebrew does not refer to a call of Gentiles but to a conquest of them by Israel.

37. Dibelius, *Studies*, 58, maintained that the speech of Paul on the Areopagus was "a hellenistic speech with a Christian ending." Haenchen, *Acts*, 527, calls special attention to the "allusive references to Socrates" in the Areopagus speech. But he also thinks that Dibelius underemphasized the OT components of the speech. He cites allusions to and use of Wisdom 14:20; 15:17; Isa 42:5; and perhaps Gen 1:28; Ps 74:17; 9:5; 95:13; 97:9. See Haenchen, *Acts*, 517–27. Gerhard Schneider finds that the theme of the unknown God reflects Isa 45:18–25. See Schneider, *Lukas, Theologe der Heilsgeschichte: Aufsätze zum lukanischen Doppelwerk*, 297–302. See also Hans Conzelmann, "The Address of Paul on the Areopagus."

38. Haenchen, *Acts*, 525, agrees, "The quotation (Aratus *Phaenomena* 5) stands as proof in the same way as biblical quotations in the other speeches of Acts."

# 8

# Paul in Jerusalem, Caesarea, and Rome

## (Acts 21:15–28:31)

In the concluding chapters of the Acts of the Apostles, the reader follows Paul as he arrives in Jerusalem, is arrested and taken to Caesarea, and then finally transferred to Rome, ostensibly to await the outcome of his appeal to the emperor. Although the geographical setting in this section of Acts changes, there is sufficient coherence in respect to images of Judaism to make it appropriate for us to treat the entire section in one chapter. We shall nevertheless respect the divisions within the narrative and treat each as a subsection of this chapter. Thus the present chapter will first investigate the section in Acts that deals with Paul in Jerusalem (Acts 21:15–23:22), and then the section on Paul in Caesarea (23:23–26:32), and finally on Paul in Rome (27–28).

### PAUL IN JERUSALEM (ACTS 21:15–23:22)

As soon as Paul and his party arrive in Jerusalem, they report to James and the elders, who inform them about the large number of Jewish believers who are disturbed by the information they have received about Paul's activity in the Diaspora. At James' suggestion, Paul participates in a ritual of purification with four other men who have made a vow, and he pays their expenses. But some seven days after this occurrence, Asian Jews, thinking that he has been teaching against the people, the law, and the Temple, and believing that he took a Greek man into the Temple, seize Paul. As a near riot ensues and Paul is in danger of being killed, the Roman tribune in Jerusalem, with a military escort, inquires about the reasons for the disturbance and arrests Paul. As he is being taken away, Paul receives permission from the tribune to speak to the people of Jerusalem, and he does so. After the speech there is a demand for Paul's execution, and the tribune prepares to torture

Paul in order to determine the reasons for the crowd's opposition, but Paul pleads that his Roman citizenship protects him from this kind of torture. So the tribune releases Paul but sends him to appear before the Sanhedrin. His appearance there ends in a riot, from which the tribune rescues him. While Paul is being held in the Roman garrison, forty Jews conspire with the chief priests and elders to capture him in an ambush and kill him. But Paul learns of the plot from a nephew, who communicates it to the tribune, who decides to send Paul to Caesarea.

After what we have read in the previous section of Acts, the section on Paul in Jerusalem contains few surprises. Luke has carefully prepared for the narration of these events by the various warnings about Paul's fate in the city, and so it is appropriate for him to present here the culmination of Jewish opposition to Paul. The role of the Jewish people and leaders here is precisely what we have been led to expect by the previous chapters. In general, Paul's Jewish opponents think that he has been teaching against Judaism, "teaching everyone everywhere against our people, our law, and this place" (21:28).

Thus the images of the Jewish people in this section are overwhelmingly negative. The disturbance that led to Paul's arrest in Jerusalem was instigated by a group of Jews from Asia.[1] They not only charge him with anti-Jewish teaching, but they think that he has taken Trophimus, a Gentile, into the Jerusalem Temple. Luke's mention of Jews from Asia raises a number of questions. We do not learn from the text of Acts if these were Jews who were visiting in Jerusalem or had long ago settled there. Perhaps we are to think of them as Jews who were in the province of Asia when Paul preached there and had returned to Jerusalem for the express purpose of bringing a halt to his activities. In any event they seem to have no difficulty in inciting the crowd in Jerusalem to come to a fever pitch in mobbing Paul. Indeed, Luke says that the entire city was aroused and that as a result Paul was dragged out of the Temple and almost killed (21:30–31). Although the crowd listens to Paul's public speech in 22:1–21, afterward they demand that he be executed: "Away with such a fellow from the earth! For he should not be allowed to live" (22:22). Their shouts are accompanied by visual signs of their hostility (22:23).

The opposition to Paul becomes so intense that the Roman tribune finally decides to escort him from Jerusalem to Caesarea in order to remove him from mortal danger. After the hearing before

the Sanhedrin in Acts 23:1–10, some Jews form a plot to ambush
Paul. The dark tones of Luke's portrait at this point are striking,
"In the morning the Jews joined in a conspiracy (*poiēsantes
systrophēn*) and bound themselves by an oath neither to eat nor
drink until they had killed Paul" (23:12). We later learn that the
plot was agreed to by "more than forty" (23:13), but the first impression is that the plot was agreed to by all "the Jews." The reference to the plot (*systrophē*) has nuances of political sedition, and
the blood oath evokes images of fanatical terrorism. Further, the
leaders—chief priests and elders—become involved in the plot
(23:14), which only fails because Paul's nephew learns of it and is
able to bring it to the attention of the tribune.

Thus the narratives about Paul in Jerusalem provide us with
an almost totally negative image of the Jewish people. They are
unruly, seditious, and fanatical. The role of the Jewish people
(called "the Jews" in 22:30; 23:12, 20) here is consistent with that of
Paul's Jewish opponents in the Diaspora. They are bloodthirsty, violent, loud, confused, and obdurate.

The character of the Roman tribune (*chiliarchos*) forms a contrast to that of the Jewish people. He, later identified as Claudius
Lysias (23:26), is shown to be fair and judicious in permitting Paul
to speak to the crowd and in halting the torture when he learns
that Paul is a Roman citizen. He fulfills his orders by attempting to
keep the peace in Jerusalem, even if it requires force. He protects
Paul from mortal danger on more than one occasion. He simply
wants to learn why there is such a disturbance surrounding this
man, and the noise and confusion of the crowd prevent him from
doing so. The reader is reminded of an earlier crowd scene at
Ephesus, where some shouted one thing and some another (19:32
cf. 21:34), and where the city magistrate calmed the crowd with his
address. It is true that the Roman tribune mistook Paul for an
Egyptian terrorist (21:38),[2] but for the most part he, as a symbol of
Roman law and order, provides a contrast to the kind of mob violence that is here associated with the Jewish people.[3]

Despite the overwhelmingly negative portrait of Jewish people in this section of Acts, there are aspects of the narrative at this
point that suggest somewhat ambivalent evaluations. For one
thing we are reminded in Acts 21:20 of the existence of a large community of Jewish believers in Jerusalem. This information is given
to Paul and hence to the reader by James. When the two characters
meet just after Paul's arrival in Jerusalem, Paul explains in detail

everything that has happened in connection with his activity among the Gentiles. James replies by calling attention to the myriad of believers from among the Jews, "You see, brother, how many thousands (*posai myriades*) of believers there are among the Jews" (Acts 21:20). James describes these believers as, like Paul, zealous for the law.

Jacob Jervell has frequently reminded us of the importance of Acts 21:20 in assessing the relationship between Jews and Christians as presented in Acts.[4] He maintains that it is incorrect to speak of a failed mission of Christians among Jews, for Acts 21:20 is the culmination of a series of passages that call attention to a successful mission among Jews. Jervell is technically correct. The mission to Jews, especially in Palestine, has not been a failure if myriads can be counted as believers. But Jervell has not paid sufficient attention to the narrative function of this group of believers. Although James maintains that these people are zealous for the law, as Paul has been described as being, they nevertheless are deeply suspicious about Paul's activity among the Gentiles (Acts 21:21). Indeed, they harbor the same suspicions as do the Asian Jews in Acts 21:28. These two verses may bear close comparison:

> *Katēchēthēsan de peri sou hoti apostasian didaskeis apo Mōyseos tous kata ta ethnē pantas Ioudaious, legōn mē peritemnein autous ta tekna mēde tois ethesin peripatein* ("They have been told about you that you teach all the Jews living among the Gentiles to forsake Moses, and that you tell them not to circumcise their children or observe the customs," Acts 21:21).
>
> *Houtos estin ho anthrōpos ho kata tou laou kai tou nomou kai tou topou toutou pantas pantachē didaskōn* ("This is the man who is teaching everyone everywhere against our people, our law, and this place," Acts 21:28).

In both cases the objection is to Paul's teaching, and one common point is the suspicion that he teaches against the law. The objection raised by the believers in 21:21 is more specific on this point than that of the Asian Jews in 21:28 and includes the charge that Paul teaches against the necessity of circumcision for Jewish sons. In order to answer the objections of the Jewish believers, James counsels Paul to join a group of four others who are fulfilling a vow and to appear with them in the Temple. Paul does so, but this event leads instead to his capture.

Close attention to the narrative at this point shows that the existence of a large number of Jewish believers is a positive factor, but it is difficult to avoid a blurring of the distinction between this group and the other Jews who suspect Paul of apostasy. There is, of course, no suggestion in the narrative that the Christians in Jerusalem were influenced by the Asian Jews or were in any way involved in the disturbance that led to Paul's arrest. But it is notable that they hold essentially the same suspicions about Paul as do the Jews from Asia and that they do nothing to protect Paul from the violence of the rest of the population. Indeed, James implies in 21:22 that Paul is in a dangerous situation vis-à-vis the Jewish believers. He suggests that something must be done to answer their objections, since they will certainly find out that Paul has come to Jerusalem, and he claims that Paul's participation with the others will show "that there is nothing in what they have been told about you, but that you yourself observe and guard the law" (21:24). In the final analysis the Christian and the non-Christian Jews play essentially the same narrative role in this section of Acts. Both are presented as opponents of Paul, and both suspect him of apostasy to Judaism. We may therefore agree with Jervell that the Christian mission to Jews has not been a failure.[5] But we must also say that those Jews who have become believers are nevertheless to be counted among Paul's opponents.

This section of Acts is also remarkable in stressing Paul's conformity to Jewish practices and beliefs. In connection with the suspicions of the Jewish believers, James makes a special effort to demonstrate that they are unfounded, and he calls attention to Paul's own zeal for the law. The reader will recall that Luke has already made it clear that Paul is not guilty of these charges (cf. esp. Acts 16:1–5). Further, James reminds the reader about the requirements for Gentile believers in 21:25, and we have read that Paul taught adherence to these requirements (16:4). Thus, we are compelled to conclude that the believers among the Jews are mistaken in their estimation of Paul and to view Paul as a believer who is zealous for the law.

Similar charges by the Jews from Asia are shown to be in error. Luke's explanation of the basis of their belief that Paul had taken a Greek into the Temple (21:29) may not be an explicit denial of the charge, but it would have that function for most readers. Luke first notes that the accusers had seen Trophimus with Paul in the city, an implicit denial that they had seen them together in the Temple. Then Luke also uses a verb (nomizō), which he has frequently used in contexts where doubt is possible (cf. Luke 3:23; Acts 16:13) or to indicate a mistaken idea (cf. Luke 2:44; Acts 7:25; 8:20; 14:19; 16:27; 17:29). The force of Acts 21:29 may be represented as saying, "For they had seen Trophimus the Ephesian with him in the city, not the Temple, and they mistakenly supposed that Paul had taken him into the Temple."

Paul's public speech in the Temple court (Acts 22:1–21) also functions to portray him as a loyal Jew. He begins, not by describing himself as a believer or a Christian, but as a Jew from Tarsus in Cilicia (22:3; cf. 21:39). Paul is still a Jew, and he will later claim still to be a Pharisee (23:6). His use of the Hebrew language (21:40; 22:2) is not just a practical means of communicating with the people of Jerusalem; it is also a way of identifying himself with these people, a point that is emphasized further when Paul says that he was brought up in Jerusalem at the feet of Gamaliel (22:3).[6] Paul describes himself as trained in Torah and zealous in its observance, so zealous in fact that he persecuted those who believed in Jesus.

Toward the end of the speech, however, Paul tells of his experience on the road to Damascus (cf. Acts 9:1–19) and of a subsequent vision that occurred when he was praying in the Temple. In this vision he is told to get out of Jerusalem immediately, "because they will not accept your testimony about me" (22:18). Paul protests that they knew him as persecutor, but the voice commands, "Go, for I will send you far away to the Gentiles" (22:21). It is this statement that touches off the demonstration of mob hostility.

The reference to a vision in the Temple (Acts 22:17–21) has several difficulties, which must be faced at this point. For one thing, this pericope appears to give the reader some information that was not contained in the narrative of Paul's conversion in Acts 9:1–19. In that narrative there was nothing about Paul's praying in the Temple of Jerusalem or about his receiving a vision there. But Acts 9:26–30 does tell of the suspicion that initially met Paul in Jerusalem. The Christians there knew of his persecuting activity, and the intervention of Barnabas was required before Paul was accepted by them. Even at that the Hellenists sought to kill Paul, and he was dispatched to Tarsus. Thus Acts 22:17–21 may be a rewriting of 9:26–30.[7]

A further difficulty is encountered in the indefinite pronouns in Acts 22:18, 19. In the vision Paul is told that "they" will not accept his testimony, and Paul replies that "they" know of his persecuting activity. If Acts 22:17–21 is a rewriting of 9:26–30, "they" must refer to the Christians in Jerusalem who were suspicious because of what they had known of Paul's persecuting activity. On the other hand, if "they" in 22:18 refers to the non-Christian Jews in Jerusalem, as suggested by the contrast with Gentiles in 21:21,

Paul's reference to his persecuting activity must be intended to counter Jewish rejection. Paul thinks that his role in persecuting the believers should give him credibility with the nonbelieving Jews. It is not possible to say which reference is intended here, and in fact the ambiguity itself has a certain rhetorical function. The reader is led to question whether the rejection of Paul comes from the Jewish Christians or from the Jews, and we have already seen that there is here a blurring of the distinction between these two groups.

Yet another difficulty is met in Acts 22:21. The voice that speaks to Paul during his vision in the Temple not only commands him to leave Jerusalem but to go far away to Gentiles. The difficulty is the inconsistency between this command and that given to Paul through Ananias in 9:15. There it was said that Paul is expected to preach to Gentiles and kings and the sons of Israel. We have also observed the way in which this verse controlled the narrative in 13:1–21:14. In the reprise of Paul's conversion experience, the comparable verse states that Paul is to be a "witness to all the world of what you have seen and heard" (22:15). A mission to Jews is implicitly included here, but Acts 22:21 would seem to mean that Paul is not to be a witness to Jews but only to Gentiles.

Considering all the difficulties in Acts 22:17–21, it seems best not to think of it simply as a rewriting of 9:26–30. Although it tells of an earlier time in Paul's life and may remind the reader of Luke's earlier description of Paul's calling, the pericope in its present location functions primarily to lead the reader to anticipate Paul's trip to Rome and the approaching end of the mission to the Jews. Paul's message has not been accepted in Jerusalem (either by Christians or by Jews), and it may now be said that he has fulfilled one portion of the divine charge of 9:15. He will soon be dispatched far away among Gentiles where, as we shall see, he will pronounce the close of the mission to the Jews.

The reaction to Paul's speech in the Temple court underlines the significance of the statement in Acts 22:21. Apparently the crowd listened to Paul intently until he uttered the last sentence (22:22). At this there was a great uproar that required the tribune to rescue him. The one thing that the crowd was not prepared to hear was that God had sent Paul to preach among Gentiles.

The effort to portray Paul as a loyal Jew also shows itself in his appearance before the Sanhedrin (Acts 23:1–10), but here the Jewish leaders are no less confused and unruly than the people. The description of the Sanhedrin session is a study in confusion. It consists of two major subsections. In the first, we have a confrontation between Paul and Ananias, the high priest (23:1–5). In the second part, Paul is able to cause a division between the Pharisaic and Sadducaic members of the Sanhedrin (23:6–10). It is misleading to think of this episode as Paul's speech before the Sanhedrin, since most of the attention is given to narrative rather than discourse. In fact, Paul addresses only one sentence (23:1) to the body before he is interrupted by the chief priest. Then he speaks again briefly (23:6) before a riot breaks out between the two groups in the Sanhedrin. The two sections of the narrative require some discussion and interpretation.

The confrontation between Paul and the high priest (Acts 23:1–5) does not present a clear image to the reader. At one level we should expect this narrative to tell of a climatic meeting between protagonist and antagonist. It might include a verbal duel between Paul and Ananias in which Paul demonstrates his superiority. What we have in Acts 23:1–5 is something of a battle, but not one with a clear victor. Paul begins by asserting his fidelity to God, but Ananias orders him to be struck on the mouth. Paul then accuses the high priest of violating the law and thus rendering himself unfit to judge the case at hand. But after he is warned about reviling the high priest, Paul pleads ignorance and quotes a verse from Exod 22:28, "You shall not speak evil of a leader of your people" (Acts 23:5).

Despite the lack of clarity in this brief narrative, we may examine the image of the high priest conveyed in it. Although he is identified by name, his characterization here is impersonal. There is no description of him and nothing about his relationship to the others who are alluded to in the narrative. He has no speaking parts, nor does he act directly. We only read that he gives an order to strike Paul on the mouth. We should probably assume that this order is intended to indicate a judgment that Paul has spoken blasphemy, but we are not told this. Due to the place that Paul holds in the narrative, the implied reader would surely be inclined to take his judgment against the high priest (23:3) quite seriously. Although he does not back up his contention that Ananias has broken the law, Paul has, by this point in the narrative, become a reliable character.[8] Thus we have in this pericope an image of the major leader of the Jewish people who does not obey Torah and is unqualified to act as judge.

The problem of understanding how Paul could have failed to recognize the high priest remains, however. We learned in Acts 9:1–2 that he had been commissioned by the high priest to search out Jewish believers, and in 22:4–5 Paul reminded us of this and claimed that the high priest and the entire council could be called to testify about his persecuting activity. In this way the reader would tend to assume that some personal relationship existed between the high priest and Paul. On the other hand, some time has passed between the persecuting activity of Paul and the hearing before the Sanhedrin in Acts 23. We are forced to assume that the present high priest is not the same as the one who had known Saul before his conversion.[9] It is worth noting that Luke knew of an earlier high priest by the name of Annas (Acts 4:6), who had participated in the examination of Peter. Thus there is little difficulty in assuming that a new high priest, unknown to Paul, is intended in Acts 23. This also means that, contrary to Paul's expectation in 22:5, Ananias would not be able to testify about Paul's persecuting Christians.

But Paul's own reliability and fidelity to Torah are indirectly affirmed in Acts 23:5. The reader is to assume that Paul would not have spoken as he did in 23:3 if he had known that it was the high priest who had given the order for him to be struck. For Paul knows the scriptures and the prohibition against reviling a leader of God's people (Exod 22:28). Thus the character Paul, who knows Torah and is faithful to God, stands in contrast to the character Ananias, who, though a leader of the people, violates God's law.

After the narrative of the confrontation between Paul and the high priest, Luke tells of Paul's hearing before the Sanhedrin proper (Acts 23:6–10). Knowing that this body is made up of both Pharisees and Sadducees, Paul intentionally identifies himself with the former and causes a riot (*stasis*). Luke explains that Sadducees deny resurrection and the existence of angels and spirits, while Pharisees believe these things (cf. Luke 20:27).[10] Paul claims it is because of his Pharisaic belief in the resurrection that he is being judged by the Sanhedrin, and the Pharisaic members of the body (literally Pharisaic scribes, 23:9) declare him innocent and speculate that an angel or spirit has communicated with him. But contention between the two parties leads to a riot, and the Roman tribune is compelled to break up the meeting and rescue Paul, who is about to be torn apart by the members of the Sanhedrin.

Two major images of Judaism emerge from this narrative. The first is the image of a judicial body in disarray. The Sanhedrin is pictured as fractious and contentious. The deep division between Pharisees and Sadducees not only impairs the council from taking action in the case of Paul, but it leads to rioting and violence, which requires the intervention of Roman military authority.

The second image that comes out of a reading of Acts 23:6–10 is a more positive one. Luke calls attention here to a certain identity of belief between Paul and the Pharisees. Indeed, Paul states that he is a Pharisee and the son of Pharisees (*egō Pharisaios eimi, hyios Pharisaiōn*, 23:6). It is startling to hear Paul identify himself this way so late in the narrative of Luke-Acts. For in the gospel of Luke we observed the many occasions on which Jesus was confronted with Pharisaic hostility, and we have read of his condemnations of this group. But we have also observed the quasi-sympathetic role that was played by Gamaliel, identified as a Pharisee in Acts 5:34, and we have encountered Pharisaic Christians in Acts 15:5. As we observed in chapter 7, there appears to be a gradual re-evaluation of Pharisees going on in Luke-Acts. In the present pericope, there is such a close relationship between the beliefs of Christians and Pharisees that Paul can be called by either name.[11] In addition, we are informed that the major item that separates Christians from non-Pharisaic Jews is the belief in the resurrection and that on this fundamental matter Christians and Pharisees are in agreement. Thus the Pharisees must be seen as exceptions to the otherwise one-dimensional portrait of Jews in this section of Acts.

In terms of Jewish religious practices and observances, Acts 21:15–23:22 is quite rich, but little new information is provided. There is some stress on the centrality of the Temple, the importance of strict observance of Torah, circumcision, and other so-called customs. We learn from Paul's quotation of Exod 22:28 that it is necessary to obey Torah even when calling attention to an injustice by a Jewish leader (23:5).

In addition, however, we are given a glimpse, albeit a veiled one, of ritual activity in the Temple.[12] Paul must undergo a ritual of purification before entering the Temple (21:26). He takes James' suggestion to accompany the four men who are fulfilling a vow, and, after purifying himself, goes with them into the Temple to report the time when the purification will be complete and when a sacrifice will be offered. We gain no concrete information from this vignette and only learn that the performance of such rituals forms an important part of Jewish practice and demonstrates one's piety. The same incident shows that Gentiles may not enter the Temple and that this prohibition is taken with utmost seriousness by Jews. The fact that Luke denies the charge that Paul took Trophimus or any other Gentile into the Temple allows the reader to sense the importance of this prohibition.

The section of Acts on Paul in Jerusalem provides us some insight into ritualistic aspects of Jewish religious life. It also contains some devastatingly negative images of Jewish people. But over against these images there is a stress on Paul as a law-observant Jew and a faithful Pharisee. What separates him from his fellows is the divine charge to carry the message of Jesus to the Gentiles. The negative images of Jews and Judaism are to some extent relieved by the presence of a Christian Jewish community in Jerusalem and by the positive support provided by Pharisees. But even these images are compromised. Any distinction between Christian and non-Christian Jews is blurred, and the positive support that Pharisees offer to Paul is not effective in rescuing him from the hostility of more formidable opponents.

### PAUL IN CAESAREA (ACTS 23:23–26:32)

The section of Acts that deals with Paul in Caesarea consists of a long series of semijudicial proceedings. Much of it is a reprise of earlier sections, with lengthy reviews of the events surrounding Paul in Jerusalem and a third telling of the narrative of his conversion. The tribune, Claudius Lysias, has decided to send Paul to Caesarea in order to remove him from the danger posed by Jewish plotters. So he writes to Felix and briefly reviews the recent events (Acts 23:26–30) and sends him under military escort to Caesarea, where he is kept under guard at Herod's praetorium (23:31–35). Five days later the high priest Ananias, accompanied by Tertullus, a rhetor, and some elders, arrives in Caesarea, and Tertullus presents to Felix the charges of Jews against Paul (24:1–9). Paul is allowed to respond to the charges (24:10–21), but Felix postpones a decision for some two years (24:22–27). Porcius Festus then succeeds Felix, begins to look into Paul's case (25:1–5), and conducts a trial, during which Paul appeals to Caesar (25:6–12). This is followed by a hearing before King Agrippa, who concludes that Paul could have been released if he had not appealed to Caesar (25:13–26:32).

Parallels with the trials of Jesus have frequently been noticed.[13] Both Jesus and Paul were subjected to a hearing before the Sanhedrin; both appeared before a Roman governor; both appeared before a Herodian. But there are striking differences between the trials of Jesus and Paul that should not be overlooked. The charges brought against Jesus are reported by Luke very briefly, but in Acts the charges against Paul are given more fully and argued extensively and repeatedly. Jesus does not offer any words in his own defense, but Paul presents his case in speeches before two procurators and a king. Jesus appeared before one Roman, while Paul argued his case before two and addressed some words in the presence of the tribune in Jerusalem. Although we know that Agrippa was a great-grandson of Herod the Great and a grand-nephew of the Herod of Jesus' trial, we are not given that information in Acts, where he is called King Agrippa.[14]

In the section of Acts on Paul in Caesarea, there continues to be great stress on Paul's fidelity to Judaism. But little new information about the religious life of the Jewish people is offered here, and so it is only necessary to examine briefly the major sections and note the pertinent passages.

**Tertullus' charges against Paul (Acts 24:1–9).** The speech of the rhetor is brief and effective. He begins with the expected *captatio benevolentiae,* flattering words to Felix, and then describes Paul as diseased, as an instigator of riots "among all the Jews throughout the world, and a ringleader of the sect of the Nazarenes (*tēs tōn Nazōraiōn haireseōs,*" 24:5). It is not clear whether Tertullus' mention of Paul's membership in the Nazarene sect is meant to be taken as a crime or forms a part of the background description. But then the rhetor continues and accuses Paul of profaning the Temple, and he states that Paul was arrested on this charge. At the end of this pericope Luke states that "the Jews," probably meaning Ananias and the elders, agreed with Tertullus' charges (24:9).

The implied reader here would probably think of Tertullus as a cultured spokesperson even if he is convinced that his charges are untrue.[15] The presence of Ananias at the hearing would, however, cause one to recall his confrontation with Paul in Jerusalem. The concluding note about "the Jews" also evokes negative images.[16]

**Paul's defense before Felix (Acts 24:10–21).** Like Tertullus, Paul also begins with a *captatio benevolentiae,* though a briefer one. He denies that he profaned the Temple, but rather affirms that he was purified when he entered it and did not stir up a mob either there or in synagogues or in the city of Jerusalem. Paul admits to being a member of a sect (*hairesis*) which he calls the Way (*ho hodos*), but he makes it clear that as such he believes in the ancestral God and the scriptures.[17] He shares the belief in the resurrection with other Jews ("I have a hope in God—a hope that they themselves also accept—that there will be a resurrection of both the righteous and the unrighteous," 24:15). Paul ends his speech with a reference to the Jews from Asia, who originally brought charges against him but are not now present at the hearing before Felix. The only violation that Paul can conceive is that in the Sanhedrin he claimed that he was being judged concerning his belief in the resurrection.

It is notable that neither Tertullus nor Paul addressed the question of Paul's taking a Gentile into the Temple. Although that had been the source of the charge by the Asian Jews and although Tertullus expressly claimed that Paul had profaned the Temple, he said nothing about Trophimus or any other Gentile. Nor does Paul in his defense make any reference to this incident. He rather seems more interested in letting Felix know that it was not he who caused the recent disturbance in Jerusalem. The implied reader, of course, knows of the Trophimus incident and of Paul's innocence in the whole matter. One effect of the speech is to refocus attention on the Jews from Asia as those who are really guilty of inciting the crowd to riot and constitute the ultimate source of all Paul's problems. There may also be nuances of cowardice in the reference to their absence from the hearing before Felix, but their absence also suggests that no one is present in this hearing who is able to substantiate their charges against Paul.

Paul's defensive speech before Felix strongly underscores his fidelity to Judaism.[18] Indeed, serious attention must be given to the affirmation in 24:14–16, which constitutes Paul's description of his religious beliefs. If we had only this statement, we would conclude that there is no distinction between Judaism and Pauline Christianity. Both have the same God, the same scriptures, and the same hope for the future. The reader knows that not all Jews accept the belief in the resurrection, but the Lukan Paul seems intent at this point on stressing the identity of Christian and Jewish belief.

**Felix's Delay (Acts 24:22–27).** We learn that Felix had some knowledge of the Way and that he had a Jewish wife. But he was replaced before he came to a final decision about Paul, and during the two-year delay he often sent for Paul and listened to his preaching. We also learn, however, that Felix had some base motives: he hoped that Paul would offer a bribe, and he kept Paul imprisoned because he wanted to grant favors to the Jews (24:27).

**Festus in Jerusalem (Acts 25:1–5).**   In Jerusalem the new governor is informed about Paul. The chief priests and the first citizens urge him to send the prisoner to Jerusalem, but Festus rejects their plea and invites any who have charges against Paul to come to Caesarea to press them. Luke reminds the reader that the Jews who spoke to Festus are part of the plot against Paul and that they still plan to ambush and kill him (23:12–15).

**Paul's trial before Festus (Acts 25:6–12).**   The Jews from Jerusalem make serious but unsubstantiated charges against Paul, who again maintains his innocence. But Festus acts surprisingly by offering to send Paul to Jerusalem for trial. Luke explains his motivation as wanting to do a favor for the Jews. But Paul rejects the Jerusalem venue and appeals to Caesar. He is told that he will go to Rome, just as it had been revealed to him in a vision in 23:11.

The image of Roman officials is tarnished in this episode.[19] After rejecting the demand of the chief priests and first citizens in 25:4, in 25:9 Festus offers to do precisely as they had urged and to send Paul to Jerusalem for trial. We now know that both he and Felix were motivated by their desires to benefit Paul's Jewish accusers (25:9; 24:27; cf. also Herod in 12:3). Although there is no hint that the corrupt practices of Festus (or Felix) should be excused, it is also clear that Jews share blame with the Roman officials in these matters.[20]

**Festus confers with Agrippa (Acts 25:13–22).**   Luke takes this opportunity to review the case of Paul, and thus little new information is to be found here. We do, however, learn that Festus thinks that Paul is innocent (25:18). He informs Agrippa that the case deals with some matters relating to religion and to the resurrected Jesus. Then Festus explains that he has offered to send Paul to Jerusalem for trial simply because he was uninformed about religious matters. The reader knows that this is not the real reason for Festus' offer but may understand that the governor needs to put the best face on his own doubtful dealings.[21]

**Paul's hearing before Agrippa (Acts 25:23–26:32).**   The hearing before King Agrippa is the culmination of this section of Acts. It is the fulfillment of the divine charge given Paul at his conversion, which included the need to speak before kings (Acts 9:15–16), and it reflects Jesus' prediction that his disciples would be brought

before kings and governors (Luke 21:12). Agrippa, with his sister
Bernice, enters with great pomp and in the company of Roman officials and leading citizens of Caesarea. Luke clearly describes
a royal audience. Agrippa is repeatedly called king (25:13, 14, 24,
26; 26:2, 7, 13, 19, 26, 27, 30) and is so addressed by both Festus
and Paul.

At the beginning of the hearing, Festus, in an obvious exag-
geration, introduces Paul as the person "about whom the whole
Jewish community petitioned me, both in Jerusalem and here,
shouting that he ought not to live any longer" (25:24). He informs
the king about Paul's legal status and about the need to provide a
list of particulars to the emperor.

Then Paul begins his defense with the customary flattering
words to the king.[22] He claims to be fortunate since the king is so
well informed about Jewish customs and issues. Then Paul reviews his life and claims that from his youth he has lived as a Pharisee, "the strictest sect of our religion" (26:5), and, as in the
hearing before the Sanhedrin, he affirms that he is on trial because
of his belief in the resurrection. He recalls his persecution of the
Christians and tells again of his conversion and divine charge
given to him at that time:

> For I have appeared to you for this purpose, to appoint you to serve
> and testify to the things in which you have seen me and to those in
> which I will appear to you. I will rescue you from your people (ek tou
> laou) and from the Gentiles—to whom I am sending you to open their
> eyes so that they may turn from darkness to light and from the power
> of Satan to God, so that they may receive forgiveness of sins and a place
> among those who are sanctified by faith in me (26:16–18).

This is the third version of the divine command, with which
may be compared 9:15–16 and 22:15. In the present version it is unclear whether Paul is being sent to Gentiles only or to both Jews
and Gentiles. The verb exaireō may be translated either as rescue,
as in the NRSV, or as select. In the latter sense the meaning is that
Paul has been selected from among Jews and Gentiles. It would
seem probable that he is being sent (apostellō) to the same people
from whom he has been selected. A similar meaning is possible if
we understand exaireō as deliver or rescue: Paul is being sent to
those from whom he has been delivered. Although it is reasonable
to read 26:17 as meaning that Paul is being sent to Gentiles, not to
the people, i.e., Jews, such a sense is inconsistent with the first

version of the divine command in 9:15–16 and, to a lesser extent, the second in 22:15. Further, it should be noted that in something of an interpretation of the command in 26:19–20 Paul cites his work among both Jews and Gentiles, and he refers to the resurrected Christ as proclaiming light to both Jews and Gentiles (26:23). If we understand all three versions of the command as requiring Paul to preach among both Jews and Gentiles, we can say that at this point in the narrative he has fulfilled this charge.

But Acts 9:15 had also required Paul to speak to kings, and although this statement is not included in either the second or the third version of the divine command, it is nevertheless being fulfilled at the moment of Paul's address to Agrippa. Thus it is entirely appropriate for Paul to claim, as he does in 26:19, "After that, King Agrippa, I was not disobedient to the heavenly vision," and to support his affirmation by citing his preaching in Damascus, Jerusalem, Judea, and among the Gentiles (26:20). At this climactic moment, Paul can say that he has fulfilled his God-given duty and preached not only to Jews and Gentiles, but also to kings, since the present speech to Agrippa is not only apologetic but also evangelistic. At the end of Paul's speech the king says, "Are you so quickly persuading me to become a Christian?" (26:28).

Included in Paul's defense is a strong affirmation of the consistency of Christian belief with the Hebrew Scriptures. Paul claims that he has preached nothing except "what the prophets and Moses said would take place" (26:22; cf. 24:14). And this means the suffering and resurrection of the Christ. As we have come to expect, no scriptural citations are included here, but the idea that the suffering of the Messiah is predicted in the scriptures has been presented several times already in Luke-Acts. Finally, Paul addresses the question to Agrippa, "Do you believe the prophets?" (26:27), and answers his own question in the affirmative.

Although there are no new images of Judaism and the Jewish people in the section of Acts on Paul in Caesarea, what we have tends to emphasize and underscore the negative images that we have observed from Acts 13:1 on. "The Jews" have unjustly accused Paul of profaning the Temple and violating Torah. They persistently press their charges against him, even though they are not able to prove them, and they obstinately continue a death threat against him. They are a corrupting influence on Roman officials. The faith of Paul is said to be in total harmony with the

Hebrew Scriptures, and Paul is portrayed as one who is aligned with Pharisees and as never doing anything against Torah or against any Jew.

The king and the governor agree at the end of the last hearing that Paul is innocent, and Agrippa says that he could have been released if he had not appealed to Caesar. But the appeal has been made, and so in Acts 27–28 Paul travels to Rome.

### PAUL IN ROME (ACTS 27–28)

Most of the space in Acts 27–28 is devoted to an exciting narrative about Paul's voyage from Caesarea to Rome, and there is little in it that is of value to our search for images of Judaism.[23] But after Paul finally arrives in Rome (Acts 28:14), we have a pericope (28:17–28) of major significance, a pericope that constitutes the last reported incident of the hero's life.[24]

It is significant that, in dealing with the Roman ministry, the only incident that Luke wants to report is one that tells of Paul's relationships with Jews. The meeting is the culmination of a long narrative in which the mission of Paul to Jews has been a matter of deep concern. The meeting is actually a double one, set on two separate days. The first incident (28:17–22) occurs three days after Paul arrives in Rome, and the second (28:23–28) at an indefinite time later. In the first, Paul summons a group of Jewish leaders and explains his legal status. The substance of the explanation is that Paul has committed no crimes against Jewish law but was nevertheless accused by Jews and turned over to Roman authorities for trial. Just when the Roman authorities were about to declare him innocent, the Jews objected to the proceedings, and Paul was forced to appeal to Caesar.[25] Paul then says to the Roman Jews that he wants to explain his situation to them since he has been imprisoned "for the sake of the hope of Israel" (28:20).[26] And the Jewish leaders respond that, although they have heard a great deal against the Christian movement, they have not heard anything about Paul himself and thus are anxious to hear him express his views.

In the second meeting (Acts 28:23–28), apparently rank-and-file Jews as well as leaders are present. It is an all-day meeting, during which Paul attempts to convince his hearers about Jesus on the basis of Torah and prophets. The result of the session is that "some were convinced by what he had said, while others refused to believe" (28:24). Then Paul makes one final statement before the group departs. The statement consists of a quotation from the LXX of Isa 6:9–10 and an application. The quotation describes Isaiah's contemporaries as lacking in understanding and perception.

> Go to this people and say,
> You will indeed listen, but never understand,
> and you will indeed look, but never perceive.
> For this people's heart has grown dull,
> and their ears are hard of hearing,
> and they have shut their eyes;
> so that they might not look with their eyes,
> and listen with their ears,
> and understand with their heart and turn—
> and I would heal them. (Acts 28:26–27)

In Isaiah the description of the people is given by Yahweh, and it functions to predetermine the rejection of the prophet's message. In the application in Acts 28:28, Paul concludes that God's salvation has been sent to the Gentiles, who will listen and presumably accept it.

The double meeting with the Jews in Rome is in some respects parallel to the meeting of Paul with Jews in Pisidian Antioch.[27] In both incidents, the first meeting is cordial and the second is marked by rejection, after which Paul quotes a passage from Isaiah to support a solemn announcement of the replacement of the mission to Jews by the mission to Gentiles. As we have seen, the solemn announcement is given again in Corinth at Acts 18:6. In addition, the narrative of Paul and Barnabas at Pisidian Antioch is the fullest narrative that makes use of a common literary pattern, in which initial acceptance by some Jews is followed by rejection by the Jews as a whole. This pattern governs the narrative in Acts 28, but with a variation. The first meeting of Paul with the Jews at Rome is not an evangelistic occasion. Paul uses it to introduce himself and to stress his fidelity to traditional Jewish beliefs and practices. His claim to be imprisoned for the hope of Israel (28:20) probably reflects the belief in the resurrection, which has been shown to be a Pharisaic belief.[28] Here, however, there is no occasion for subtleties, since the Lukan Paul wants to present himself as a loyal Jew. It is in the second meeting that Paul presents the message about the kingdom of God and Jesus, and the reaction of the Jews is not one of total rejection, but of partial acceptance: "Some were convinced by what he had said, while others refused to believe" (28:24).[29] Despite the partial acceptance, Paul quotes the words of Isaiah against them. Acts 28:25 contains a small clue about a significant difference between the two meetings of Paul with the Roman Jews. In the first, Paul speaks of "the customs of *our* ancestors" (28:17), but at the end of the second meeting he speaks of "*your* ancestors" (28:25) as those condemned by Isaiah. The different pronouns indicate a subtle distancing of Paul from the Jews, who have rejected his preaching. So Paul finally announces that "this salvation of God has been sent to the Gentiles; they will listen" (28:28).

There has recently been a great deal of discussion about the meaning of this concluding section of Acts and its bearing on the treatment of the Jews in Luke-Acts. Jacob Jervell maintains that Luke has, at the end of Acts, declared an end to the Jewish mission but not because it was a failure.[30] On the contrary, according to Jervell, Luke shows that the Gentile mission can begin because the Jewish mission was a success. In his view the quotation from Isaiah in Acts 28:26–27 is directed against the unrepentant Jews and is not in conflict with 28:24, which distinguishes between the repentant and the unrepentant. Jervell calls attention to the similarities between the description of Paul's mission in Rome and many earlier narratives, in which a distinction is made between those Jews who accept the Christian message and those who do not. The result of Paul's preaching in Rome is both positive and negative, as it had been all along. Robert Tannehill has written that the ending of Acts does not categorically mark the end of the mission to the Jews.[31] Although, after the end of the Acts narrative, the church's work will be predominantly among Gentiles, Jews are always to be welcomed into Christian fellowship. Tannehill observes that in the concluding summary statement in Acts 28:30, Paul welcomes *all* who come to him and continues to preach to them about Jesus and the kingdom. Tannehill insists that "all" in Acts 28:30 must include Jews as well as Gentiles.

Other scholars, however, have concluded that Luke narrates a failed mission to the Jews, the termination of which is announced in Acts 28:28.[32]

The failure of modern scholars to agree about the meaning of these verses suggests that Luke's presentation is more complex than is usually recognized. Although there are a number of exegetical problems in Acts 28:17–28, the major one appears to be the inappropriateness of Paul's concluding remarks.[33] The quotation from Isaiah, together with the application, shows Jews to be unhearing, unperceptive, and unreceptive of God's messenger. In a quite literal sense, these remarks appear to be inappropriate to the situation that Luke has described. Although Paul applies Isaiah's condemnation to Jews generally, some of his Jewish hearers have accepted his message. Jervell is correct to observe that the condemnation applies only to those who did not accept Paul's message, but the quotation speaks of the people (*ho laos*) as a whole. It is the people who lack understanding and perception, whose hearing is defective and whose eyes have closed. As Nils Dahl has shown, the term *ho laos* in Luke-Acts almost always designates the Jewish people, and Luke clearly understands the quotation from Isaiah to refer to them (cf. "your ancestors" in 28:25).[34] This understanding is particularly compelling when we relate the quotation to its application in Acts 28:28, which implicitly contrasts the expected attitude of Gentiles with the lack of understanding and perception found among Jews.

But there is one condition under which Paul's concluding words may be appropriate. If we should proceed from the view that the acceptance that is mentioned in Acts 28:24 is, for the implied author, an example of individual Jewish response, while the rejection in 28:25–28 designates the corporate Jewish response, we would be in a position to understand the passage as internally consistent. Under this view, there is a fundamental distinction between the collective response of Jews as a whole and the response of individual Jews. Given this distinction, we may say that, although Luke feels that positive responses from individual Jews should be noted and celebrated, such responses are not sufficient, since what is intended is the conversion of the people as a whole, and that, since this wholesale conversion has not occurred, the Pauline mission will hereafter be directed toward Gentiles. Although there is nothing to prohibit individual Jews from accepting the Christian message in the post-Pauline period, the passage leaves no hint that there will be a return to the Jewish mission, and it gives every indication that the previous mission to the Jews, which Luke has so abundantly described, has been a failure. As we have seen, Acts 28:28 is the last of three announcements about turning to Gentiles (cf. 13:46; 18:6). It is true that after both of the first two announcements Paul returned to present the Christian message to Jews. But, due to its location at the end of Luke-Acts, the third announcement carries special narrative weight. It functions as the culminating announcement, justification for which draws not only on Paul's immediate experience in Rome, but also on all those previous occasions of Jewish rejection. The announcements at Pisidian Antioch and Corinth now turn out to be anticipations of this final proclamation of the termination of the Pauline mission to the Jews.

This way of understanding the passage provides some insight into the tension and ambivalence that we have seen to be characteristic of Luke's entire narrative. There seems to be no hesitancy in reporting that some of Paul's Jewish hearers responded positively nor any reluctance in condemning the Jews as a whole for their rejection of Paul's message. Luke's narrative treats the retail acceptance of the gospel as positive but insufficient. What has been called for is the wholesale repentance of the Jewish people and their turning to accept Jesus as the Christ sent for them. That acceptance has not been forthcoming, so the mission to the Jews must be declared to be a failure, and it is terminated in favor of a successful mission to Gentiles.[35]

NOTES

1. Luke also notes in Acts 6:9 that foreign Jews were among those who brought accusations against Stephen.
2. It is probably the Egyptian described in Josephus, *Jewish War* 2:261–63; *Antiquities* 20:169–72, who is intended here.
3. Robert C. Tannehill, *The Narrative Unity of Luke-Acts: A Literary Interpretation,* 2:294–96, rightly points out that the characterization of Lysias here is complex. He calls attention to the discrepancies between the narrator's description of the events surrounding Paul and Lysias's version in his report (Acts 23:26–30), and comments, "He is decisive and perceptive (positive traits) but shares the tendency of those in political power structures to shade the truth for self-protection (a negative trait)" (295).
4. See Jacob Jervell, "The Divided People of God," in *Luke and the People of God: A New Look at Luke-Acts,* 41–74; idem., "The Mighty Minority," in *The Unknown Paul: Essays on Luke-Acts and Early Christian History,* 26–51. For a different reading, see Michael J. Cook, "The Mission to the Jews in Acts: Unraveling Luke's 'Myth of the "Myriads.' "
5. See Jervell, "Divided People."
6. Apparently we are to think of the Gamaliel who had appeared in Acts 5:33–39.
7. Tannehill's comments at this point are helpful. He points out that this version of the Damascus road experience is told from Paul's point of view, while that in Acts 9 is from the point of view of the narrator. See Tannehill, *Narrative Unity,* 2:275–76.
8. Paul's charge could have been based on Lev 19:15.
9. Ananias' high priesthood began c. 48 CE. See Josephus, *Antiquities* 20:103.
10. Hans Conzelmann observes: "Luke knows that the Sadducees reject belief in the resurrection (Luke 20:27–33; cf. Josephus *Bell.* 2.165), but he does not know why—namely their limiting Scripture to the Torah and their rejection of tradi-

tion. Thus he alters the picture of them by depicting them as skeptics. In his opinion they are not true Jews." *Acts of the Apostles*, 192.

11. Note, however, that Paul is distinguished from those Pharisaic Christians of Acts 15:5.

12. On the ritualistic aspects of the Nazirate and Luke's treatment of it, see Ernst Haenchen, *The Acts of the Apostles: A Commentary*, 612. Conzelmann, *Acts*, 180, comments, "The account which follows certainly raises difficulties if we look closely at Jewish prescriptions about vows, but these result from Luke's inexact knowledge of these prescriptions."

13. See esp. Walter Radl, *Paulus und Jesus im lukanischen Doppelwerk: Untersuchungen zu Parallelmotiven im Lukasevangelium und in der Apostelgeschichte*, 169–221; Charles H. Talbert, *Literary Patterns, Theological Themes and the Genre of Luke-Acts*.

14. Haenchen, *Acts*, 674, comments: "Agrippa of course did not rule over Judaea. But to him was entrusted the keeping of the High-Priestly vestments, and it was he who now could depose and nominate the High Priest. In this capacity he could be claimed as an authority on Jewish problems."

15. Haenchen, *Acts*, 657, notes, "Through vv. 2–4 Luke allows us to detect that Tertullus knows his trade and is a dangerous opponent."

16. For an examination of the trials of Paul in Acts 22, 24, and 26, see William R. Long, "The Trial of Paul in the Book of Acts: Historical, Literary, and Theological Considerations." Long makes use of ancient rhetorical theory to illuminate these trials. See also Martin Dibelius, *Studies in the Acts of the Apostles*, 138–85; Jerome Neyrey, "The Forensic Defense Speech and Paul's Trial Speeches in Acts 22–26: Form and Function"; Fred Veltman, "The Defense Speeches of Paul in Acts."

17. On the use of the term *the Way*, Haenchen, *Acts*, 658, comments, "We see here why Luke so readily uses the concept of the 'Way'; this concept describes the new religion of Jesus as an entity in itself and yet does not divorce it from Judaism: indeed it is strongly reminiscent of such OT expressions as 'the ways of the Lord', which represented Judaism as the beloved true religion." We should also note the use of the term *Halakhah* to designate the way of walking before God in true obedience.

18. Long's study of the rhetorical aspects of Paul's speeches has shown that the question of Paul's fidelity to Judaism is the chief issue throughout. See Long, "Trial of Paul," 159–256.

19. For a study of the political aspects of Paul's trials see Richard J. Cassidy, *Society and Politics in the Acts of the Apostles*, 96–116. Cassidy concludes that, as presented in Acts, both Felix and Festus mishandled Paul's case.

20. On the character of Festus as portrayed here, see Tannehill, *Narrative Unity* 2:305–308.

21. Cassidy, *Society and Politics*, 111, is not so charitable to the Lukan Festus, "For here [Acts 25:20–21], by virtue of a crucial omission and a serious misrepresentation, Festus is unmistakably portrayed presenting a summary that is decidedly biased in his own self-interest."

22. Long, "Trial of Paul," 236–44, treats the *captatio benevolentiae* as an essential part of the exordium, with which a defensive speech opens, but he also points out that the more effective speeches link "the praise of the judge with the furtherance of one's own case" (240). Long says that the exordium in Acts 26:2–4 is the best example of this principle among the defensive speeches of Paul: "Following the sense of Quintillian's advice, we recognize that Paul's statement that Herod is 'especially familiar with all customs and controversies of the Jews' (26:3) is intended to link Herod's knowledge with the desired outcome of the case. A declaration of innocence by a king with an intimate knowledge of Judaism will vindicate the claim of Paul made in all the defense speeches that he is still a faithful Jew" (240). For a theological study of Paul's

speech before Agrippa, see Robert F. O'Toole, *Acts 26: The Christological Climax of Paul's Defense (Ac 22:1–26:32)*.

23. Acts 27:9 may, however, contain a reference to the Day of Atonement. On this verse, Conzelmann, *Acts*, 216, comments, "The rabbis counted the beginning of the time when sailing was dangerous from the time of the feast of the booths." Conzelmann notes that the Feast of Booths comes five days after the Day of Atonement.

24. Acts 28:30–31 does not report an incident but rather a summary of a two-year period of Paul's activities in Rome. For a study of Acts 28:16–31, see Charles B. Puskas, Jr., "The Conclusion of Luke-Acts: An Investigation of the Literary Function and Theological Significance of Acts 28:16–31."

25. Paul's statement in Acts 28:18–19 is not consistent with the procedure described earlier in Acts. The appeal to Caesar came during Paul's trial before Festus when he was given the alternative to be tried in Jerusalem rather than Caesarea (25:9–12). At a later hearing Festus and Agrippa express the judgment that Paul is innocent (26:31–32).

26. On this theme see Klaus Haacker, "Das Bekenntnis des Paulus zur Hoffnung Israels nach der Apostelgeschichte des Lukas."

27. See Haenchen, *Acts*, 729.

28. Haacker, "Das Bekenntnis," shows that the Pharisaic and Pauline belief in resurrection cannot be separated from political eschatological expectation.

29. But F. F. Bruce, *The Acts of the Apostles: The Greek Text with Introduction and Commentary*, 479, notes that "the imperf. does not necessarily imply that they were actually persuaded." He translates *epeithonto* as "gave heed" (479). Tannehill, *Narrative Unity*, 2:347, understands the verb to mean that some of Paul's hearers "were in process of being persuaded but had made no lasting decision."

30. See Jervell, "Divided People," esp. 63–69.

31. See Robert C. Tannehill, "Rejection by Jews and Turning to Gentiles: The Pattern of Paul's Mission in Acts." See also idem., "Israel in Luke-Acts: A Tragic Story"; idem., *Narrative Unity* 2:344–57. For similar approaches, see J. Bradley Chance, *Jerusalem, the Temple, and the New Age in Luke-Acts*; David P. Moessner, "Paul in Acts: Preacher of Eschatological Repentance to Israel"; David L. Tiede, " 'Glory to Thy People Israel': Luke-Acts and the Jews."

32. See Ernst Haenchen, "Judentum und Christentum in der Apostelgeschichte"; see also Haenchen, *Acts*, 721–32; Conzelmann, *Acts*, 227–28. A similar position has been maintained by Stephen G. Wilson, *The Gentiles and the Gentile Mission in Luke-Acts*, 219–38. See also idem., "The Jews and the Death of Jesus in Acts." See also Lloyd Gaston, "Anti-Judaism and the Passion Narrative in Luke and Acts." See also Jack T. Sanders, "The Salvation of the Jews in Luke-Acts"; idem., "The Jewish People in Luke-Acts"; idem., *The Jews in Luke-Acts*, especially pp. 296–99; Robert L. Maddox, *The Purpose of Luke-Acts*, especially pp. 31–65. Robert L. Brawley takes a mediating position in "Paul in Acts: Lucan Apology and Conciliation." See also idem., *Luke-Acts and the Jews: Conflict, Apology, and Conciliation*.

33. See Haenchen, *Acts*, 721–32, for an analysis of other exegetical problems.

34. See Nils Dahl, "A People for His Name." Dahl lists only two exceptions, Acts 15:14 and 18:10.

35. See further Joseph B. Tyson, "The Problem of Jewish Rejection in Acts," in *Luke-Acts and the Jewish People*, 124–37. The ambivalence of Luke's treatment of the Jews is recognized by Wilson, "The Jews and the Death of Jesus," and *The Gentiles*, 219–38, as well as by Gaston, "Anti-Judaism and the Passion Narrative," and Maddox, *Purpose of Luke-Acts*. Gaston, p. 153, writes, "In any case the paradox remains that Luke-Acts is one of the most pro-Jewish and one of the most anti-Jewish writings in the New Testament."

# 9

# Judaism in Luke-Acts

This quest began with a series of questions about the role that the Jewish people play in Luke-Acts and the consequent images of Judaism embedded within these texts. We were impressed with the attention accorded to Jewish religious life and institutions in Luke-Acts and interested to learn what light this fact may shed on the question of the purpose of these documents. Since some modern critics have cited reasons for thinking that Luke-Acts and other NT documents played a role in the development of Christian anti-Judaism, the task of assessing the images of Judaism in our texts has taken on a dimension of contemporary social and theological significance.

The reading of Luke-Acts represented in the preceding chapters has been controlled by the concept of the implied reader, i.e., the reader within the text. We have therefore searched for clues embedded within Luke-Acts that would lead the implied reader to reach his or her own assessment of Jewish people and their religious life. Thus the reading has been based upon a profile of the implied reader, who is represented within the text as a Godfearer, a Gentile who is positively attracted to Judaism but has not made a total commitment by accepting circumcision and the obligations of Torah. In Luke-Acts, Godfearers are shown to be not only associated with synagogues but also positively attracted to Christian preachers. The centurions in Luke 7 and Acts 10–11, who observe some Jewish ways and are held in deep respect by Jews, are model Godfearers.

Although this kind of reading does not afford us a basis for making a determination about the intent of the flesh-and-blood author, some judgment can be made about the probable purpose of the implied author and the probable effect of Luke-Acts on the implied reader. If the implied author is speaking to one who is thought of as a Godfearer, he seems to be attempting to gain from him positive support for the Christian way. This reader, who is assumed to be favorably disposed toward Judaism, is being shown that what is good about Judaism may be found in Christianity without the burden of circumcision and full Torah obedience. He learns that the first Jewish converts to Christianity regularly adhered to Torah, even if they were persecuted by Jewish leaders. Christianity is shown to be the fulfillment of the Hebrew Scriptures and long-held Jewish hopes and expectations. The belief in the resurrection is precisely the same belief as held by Pharisees, the party of Paul and the strictest party among the Jews. As Hans Conzelmann said, in commenting on Acts 26:6–7, "The true Jew must become a Christian, in order to remain a true Jew."[1] Thus, without invoking problematic language about the intention of a flesh-and-blood author, we may say that the purpose of Luke-Acts is to persuade Godfearers to accept the Christian message about Jesus rather than accepting Judaism.

Luke-Acts must also deal with a historical problem, namely the problem that most Jews did not become Christians. The implied author must make clear to the implied reader the issues at stake in the failure of the Christian mission to Jews, and this need is met through a historical narrative approach. It is striking to recognize the contrast between images of Judaism at the beginning of Luke-Acts and at the end. The narrative begins with highly positive images of individual Jewish piety and reverence for the Temple and ends with images of Jewish leaders and people who are hostile, vicious, and obdurate. But no less striking is the stress at the end of Acts on Paul's fidelity to Judaism and the harmony between Christian and Pharisaic beliefs. The fact is that deeply ambivalent expressions about Jewish people and religious life pervade Luke's writings. Although the infancy narratives are dominated by the sense that long-held expectations of pious Jewish people are about to be met through the work of John the Baptist and Jesus, the prophecy of Simeon (Luke 2:34–35) warns of controversy and division among the people of Israel. In the early ministry of Jesus, the reader is given a sense of the common heritage that exists between Jesus and the Jewish people, but she also learns of controversies about Torah obedience. In the passion narrative, Jesus is shown to be the one sent by God to reorient Israel, but he is rejected by the Jewish leaders and executed. His followers initially gain wide support among Palestinian Jews but nevertheless remind the reader of the guilt of Jews in putting Jesus to death. Stephen, reciting a span of history recorded in the Hebrew Scriptures, accuses the Jewish people of continuous rebellion against God and claims that Solomon's building of the Temple was an act of disobedience. Admission of the first Gentile requires a modification of dietary restrictions and abandonment of the concept of divine partiality toward Israel. Admission of Gentiles generally requires the observance of some minimal dietary regulations but not circumcision. Paul's missionary efforts are met with a positive response from some Jews but with rejection and opposition from most. Throughout his trials Paul insists not only on his innocence but also on the near identity of the Christian way with the ancestral religion. Even at the end of Acts, the Roman Jews first greet Paul cordially, but he finally announces the termination of the Christian mission to Jews.

If one intent of the implied author is to wean the implied reader away from Judaism and convince him to accept the Christian message, the ambivalence in Luke-Acts in regard to the images of Judaism can be understood. The positive images of Judaism are consistent with the assumed attitudes of a Godfearer. Negative images both show the inferiority of Judaism to Christianity and help to explain Jewish rejection of the Christian message.

Three special problems require our attention in the conclusion to our study. We have been able to address these problems in fragmentary fashion in the preceding chapters, but it is now necessary to examine them in a more comprehensive overview. The problems are: the image of the Temple; the image of the Hebrew Scriptures; and, finally, the question, is Luke-Acts anti-Jewish?

### THE TEMPLE

For the most part, images of the Temple run in tandem with images of Judaism generally. At the opening of the gospel, the Temple is shown to be the focal center of pious and hopeful people as well as a scene of prophecy. Its rituals and sacrifices are expressive of humble and genuine devotion. But before the narrative in Luke-Acts is over, the Temple has become a scene of controversy and a point of contention. It loses its significance as a religious shrine and becomes a base for priestly political power. Several points along the way are worthy of note.

We saw that in the passion narrative of the gospel, the parable of the vineyard (Luke 20:9–19) leads the reader to expect Jesus and his followers to take control of the Temple. We saw further that

Jesus, in his act of cleansing the Temple and teaching in it, attempted to make of it what God had intended, namely a house of prayer. Likewise, the apostles gathered in the Temple at the end of the gospel and occupied the Portico of Solomon in the first chapters of Acts. The activity of Peter and the apostles in Acts 1–5 may be read, in part, as their attempt to take control of the Temple. The Temple is the scene of a major miracle of healing (Acts 3:1–10), and Peter uses Solomon's portico as the location of teaching and preaching (3:11; 5:12). At one point the apostles are commanded by an angel to teach in the Temple (5:19–20), but they are arrested in the act of doing go (5:26) and saved only by the intervention of the Pharisee Gamaliel (5:34–39). At the end of Acts 5, however, the apostles are still using the Temple as a place of teaching and preaching (5:42). A drastic turn in the evaluation of the Temple occurs with the speech of Stephen, who claims that God does not live in edifices built by human beings and considers Solomon's building of the Temple to be an act of disobedience and idolatry (7:47–50). When we consider Stephen's speech in its context after the teaching of Jesus and the apostles in the Temple, we are led to the conviction that the efforts of Jesus and his apostles were unsuccessful. Although they taught in the Temple, they were unable to reclaim it for God. Thus, Stephen pronounces its very construction as an act of disobedience to God.

But there is a final attempt to return the Temple to its proper use when Paul enters it (21:26), after undergoing a ritual of purification. However, Paul is believed to have profaned the Temple instead of participating in its sanctity, and his visit to the Temple leads to his arrest. A crowd of Jews seizes Paul and drags him out of the Temple, after which the gates are shut (21:30). Perhaps we should understand that the gates are closed to prevent further damage, but the closing of the gates also has powerful symbolic significance at this point in Acts. From this point on, no Christian enters the Temple, nor does it function in any way in the following narratives.

How are we to read the story of the Temple in Luke-Acts? Just before the coming of Jesus, it is portrayed in positive ways, but through Jesus himself we learn that it has become a den of robbers. Its priestly tenants have not returned to God his due. Jesus and his followers attempted to make of it a house of prayer, but they were not successful. Thus Jesus predicts its destruction, Stephen claims that it is not God's house, and with Paul its gates are finally closed. The closing may be taken as Luke's description of the symbolic break between Judaism and Christianity. It also serves to show that Judaism rejected Christianity, not vice versa.

## THE SCRIPTURES

While the Temple may be regarded in Luke-Acts as an institution given over to Jews and no longer of any theological significance, just the opposite is the case with the scriptures. The function of the scriptures is to point to the ministry and passion of Jesus the Christ and to the history of his earliest followers. But it is only those who believe in Jesus who understand the scriptures correctly. Unbelieving Jews have heard the scriptures every Sabbath. They have Moses and the prophets, but they have not interpreted them correctly, i.e., Christologically. Thus the scriptures may be said to belong to those who understand them and not to the Jews.

The authority of the Hebrew Scriptures is assumed throughout Luke-Acts, where, with proper interpretation, they provide support for a wide variety of events and concepts. Most notable is the scriptural basis for the suffering and death of Jesus as the Christ. Rarely is a scriptural passage actually quoted to show the necessity of the passion (e.g., Luke 22:37; Acts 8:32–33), but the author seems totally convinced that it is predicted throughout. The major point is not that individual passages may be found and interpreted to foretell the suffering of Jesus, but that scripture as a whole shows the necessity of the Christ's suffering.

Although Paul can claim to believe "everything laid down according to the law or written in the prophets" (Acts 24:14) and to say "nothing but what the prophets and Moses said would take place" (26:22), there are in fact limitations to the authority of scripture in Luke-Acts. Many parts of scripture are, of course, neglected, but some parts are actually jettisoned. One may argue that in scripture the requirement of circumcision was meant only for Jews and thus the dropping of this rite for Gentiles does not imply a variation from scripture. For this reason Luke can in good conscience report Paul's circumcision of Timothy in Acts 16. But in Acts 15, Peter and James regard not only circumcision but Torah obedience as a whole as a burden which Jews have not been able to bear and which should not be imposed on Gentiles. Earlier in Acts 10 Peter has been told that the dietary regulations have been annulled, but Luke never gives any indication that these regulations are contained in scripture. For Luke, the fundamental authority of

the scripture as predictor of Jesus and his followers is not compromised by Christian nonobservance of major parts of it. In any
event, it is important to note that not all of the Hebrew Scriptures
are accepted as authoritative.

Nor does scripture appear to be the only authority. Although
Paul can quote a passage from Isaiah to support the concept of the
Gentile mission (Acts 13:47), the scripture appears to be inopera-
tive at the point where the first Gentile was brought into Christian
faith (10:1–11:18). Peter claims that all the prophets have borne witness to Jesus (Acts 10:43), but there appears to be no need to appeal
to scripture to defend the abolition of the dietary regulations. The
divine voice that spoke to Peter (10:9–16) is sufficient for this. And
the receipt of the spirit by Cornelius and his household is a sufficient justification for Peter's visiting and eating with Gentiles
(11:17).

Nor does scripture seem to have any significant function
among Gentiles, as is indicated by the lack of any quotations in
Paul's speech at Athens (Acts 17:22–31). Paul may there quote Aratus (17:28) in the same way in which, in speeches to Jews and Godfearers, he quotes Isaiah or another prophet. At another level,
however, if the narrative is addressed to Gentile Godfearers, there
is an assumption that they are not only acquainted with scripture
but that they also acknowledge its authority.

We earlier confronted the problem of the continuing validity
of scripture. Luke 16:16 seems to limit the significance of scripture
to the time before Jesus. At the transfiguration (Luke 9:28–36),
Moses and Elijah, as symbols of law and prophets, retreat to leave
Jesus alone, and the heavenly voice commands the disciples to listen to him. But Luke 16:17 announces the eternal validity of Torah,
down to its finest point, and throughout the book of Acts the scriptures are used to support decisions made by the apostles and Paul,
including the initiation of the Gentile mission, the terms of admission of Gentiles, and the termination of the mission to Jews.

There is no easy way to solve this problem, for Luke seems
genuinely ambivalent on the question of the continuing authority
of the scriptures. It is clear, however, that it is only in their predictions about Jesus and his followers that the scriptures retain authority and that Jesus himself, together with his spirit-led
followers, is the authoritative interpreter of scripture. One may
formulate Luke's probable view thusly: law and prophets have no

continuing significance without the authentic interpretation provided through Jesus (see Luke 16:16); under Christian interpretation scripture has eternal validity (see Luke 16:17).

We began with a concern, expressed most vigorously by Rosemary
Ruether, that the roots of negative Christian attitudes toward Jews
may be found in certain anti-Jewish attitudes in the NT, and our
study of Luke-Acts has been partly motivated by this concern.[2] But
we may now formulate our question in a somewhat different fashion: Do the images that are embedded in Luke-Acts convey to the
implied reader positive or negative impressions of Jewish religious
life and the Jewish people? The answer, of course, is that they convey both.

Aspects of Jewish religious life are often portrayed in positive
ways. There are images of individual Jewish piety that elicit deep
admiration. Jewish monotheism is assumed to be superior to the
worship of many Gods, the scriptures are holy, and many ancient
Hebrews—among them Abraham, Moses, and David—command
respect. The rising status of the Pharisees that we have observed,
from their opposition to Jesus to their support of Paul, must
be counted as at least a quasi-positive image of a significant group
of Jews.

The relationship of Jewish life and faith to Christian life and
faith is also treated in ways that express no anti-Jewish sentiments.
The initially positive reception of the preaching of Peter and the
apostles is a demonstration of the harmony that is seen to exist between Christianity and Judaism. Of fundamental importance is
the effort to show that Paul as a Christian is nevertheless a faithful
Jew. This effort is supported by Paul's claim that Christian belief in
resurrection is identical to Pharisaic belief and his claim to be a
Pharisee who adheres to the Way.

But there are powerfully negative images of Judaism and the
Jewish people as well. The Jewish priestly leaders seem to have no
redeeming features, and they are pictured as unworthy stewards
of the Temple. Despite the fact that Paul is shown to observe it, the
Torah is sometimes portrayed as dealing in trivial matters and
sometimes as an unnecessary burden. For the most part, the Jewish people are cast in the role of opponents of the Christian
preachers. Not only do they reject the message that ostensibly was

meant for them, but they frequently oppose the preachers in violent ways. They engage in plots; they incite riots; they bring accusations in Roman courts and call for executions. The negative images tend to increase as the narrative progresses, and the reader is drawn to join in the condemnation of Jews for their rejection of the Christian message.[3]

It is appropriate here, as it was in chapter 1, to refer to Lloyd Gaston's paradoxical assessment, "Luke-Acts is one of the most pro-Jewish and one of the most anti-Jewish writings in the New Testament."[4] Although our study does not contain comparisons between Luke-Acts and other NT documents, it nevertheless tends to confirm Gaston's judgment. In order to assess the significance of Luke-Acts in terms of the images of Judaism, it is essential to avoid an oversimplification that would eliminate the tension between these polarities. It is incorrect to maintain that Luke is simply pro-Jewish or simply anti-Jewish. He is both.

But the matter cannot be allowed simply to rest with this tension. Although it is necessary to recognize that Luke is pro-Jewish and anti-Jewish and both in profound ways, it is essential finally to determine which set of images appears to dominate the narrative. Although efforts to read Luke-Acts and other NT texts in basically positive ways are understandable, for me the images that seem more powerful are the negative ones. This is so for several reasons. For one thing, the narrative moves in the direction of the negative. Those benign portraits of individual Jewish piety in Luke 1–2 have, long before the end of Acts, given way to descriptions of Jewish people as fanatic, hostile, and vindictive. For another, the ending of Acts, like narrative endings generally, functions to ease the reader out of the narrative and back into the real world.[5] With its quotation from Isaiah and its application to the Roman Jews (Acts 28:25–28), this ending leaves the reader with a memorable portrait of the Jewish people as obstinately imperceptive and unheeding.

Because of the dominance of these negative images, it has been possible for flesh-and-blood readers to use Luke-Acts as a justification for negative Christian attitudes toward Jewish people and their religious life. In this sense these documents have played a role in a tragic history. But, if the analysis here is correct, the use of Luke-Acts as a justification for Christian anti-Judaism is based on a misreading of these texts. It is a misreading in which the profound tension that exists between positive and negative images of Judaism has, for the most part, been resolved in favor of a negativity that has been used to support anti-Jewish sentiments. It is to be hoped that a more balanced reading, one that recognizes the tension in these texts, will not only provide us with a better understanding of Luke's narrative within its own historical context but will also support more benign convictions about Jewish-Christian relationships in our own time.

## NOTES

1. Hans Conzelmann, *Acts of the Apostles*, 210.
2. See Rosemary R. Ruether, *Faith and Fratricide: The Theological Roots of Anti-Semitism*, and the discussion of her work in chapter 1 of this book.
3. I have not attempted to classify these negative images in terms suggested by Douglas R. A. Hare, i.e., prophetic, Jewish Christian, and gentilizing Anti-Judaism. See Hare, "The Rejection of the Jews in the Synoptic Gospels and Acts." See also the discussion of Hare in chapter 1. The categories employed by Hare, while useful for his purposes, require extratextual concepts and assumptions that are inappropriate for the kind of reading that I have used here.
4. Lloyd Gaston, "Anti-Judaism and the Passion Narrative in Luke and Acts," in *Anti-Judaism in Early Christianity*, 1:153.
5. See Boris Uspensky, *A Poetics of Composition: The Structure of the Artistic Text and Typology of a Compositional Form*, 137–51; Mikeal C. Parsons, *The Departure of Jesus in Luke-Acts: The Ascension Narratives in Context*, 96–102.

# Bibliography

Achtemeier, Paul. "An Elusive Unity: Paul, Acts, and the Early Church." *CBQ* 48 (1986):1–26.

Alexander, Loveday. "Luke's Preface in the Context of Greek Preface-Writing." *NovT* 28 (1986):48–74.

Arai, Sasagu. "Zum 'Tempelwort' Jesu in Apostelgeschichte 6.14." *NTS* 34 (1988):397–410.

Aune, David E. *The New Testament in Its Literary Environment*. Library of Early Christianity 8. Philadelphia: Westminster Press, 1987.

Bachmann, Michael. *Jerusalem und der Tempel: Die geographisch-theologischen Elemente in der lukanischen Sicht des jüdischen Kultzentrums*. Stuttgart: W. Kohlhammer, 1980.

Balzer, K. "The Meaning of the Temple in the Lukan Writings." *HTR* 58 (1965):263–77.

Barclay, William. *The Gospel of Luke*. Daily Study Bible. Revised edition. Philadelphia: Westminster Press, 1975.

Bassler, Jouette M. "Luke and Paul on Impartiality." *Bib* 66 (1985):546–52.

Bauernfeind, Otto. *Kommentar und Studien zur Apostelgeschichte*. Ed. Volker Metelmann. Tübingen: J. C. B. Mohr, 1980.

Baur, Ferdinand C. "Über Zweck und Veranlassung des Römerbriefs und die damit zusammenhangenden Verhältnisse der römischen Gemeinde." *Tübinger Zeitschrift für Theologie* (1836):59–178.

———. *The Church History of the First Three Centuries*, vol. 1. Translated by Allan Menzies. 3d ed. London: Williams and Norgate, 1878.

Beardsley, Monroe C. "Textual Meaning and Authorial Meaning." *Genre* 1 (1968):169–81.

Beck, Norman A. *Mature Christianity: The Recognition and Repudiation of the Anti-Jewish Polemic of the New Testament*. London and Toronto: Associated University Presses, 1985.

Bellinzoni, Arthur J., Jr., ed. *The Two-Source Hypothesis: A Critical Appraisal*. Macon: Mercer University Press, 1985.

Bemile, Paul. *The Magnificat Within the Context and Framework of Lukan The-*

ology: An Exegetical Theological Study of Lk 1:46–55. Frankfurt: Peter Lang, 1986.

Blomberg, Craig L. "Midrash, Chiasmus, and the Outline of Luke's Central Section." In *Gospel Perspectives: Studies in Midrash and Historiography*, edited by R. T. France and David Wenham, 3:217–61. Sheffield: University of Sheffield, 1983.

————. "The Law in Luke-Acts." *JSNT* 22 (1984):53–80.

Bock, Darrell L. *Proclamation from Prophecy and Pattern: Lucan Old Testament Christology*. JSNTSup 12. Sheffield: JSOT Press, 1987.

Booth, Wayne. *The Rhetoric of Fiction*. 2d ed. Chicago: University of Chicago Press, 1983.

Boucher, Madeleine. *The Mysterious Parable: A Literary Study*. Washington, D.C.: Catholic Biblical Association, 1977.

Bovon, F. "Du côte de chez Luc." *RTP* 115 (1983):175–89.

Brawley, Robert L. "Paul in Acts: Lucan Apology and Conciliation." In *Luke-Acts: New Perspectives from the Society of Biblical Litarature Seminar*, edited by Charles H. Talbert, 129–47. New York: Crossroad Books, 1984.

————. *Luke-Acts and the Jews: Conflict, Apology, and Conciliation*. SBLMS 33. Atlanta: Scholars Press, 1987.

Brown, Raymond E. *The Birth of the Messiah: A Commentary on the Infancy Narratives in Matthew and Luke*. Garden City: Doubleday & Co., 1977.

Brown, Schuyler. "Precis of Eckhard Plümacher, Lukas als hellenistischer Schriftsteller," in *SBLSP*, edited by George W. MacRae, 2:103–13. Cambridge, MA: Society of Biblical Literature, 1974.

Bruce, F. F. *The Acts of the Apostles: The Greek Text with Introduction and Commentary*. Grand Rapids: William B. Eerdmans, 1951.

————. *The Book of Acts*. NICNT. Grand Rapids: William B. Eerdmans, 1981.

Bultmann, Rudolf. *The History of the Synoptic Tradition*. Translated by John Marsh. New York: Harper & Row, 1963.

Burton, Ernest D. "The Book of Acts." *Biblical World* 6 (1895):39–44.

Cadbury, Henry J. "Commentary on the Preface of Luke." In *The Beginnings of Christianity*, edited by F. J. Foakes Jackson and Kirsopp Lake, 2:489–510. London: Macmillan and Co., 1920–32.

————. "The Hellenists." In *The Beginnings of Christianity*, edited by F. J. Foakes Jackson and Kirsopp Lake, 5:59–74. London: Macmillan and Co., 1920–32.

————. "The Speeches in Acts." In *The Beginnings of Christianity*, edited by F. J. Foakes Jackson and Kirsopp Lake, 5:402–27. London: Macmillan and Co., 1920–32.

————. *The Making of Luke-Acts*. 2d ed. London: S. P. C. K., 1958.

Caird, George B. *Saint Luke*. Pelican New Testament Commentaries. New York: Penguin Books, 1963.

Callan, Terrance. "The Preface of Luke-Acts and Historiography." *NTS* 31 (1985):576–81.

Carroll, John T. *Response to the End of History: Eschatology and Situation in Luke-Acts.* SBLDS 92. Atlanta: Scholars Press, 1988.

Cassidy, Richard J. *Jesus, Politics, and Society.* Maryknoll, NY: Orbis Books, 1978.

——— . "Luke's Audience, the Chief Priests, and the Motive for Jesus' Death." In *Political Issues in Luke-Acts,* edited by Richard J. Cassidy and Philip J. Scharper, 146–67. Maryknoll, NY: Orbis Books, 1983.

——— . *Society and Politics in the Acts of the Apostles.* Maryknoll, NY: Orbis Books, 1987.

——— , and Philip J. Scharper, eds. *Political Issues in Luke-Acts.* Maryknoll, NY: Orbis Books, 1983.

Chance, J. Bradley. *Jerusalem, the Temple, and the New Age in Luke-Acts.* Macon: Mercer University Press, 1988.

Charlesworth, James H., ed. *The Old Testament Pseudepigrapha.* 2 vols. Garden City: Doubleday & Co., 1983, 1985.

Chatman, Seymour. *Story and Discourse: Narrative Structure in Fiction and Film.* Ithaca: Cornell University Press, 1978.

Chilton, Bruce. "Announcement in Nazara: An Analysis of Luke 4:16–21." In *Gospel Perspectives: Studies of History and Tradition in the Four Gospels,* edited by R. T. France and David Wenham, 2:147–72. Sheffield: JSOT Press, 1981.

Cohen, Shaye J. D. "Was Timothy Jewish (Acts 16:1–3)? Patristic Exegesis, Rabbinic Law, and Matrilineal Descent." *JBL* 105 (1986):251–68.

——— . "Crossing the Boundary and Becoming a Jew." *HTR* 82 (1989):13–33.

Conzelmann, Hans. *The Theology of St. Luke.* Translated by Geoffrey Buswell. New York: Harper and Bros., 1960.

——— . "The Address of Paul on the Areopagus." In *Studies in Luke-Acts,* edited by Leander E. Keck and J. Louis Martyn, 217–30. Nashville: Abingdon Press, 1966.

——— . *Acts of the Apostles.* Translated from 2d German edition (1972) by James Limburg, A. Thomas Kraabel, and Donald H. Juel. Hermeneia. Philadelphia: Fortress Press, 1987.

Cook, Michael J. "The Mission to the Jews in Acts: Unraveling Luke's 'Myth of the "Myriads.' ' " In *Luke-Acts and the Jewish People: Eight Critical Perspectives,* edited by Joseph B. Tyson, 102–23. Minneapolis: Augsburg Publishing House, 1988.

Corley, Bruce, ed. *Colloquy on New Testament Studies: A Time for Reappraisal and Fresh Approaches.* Macon: Mercer University Press, 1983.

Cosgrove, C. H. "The Divine *DEI* in Luke-Acts." *NovT* 26 (1984):168–90.

Creed, John Martin. *The Gospel According to St. Luke.* London: Macmillan & Co., 1930.

Crockett, L. C. "The Old Testament in the Gospel of Luke with Emphasis on the Interpretation of Isaiah 61:1–2." Ph.D. diss., Brown University, 1966.

———. "Luke 4:25–27 and Jewish-Gentile Relations in Luke-Acts." *JBL* 88 (1969):177–83.

Culpepper, R. Alan. *Anatomy of the Fourth Gospel: A Study in Literary Design.* Philadelphia: Fortress Press, 1983.

Dahl, Nils A. "A People for his Name." *NTS* 4 (1958):319–27.

———. "The Story of Abraham in Luke-Acts." In *Studies in Luke-Acts,* edited by Leander E. Keck and J. Louis Martyn, 139–58. Nashville: Abingdon Press, 1966.

Daube, David. "A Reform in Acts and Its Models." In *Jews, Greeks and Christians: Religious Cultures in Later Antiquity: Essays in Honor of William David Davies,* edited by Robert Hamerton-Kelly and Robin Scroggs, 151–63. Leiden: E. J. Brill, 1976.

Davies, Alan T., ed. *Antisemitism and the Foundations of Christianity.* New York: Paulist Press, 1979.

Dawsey, James M. *The Lukan Voice: Confusion and Irony in the Gospel of Luke.* Macon: Mercer University Press, 1986.

Derrett, J. Duncan M. "Fresh Light on St Luke XVI: II. Dives and Lazarus and the Preceding Sayings." *NTS* (1960–61):364–80.

———. "Daniel and Salvation History." *Downside Review* 100 (1982):62–68.

———. "Clean and Unclean Animals (Acts 10:15, 11:9): Peter's Pronouncing Power Observed." *HeyJ* 29 (1988):205–21.

Dibelius, Martin. *Studies in the Acts of the Apostles.* Translated by Mary Ling. Edited by Heinrich Greeven. New York: Charles Scribner's Sons, 1956.

Dillon, R. J. "The Prophecy of Christ and his Witnesses according to the Discourses of Acts." *NTS* 32 (1986):544–56.

Dobschütz, E. von. *The Apostolic Age.* Translated by F. L. Pogson. Boston: American Unitarian Association, 1910.

Dodd, C. H. "The History and Doctrine of the Apostolic Age." In *A Companion to the Bible,* edited by T. W. Manson, 390–417. Edinburgh: T. & T. Clark, 1942.

Easton, Burton S. *The Gospel According to Luke.* New York: Charles Scribner's Sons, 1926.

———. *The Purpose of Acts.* London: S. P. C. K., 1936.

———. *Early Christianity: The Purpose of Acts and Other Papers.* Greenwich, CT: Seabury Press, 1954.

Elliott, J. K. "Does Luke 2:41–52 Anticipate the Resurrection?" *ExpTim* 83 (1971–72):87–89.

Ellis, E. Earle. *The Gospel of Luke.* New Century Bible Commentary. Greenwood, SC: Attic Press, 1977.

Ellis, John M. *The Theory of Literary Criticism.* Berkeley: University of California Press, 1974.

Eltester, Walther, ed. *Jesus in Nazareth*. Berlin: Walter de Gruyter, 1972.

Epp, Eldon Jay. *The Theological Tendency of Codex Bezae Cantabrigiensis in Acts*. SNTSMS 3. Cambridge: Cambridge University Press, 1966.

Esler, Philip F. *Community and Gospel in Luke-Acts: The Social and Political Motivations of Lucan Theology*. SNTSMS 57. Cambridge: Cambridge University Press, 1987.

Farris, Stephen C. "On Discerning Semitic Sources in Luke 1–2." In *Gospel Perspectives: Studies of History and Tradition in the Four Gospels*, edited by R. T. France and David Wenham, 2:201–37. Sheffield: JSOT, 1981.

Ferguson, Everett. "The Hellenists in the Book of Acts." *ResQ* 12 (1969):159–80.

Fish, Stanley. *Is There a Text in This Class? The Authority of Interpretive Communities*. Cambridge, MA: Harvard University Press, 1980.

Fitzmyer, Joseph A. "Jewish Christianity in Acts in Light of the Qumran Scrolls." In *Studies in Luke-Acts*, edited by Leander E. Keck and J. Louis Martyn, 233–57. Nashville: Abingdon Press, 1966.

———. "The Composition of Luke, Chapter 9." In *Perspectives on Luke-Acts*, edited by Charles H. Talbert, 139–52. Danville, VA: Association of Baptist Professors of Religion, 1978.

———. *The Gospel According to Luke (I–IX)*. AB. Garden City: Doubleday, 1981.

———. *The Gospel According to Luke X–XXIV*. AB. Garden City: Doubleday, 1985.

Ford, J. Massyngbaerde. *My Enemy is My Guest: Jesus and Violence in Luke*. Maryknoll, NY: Orbis Books, 1984.

Fowler, Robert M. "Who is 'the Reader' in Reader Response Criticism?" In *Semeia* 31, edited by Robert Detweiler, 5–23. Decatur: Scholars Press, 1985.

Fox, Douglas J. *The "Matthew-Luke Commentary" of Philoxenus: Text, Translation and Critical Analysis*. SBLDS 43. Missoula: Scholars Press, 1979.

Gager, John G. *The Origins of Anti-Semitism: Attitudes Toward Judaism in Pagan and Christian Antiquity*. New York: Oxford University Press, 1983.

Garrett, Susan R. *The Demise of the Devil: Magic and the Demonic in Luke's Writings*. Minneapolis: Fortress Press, 1989.

Gaston, Lloyd. "Anti-Judaism and the Passion Narrative in Luke and Acts." In *Anti-Judaism in Early Christianity*, edited by Peter Richardson with David Granskou, 1:127–53. Waterloo: Wilfrid Laurier University Press, 1986.

Gaventa, Beverly R. *From Darkness to Light: Aspects of Conversion in the New Testament*. Philadelphia: Fortress Press, 1986.

Geiger, Ruthild. *Die lukanischer Endzeitreden: Studien zur Eschatologie des Lukas-Evangeliums*. Europäische Hochschulschriften 16. Frankfurt: Peter Lang, 1976.

George, Augustin. "Israel dans l'oeuvre de Luc." *RB* 75 (1968):481–525.

Giblin, Charles H. *The Destruction of Jerusalem According to Luke's Gospel.* AnBib 107. Rome: Biblical Institute Press, 1985.

Gilmour, S. MacLean. "Exegesis of the Gospel According to St. Luke." In *IB*, 8:26–434. Nashville, Abingdon Press, 1952.

Glockner, Richard. *Die Verkündigung des Heils beim Evangelisten Lukas.* Mainz: Grüneweld, 1976.

Goulder, Michael D. *The Evangelist's Calendar.* London: S. P. C. K., 1978.

Grant, F. C. "Luke the Historian." In *The Growth of the Gospels*, 151–75. New York: Abingdon Press, 1953.

Grundmann, Walter. *Das Evangelium nach Lukas.* THKNT 3. 2d ed. Berlin: Evangelische Verlag, 1966.

Haacker, Klaus. "Dibelius und Cornelius: Ein Beispiel formgeschichtlicher Überlieferungskritik." *BZ* 24 (1980):234–51.

———. "Das Bekenntnis des Paulus zur Hoffnung Israels nach der Apostelgeschichte des Lukas," *NTS* 31 (1985):437–51.

Haenchen, Ernst. "Judentum und Christentum in der Apostelgeschichte." *ZNW* 54 (1963):155–87.

———. *The Acts of the Apostles: A Commentary.* Translated from the 14th (1965) German edition by Bernard Noble and Gerald Shinn. Oxford: Basil Blackwell, 1971.

Hare, Douglas R. A. "The Rejection of the Jews in the Synoptic Gospels and Acts." In *Antisemitism and the Foundations of Christianity*, edited by Alan T. Davies, 27–47. New York: Paulist Press, 1979.

Harnack, Adolf. *The Expansion of Christianity in the First Three Centuries*, vol. 1. Translated by James Moffatt. New York: G. P. Putnam's Sons, 1904.

———. *Luke the Physician.* Translated by J. R. Wilkinson. New York: G. P. Putnam's Sons, 1907.

———. *The Acts of the Apostles.* Translated by J. R. Wilkinson. New York: G. P. Putnam's Sons, 1909.

———. *Marcion: Das Evangelium vom Fremden Gott.* Leipzig: J. C. Hinrichs, 1921.

Hasler, Victor. "Judenmission und Judenschuld." *TZ* 24 (1968):273–90.

Hausrath, A. *A History of New Testament Times.* London: Williams and Norgate, 1895.

Heinrici, C. F. Georg. *Das Urchristentum.* Göttingen: Vandenhoeck und Ruprecht, 1902.

Hemer, C. J. *The Book of Acts in the Setting of Hellenistic History.* Tübingen: Mohr-Siebeck, 1989.

Hengel, Martin. *Between Jesus and Paul: Studies in the Earliest History of Christianity.* Translated by John Bowden. Philadelphia: Fortress Press, 1983.

Hill, David. "The Rejection of Jesus at Nazareth." *NovT* 13 (1971):161–80.

Hock, Ronald F. "Lazarus and Micyllus: Greco-Roman Backgrounds to Luke 16:19–31." *JBL* 106 (1987):447–63.

Hoennicke, Gustav. *Das Judenchristentum im ersten und zweiten Jahrhundert.* Berlin: Trowitzsch, 1908.

Holtz, Traugott. *Untersuchungen über die alttestamentlichen Zitate bei Lukas.* Berlin: Akademie Verlag, 1968.

Holtzmann, H. J. *Die Apostelgeschichte.* HKNT 1,2. Freiburg: J. C. B. Mohr, 1901.

Horsley, G. H. R. "Speeches and Dialogue in Acts." *NTS* 32 (1986):609–14.

Houlden, J. J. "The Purpose of Luke," *JSNT* 21 (1984):53–65.

Isaac, Jules. *The Teaching of Contempt: Christian Roots of Anti-Semitism.* Translated by Helen Weaver. New York: Holt, Rinehart & Winston, 1964.

———. *Jesus and Israel.* Translated by Sally Gran. New York: Holt, Rinehart & Winston, 1971.

Iser, Wolfgang. *The Implied Reader: Patterns of Communication in Prose Fiction from Bunyan to Beckett.* Baltimore: Johns Hopkins University Press, 1974.

———. *The Act of Reading: A Theory of Aesthetic Response.* Baltimore: Johns Hopkins University Press, 1974.

Jackson, F. J. Foakes. *The Acts of the Apostles.* MNTC. New York: Harper and Bros., 1931.

Jackson, F. J. Foakes, and Kirsopp Lake. *The Beginnings of Christianity.* 5 vols. London: Macmillan & Co., 1920–32.

Jervell, Jacob. *Luke and the People of God: A New Look at Luke-Acts.* Minneapolis: Augsburg Publishing House, 1972.

———. "Das Volk des Geistes." In *God's Christ and His People: Studies in Honour of Nils Alstrup Dahl,* edited by Jacob Jervell and Wayne A. Meeks, 87–106. Oslo: Universitetsforlaget, 1977.

———. "The Acts of the Apostles and the History of Early Christianity." *ST* 37 (1983):17–32.

———. *The Unknown Paul: Essays on Luke-Acts and Early Christian History.* Minneapolis: Augsburg Publishing House, 1984.

———. "Paulus in der Apostelgeschichte und die Geschichte der Urchristentums." *NTS* 32 (1986):378–92.

———. "The Church of Jews and Godfearers." In *Luke-Acts and the Jewish People: Eight Critical Perspectives,* edited by Joseph B. Tyson, 11–20. Minneapolis: Augsburg Publishing House, 1988.

Johnson, Luke Timothy. *Luke-Acts: A Story of Prophet and People.* Chicago: Franciscan Herald, 1981.

———. "The Lukan Kingship Parable (Lk. 19:11–27)." *NovT* 24 (1982):139–59.

Juel, Donald. *Luke-Acts: The Promise of History.* Atlanta: John Knox Press, 1983.

Kany, R. "Der lukanische Bericht von Tod und Auferstehung Jesu aus der Sicht eines hellenistischen Romanlesers." *NovT* 28 (1986):75–90.

Kariamadam, Paul. *The Zacchaeus Story: A Redaction-Critical Investigation.* Alwaye, India: Pontifical Institute of Theology and Philosophy, 1985.

Karris, Robert J. *Luke: Artist and Theologian.* New York: Paulist Press, 1985.

——. "Luke 23:47 and the Lucan View of Jesus' Death." *JBL* 105 (1986):65–74.

Käsemann, Ernst. "Paul and Nascent Catholicism." *JTC* 3 (1967):14–27.

Keck, Leander E., and J. Louis Martyn, eds. *Studies in Luke-Acts.* Nashville: Abingdon Press, 1966.

Kelber, Werner. *The Oral and the Written Gospel: The Hermeneutics of Speaking and Writing in the Synoptic Tradition, Mark, Paul, and Q.* Philadelphia: Fortress Press, 1983.

Kelly, J. G. "Lucan Christology and the Jewish-Christian Dialogue." *JES* 21 (1984):688–708.

Kent, Charles F. *The Work and Teachings of the Apostles.* New York: Charles Scribner's Sons, 1916.

Kilgallen, John. *The Stephen Speech: A Literary and Redactional Study of Acts 7:2–53.* AnBib 67. Rome: Biblical Institute Press, 1976.

——. "The Function of Stephen's Speech (Acts 7:2–53)." *Bib* 70 (1989):173–93.

Kimelman, Reuven. "Birkat Ha-Minim and the Lack of Evidence for an Anti-Christian Jewish Prayer in Late Antiquity." In *Jewish and Christian Self-Definition,* edited by E. P. Sanders, 2:226–44. Philadelphia: Fortress Press, 1981.

Klauck, H. J. "Die heilige Stadt: Jerusalem bei Philo und Lukas." *Kairos* 28 (1986):129–51.

Klausner, Joseph. *From Jesus to Paul.* Translated by William F. Stinespring. New York: The Macmillan Co., 1943.

Klostermann, Erich. *Das Evangelium nach Lukas.* 2d ed. HNT 5. Tübingen: J. C. B. Mohr, 1929.

Knox, John. *Marcion and the New Testament: An Essay in the Early History of the Canon.* Chicago: University of Chicago Press, 1942.

——. "Acts and the Pauline Letter Corpus." In *Studies in Luke-Acts,* edited by Leander E. Keck and J. Louis Martyn, 279–87. Nashville: Abingdon Press, 1966.

——. *Chapters in a Life of Paul.* 2d ed. Macon: Mercer University Press, 1987.

Knox, Wilfred. *The Acts of the Apostles.* Cambridge: Cambridge University Press, 1948.

Koch, Dietrich-Alex. "Geistbesitz, Geistverleihung und Wundermacht: Erwägungen zur Tradition und zur lukanischen Redaktion in Act 8:5–25," *ZNW* 77 (1986):64–82.

Kodell, Jerome. "Luke's Use of LAOS, 'People,' Especially in the Jerusalem Narrative (Lk 19,28–24,53)." *CBQ* 31 (1969):323–43.

Kraabel, A. Thomas. "The Disappearance of the 'God-fearers.'" *Numen* 28 (1981):113–26.

——. "Greeks, Jews, and Lutherans in the Middle Half of Acts." *HTR* 79 (1986):147–57.

Kremer, J., ed. *Les Actes des Apôtres: Traditions, Rédaction, Théologie.* BETL 48, Leuven: Leuven University Press, 1979.

Krodel, Gerhard A. *Acts.* Augsburg Commentary on the New Testament. Minneapolis: Augsburg Publishing House, 1986.

Lagrange, M. J. *Évangile selon St. Luc.* EBib. Paris: Gabalda, 1941.

Lambrecht, J. "Paul's Farewell-Address at Miletus (Acts 20,17–38)." In *Les Actes des Apôtres: Traditions, Rédaction, Théologie,* edited by J. Kremer, 307–37. BETL 48. Leuven: Leuven University Press, 1979.

LaVerdiere, Eugene. *Luke.* New Testament Message 5. Wilmington, DE: Michael Glazier, 1980.

————. "The Passion-Resurrection of Jesus According to St. Luke." *Chicago Studies* 25 (1986):35–50.

Leaney, A. R. C. *The Gospel According to St. Luke.* Black's New Testament Commentaries. London: A. & C. Black, 1966.

Leon-Dufour, Xavier. "Das letzte Mahl Jesu und die testamentarische Tradition." *ZKT* 103 (1981):35–55.

Levinsohn, Stephen H. *Textual Connections in Acts.* SBLMS 31. Atlanta: Scholars Press, 1987.

Lietzmann, Hans. *The Beginnings of the Christian Church.* Translated by Bertram L. Woolf. 2d ed. New York: Meridian Books, 1949.

Lindars, Barnabas. *New Testament Apologetic.* Philadelphia: Westminster Press, 1961.

Lohfink, Gerhard. *Die Sammlung Israels: Eine Untersuchung zur lukanischen Ekklesiologie.* SANT 39. Munich: Kösel-Verlag, 1975.

Loisy, Alfred F. *L'Évangile selon Luc.* Paris: Emile Nourry, 1924.

————. *The Birth of the Christian Religion.* Translated by L. P. Jacks. New Hyde Park, NY: University Books, 1962.

Long, William R. "The Trial of Paul in the Book of Acts: Historical, Literary, and Theological Considerations." Ph.D. diss., Brown University, 1983.

Longstaff, Thomas Richmond Willis, and Page A. Thomas, eds. *The Synoptic Problem: A Bibliography, 1716–1988.* New Gospel Studies 4. Macon: Mercer University Press, 1988.

Lowe, Malcolm. "From the Parable of the Vineyard to a Pre-Synoptic Source." *NTS* 28 (1982):257–63.

Luck, Ulrich. "Kerygma, Tradition und Geschichte Jesu bei Lukas." *ZTK* 57 (1960):51–66.

Lüdemann, Gerd. *Early Christianity According to the Traditions in Acts: A Commentary.* Translated by John Bowden. Philadelphia: Fortress Press, 1989.

MacGregor, G. H. C. "Exegesis of the Acts of the Apostles." In *IB* 9:23–352. Nashville: Abingdon Press, 1954.

Maddox, R. *Witnesses to the End of the Earth.* Enfield, NSW: United Theological College, 1980.

Maddox, Robert L. *The Purpose of Luke-Acts.* Edinburgh: T. & T. Clark, 1982.

Malherbe, A. J. " 'Not in a Corner': Early Christian Apologetic in Acts 26:26." *SecCenι* 5 (1985/86):193–210.

Maly, E. M. "Women and the Gospel of Luke." *BTB* 10 (1980):99–104.

Manson, William. *The Gospel of Luke*. MNTC. New York: Harper and Bros., 1930.

Marshall, I. Howard. *The Gospel of Luke: A Commentary on the Greek Text*. NIGTC. Grand Rapids: William B. Eerdmans, 1978.

————. *The Acts of the Apostles: An Introduction and Commentary*. The Tyndale New Testament Commentaries. Grand Rapids: William B. Eerdmans, 1980.

Martyn, J. Louis. *History and Theology in the Fourth Gospel*. 2d ed. Nashville: Abingdon, 1979.

Mattill, A. J., Jr. *Luke and the Last Things: A Perspective for the Understanding of Lukan Thought*. Dillsboro, NC: Western North Carolina Press, 1979.

McGiffert, Arthur C. *A History of Christianity in the Apostolic Age*. New York: Charles Scribner's Sons, 1897.

McGown, C. C. "Gospel Geography: Fiction, Fact, and Truth." *JBL* 60 (1941):1–25.

McKnight, Edgar V., ed. *Semeia* 48. Atlanta: Scholars Press, 1989.

Menoud, P. H. "The Acts of the Apostles and the Eucharist." In *Jesus Christ and the Faith: A Collection of Essays*, translated by Eunice M. Paul, 84–106. Pittsburgh Theological Monograph Series 18. Pittsburgh: Pickwick Press, 1978.

Metzger, Bruce M. *A Textual Commentary on the Greek New Testament*. London: United Bible Societies, 1971.

Meyer, Eduard. *Ursprung und Anfänge des Christentums*. 3 vols. Stuttgart: J. G. Cotta, 1923–24.

Mills, Watson E. *A Bibliography of the Periodical Literature on the Acts of the Apostles: 1962–1984*. Leiden: E. J. Brill, 1986.

Minear, Paul S. "Luke's Use of the Birth Stories." In *Studies in Luke-Acts*, edited by Leander E. Keck and J. Louis Martyn, 111–30. Nashville: Abingdon Press, 1966.

————. "Jesus' Audiences According to Luke." *NovT* 16 (1974):81–109.

Moessner, David P. "'The Christ Must Suffer': New Light on the Jesus—Peter, Stephen, Paul Parallels in Luke-Acts." *NovT* 28 (1986):220–56.

————. "The Ironic Fulfillment of Israel's Glory." In *Luke-Acts and the Jewish People: Eight Critical Perspectives*, edited by Joseph B. Tyson, 35–50. Minneapolis: Augsburg Publishing House, 1988.

————. "Paul in Acts: Preacher of Eschatological Repentance to Israel." *NTS* 34 (1988):96–104.

————. *Lord of the Banquet: The Literary and Theological Significance of the Lukan Travel Narrative*. Minneapolis: Fortress Press, 1989.

Morgenthaler, Robert. *Lukanische Geschichtsschreibung als Zeugnis*. Zurich: Gotthef Verlag, 1949.

————. *Statistik des N. T. Wortschatzes*. Zurich: Gotthelf Verlag, 1958.

Moule, C. F. D. *Christ's Messengers*. New York: Association Press, 1957.

Munck, Johannes. *The Acts of the Apostles*. AB. Garden City: Doubleday, 1967.

Navonne, John. *Themes of St. Luke*. Rome: Gregorian University, 1970.

Neirynck, Frans. "Le Livre des Actes: 6. Ac. 10,36–43 et l'Évangile." *ETL* 60 (1984):109–17.

Neyrey, Jerome. "The Forensic Defense Speech and Paul's Trial Speeches in Acts 22–26: Form and Function." In *Luke-Acts: New Perspectives from the Society of Biblical Literature Seminar*, edited by Charles H. Talbert, 210–24. New York: Crossroad Books, 1984.

———. *The Passion According to Luke: a Redaction Study of Luke's Soteriology*. New York: Paulist Press, 1985.

Nolland, J. L. "A Fresh Look at Acts 15:10." *NTS* 27 (1980):105–15.

Oliver, H. H. "The Lucan Birth Stories and the Purpose of Luke-Acts." *NTS* 10 (1964):202–26.

O'Neill, J. C. *The Theology of Acts in Its Historical Setting*. 2d ed. London: S. P. C. K., 1970.

O'Toole, Robert F. *Acts 26: The Christological Climax of Paul's Defense (Ac 22:1–26:32)*. AnBib 78. Rome: Biblical Institute Press, 1978.

———. *The Unity of Luke's Theology*. Wilmington, DE: Michael Glazier, 1984.

Overbeck, Franz. *Kürze Erklärung der Apostelgeschichte*. Leipzig: Hirzel, 1870.

Parsons, Mikeal C. *The Departure of Jesus in Luke-Acts: The Ascension Narratives in Context*. JSNTSup 21. Sheffield: JSOT Press, 1987.

Pereira, Francis. *Ephesus: Climax of Universalism in Luke-Acts*. Anand, India: Gujarat Sahitya, 1983.

Perpich, Sandra W. *A Hermeneutic Critique of Structuralist Exegesis with Specific Reference to Lk 10, 29–37*. Lanham, MD: University Press of America, 1984.

Pervo, Richard I. *Profit with Delight: The Literary Genre of the Acts of the Apostles*. Philadelphia: Fortress Press, 1987.

———. *Luke's Story of Paul*. Minneapolis: Fortress Press, 1990.

Pfleiderer, Otto. *Christian Origins*. London: T. Fisher Unwin, 1906.

———. *Primitive Christianity: Its Writings and Teachings in their Historical Connections*, Vol. 1. New York: G. P. Putnam's Sons, 1906.

Pilgrim, Walter E. *Good News to the Poor: Wealth and Poverty in Luke-Acts*. Minneapolis: Augsburg Publishing House, 1981.

Plümacher, Eckhard. *Lukas als Hellenistischer Schriftsteller*. Göttingen: Vandenhoeck & Ruprecht, 1972.

Plummer, Alfred. *A Critical and Exegetical Commentary on the Gospel of Luke*. ICC. Edinburgh: T. & T. Clark, 1922.

Preuschen, Erwin. *Die Apostelgeschichte*. HNT 4,1. Tübingen: J. C. B. Mohr, 1912.

Puskas, Charles B., Jr. "The Conclusion of Luke-Acts: An Investigation of the Literary Function and Theological Significance of Acts 28:16–31." Ph.D. diss., Saint Louis University, 1980.

Radl, Walter. *Paulus und Jesus im lukanischen Doppelwerk: Untersuchungen zu Parallelmotiven im Lukasevangelium und in der Apostelgeschichte.* Europäische Hochschulschriften 49. Bern: Herbert Lang, 1975.

Ramsay, W. M. *Luke the Physician and Other Studies.* New York: G. H. Doran, 1908.

Ravens, D. A. S. "The Setting of Luke's Account of the Anointing: Luke 7.2–8.3." *NTS* 34 (1988):282–92.

Reicke, Bo. "Jesus, Simeon, and Anna (Luke 2:21–40)." In *Saved by Hope: Essays in Honor of Richard C. Oudersluys,* edited by James I. Cook, 96–108. Grand Rapids: William B. Eerdmans, 1978.

Rengstorf, K. H. *Das Evangelium nach Lukas.* 5th ed. NTD 3. Göttingen: Vandenhoeck und Ruprecht, 1949.

Rese, Martin. *Alttestamentliche Motive in der Christologie des Lukas.* SNT 1. Gütersloh: Gerd Mohn, 1969.

———. "Einige Überlegungen zu Lukas xiii. 31–33." In *Jesus aux Origines de la Christologie,* edited by J. Dupont, 201–25. BETL 40. Gembloux: J. Duculot, 1975.

———. "Die Funktion der alttestamentlichen Zitate und Anspielungen in den Reden der Apostelgeschichte." In *Les Actes des Apôtres: Traditions, Rédaction, Théologie,* edited by J. Kemer, 61–79. Leuven: University of Leuven, 1979.

———. "Die Aussagen über Jesu Tod und Auferstehung in der Apostelgeschichte—ältestes Kerygma oder lukanische Theologumena?" *NTS* 30 (1984):335–53.

———. "Das Lukas Evangelium. Ein Forschungsbericht." In *ANRW,* edited by Hildegard Temporini and Wolfgang Haase, II.25.3:2258–2328. Berlin: Walter de Gruyter, 1985.

Richard, Earl. "The Divine Purpose: The Jews and the Gentile Mission (Acts 15)." In *Luke-Acts: New Perspectives from the Society of Biblical Literature Seminar,* edited by Charles H. Talbert, 188–209. New York: Crossroad Books, 1984.

Richards, I. A. *Principles of Literary Criticism.* New York: Harcourt, Brace & Co., 1924.

Richardson, Neil. *The Panorama of Luke: An Introduction to the Gospel of Luke and the Acts of the Apostles.* London: Epworth Press, 1982.

Richardson, Peter. *Israel in the Apostolic Church.* SNTSMS 10. Cambridge: Cambridge University Press, 1969.

Richardson, Peter, David Granskou, and Stephen G. Wilson, eds. *Anti-Judaism in Early Christianity.* 2 vols. Studies in Christianity and Judaism 2. Waterloo: Wilfrid Laurier University Press, 1986.

Riddle, Donald W. "The Occasion of Luke-Acts." *JR* 10 (1930):545–62.

———. *Paul, Man of Conflict: A Modern Biographical Sketch*. Nashville: Cokesbury Press, 1940.

Ringe, Sharon H. *Jesus, Liberation, and the Biblical Jubilee: Images for Ethics and Christology*. OBT 19. Philadelphia: Fortress Press, 1985.

Ringgren, H. "Luke's Use of the Old Testament." *HTR* 79 (1986):227–35.

Robbins, Vernon K. "Prefaces in Greco-Roman Biography and Luke-Acts." *Perspectives in Religious Studies* 6 (1979):94–108.

Robertson, A. T. *Luke the Historian in the Light of Research*. New York: Charles Scribner's Sons, 1920.

Robinson, B. P. "The Place of the Emmaus Story in Luke-Acts." *NTS* 30 (1984):481–97.

Roloff, Jürgen. *Die Apostelgeschichte Übersetzt und Erklärt*. NTD 5. Göttingen: Vandenhoeck und Ruprecht, 1981.

Ropes, James H. *The Apostolic Age in the Light of Modern Criticism*. New York: Charles Scribner's Sons, 1906.

Ruether, Rosemary R. *Faith and Fratricide: The Theological Roots of Anti-Semitism*. New York: Crossroad Books, 1974.

Sanders, E. P., ed. *Jewish and Christian Self-Definition*. 3 vols. Philadelphia: Fortress Press, 1980, 1981, 1982.

Sanders, Jack T. "The Parable of the Pounds and Lucan Anti-Semitism," *TS* 42 (1981):660–68.

———. "The Salvation of the Jews in Luke-Acts." In *Luke-Acts: New Perspectives from the Society of Biblical Literature Seminar*, edited by Charles H. Talbert, 104–28. New York: Crossroad Books, 1984.

———. "The Prophetic Use of the Scriptures in Luke-Acts." In *Early Jewish and Christian Exegesis: Studies in Memory of William Hugh Brownlee*, edited by Craig A. Evans and William F. Stinespring, 191–98. Scholars Press Homage Series. Atlanta: Scholars Press, 1987.

———. *The Jews in Luke-Acts*. Philadelphia: Fortress Press, 1987.

———. "The Jewish People in Luke-Acts." In *Luke-Acts and the Jewish People: Eight Critical Perspectives*, edited by Joseph B. Tyson, 51–75. Minneapolis: Augsburg Publishing House, 1988.

Sanders, James A. "From Isaiah 61 to Luke 4." In *Christianity, Judaism and Other Greco-Roman Cults: Studies for Morton Smith at Sixty*, edited by Jacob Neusner, 1:75–106. SJLA 12. Leiden: E. J. Brill, 1975.

Schaff, Philip. *History of the Christian Church*, Vol. 1. New York: Charles Scribner's Sons, 1889.

Schenk, Wolfgang. "The Roles of the Readers or the Myth of the Reader." In *Semeia* 48, edited by Edgar V. McKnight, 55–80. Atlanta: Scholars Press, 1989.

Schille, Gottfried. *Die Apostelgeschichte des Lukas*. THKNT 5. Berlin: Evangelische Verlangsanstalt, 1983.

Schlatter, Adolf. *The Church in the New Testament Period*. Trans. by Paul A. Levertogg. London: S. P. C. K., 1955.

Schmeichel, Waldemar. "Christian Prophecy in Lukan Thought: Luke 4:16–30 as a Point of Departure." In *SBLSP*, edited by George W. MacRae, 293–304. Missoula: Scholars Press, 1976.

Schmidt, Daryl. "Luke's 'Innocent' Jesus: A Scriptural Apologetic." In *Political Issues in Luke-Acts*, edited by Richard J. Cassidy and Philip J. Scharper, 111–21. Maryknoll, NY: Orbis Books, 1983.

Schmithals, Walter. *Das Evangelium nach Lukas.* Zürcher Bibelkommentare. Zurich: Theologischen Verlag, 1980.

Schneider, Gerhard. *Das Evangelium nach Lukas.* 2 vols. Ökumenischer Taschenbuchkommentar zum Neuen Testament 3. Gütersloh: Gerd Mohn, 1977.

———. "Stephanus, die Hellenisten und Samaria." In *Les Actes des Apôtres: Traditions, Rédaction, Théologie*, edited by J. Kremer, 215–40. BETL 48. Leuven: Leuven University Press, 1979.

———. *Die Apostelgeschichte.* 2 vols. HTKNT 5. Frieburg: Herder, 1980, 1982.

———. *Lukas, Theologe der Heilsgeschichte: Aufsätze zum lukanischen Doppelwerk.* BBB 59. Königstein: Peter Hanstein, 1985.

Schubert, Paul. "The Structure and Significance of Luke 24." In *Neutestamentliche Studien für Rudolf Bultmann*, edited by Walther Eltester, 165–86. Berlin: Alfred Töpelmann, 1957.

———. "The Place of the Areopagus Speech in the Composition of Acts." In *Transitions in Biblical Scholarship*, edited by J. Coert Rylaarsdam, 235–61. Chicago: University of Chicago Press, 1968.

Schürmann, Heinz. *Das Lukasevangelium, Erster Teil, Kommentar zu Kap. 1, 1–9,50.* HTKNT 3. Freiburg: Herder, 1969.

Schweizer, Eduard. "Concerning the Speeches in Acts." In *Studies in Luke-Acts*, edited by Leander E. Keck and J. Louis Martyn, 208–16. Nashville: Abindgon Press, 1966.

———. *Luke: A Challenge to Present Theology.* Atlanta: John Knox Press, 1982.

Secombe, David Peter. *Possessions and the Poor in Luke-Acts.* Linz: NT und Umwelt, 1982.

Seifrid, M. A. "Messiah and Mission in Acts: A Brief Response to J. B. Tyson." *JSNT* 36 (1989):47–50.

Sevenster, J. N. *The Roots of Pagan Anti-Semitism in the Ancient World.* NovTSup 41. Leiden: E. J. Brill, 1975.

Siegert, Folker. "Gottesfürchtige und Sympathisanten." *JSJ* 4 (1973): 109–64.

Slingerland, Dixon. " 'The Jews' in the Pauline Portion of Acts." *JAAR* 54 (1986):305–21.

———. "The Composition of Acts: Some Redaction-Critical Observations." *JAAR* 56 (1988):99–113.

Smith, Dennis E. "Table Fellowship as a Literary Motif in the Gospel of Luke." *JBL* 106 (1987):613–38.

Staley, Jeffrey Lloyd. *The Print's First Kiss: A Rhetorical Investigation of the Implied Reader in the Fourth Gospel*. SBLDS 82. Atlanta: Scholars Press, 1988.

Stoops, Robert F., Jr. "Riot and Assembly: The Social Context of Acts 19:23–41." *JBL* 108 (1989):73–91.

Stowers, S. "The Synagogue in the Theology of Acts." *ResQ* 17 (1974):129–43.

Streeter, B. H. "Fresh Light on the Synoptic Problem." *Hibbert Journal* 20 (1921):103–12.

——— . *The Four Gospels: A Study of Origins*. London: Macmillan & Co., 1924.

Sylva, Dennis D. "The Meaning and Function of Acts 7:46–50." *JBL* 106 (1987):261–75.

——— . "The Temple Curtain and Jesus' Death in the Gospel of Luke." *JBL* 105 (1986):239–50.

Sylva, Dennis D., ed. *Reimagining the Death of the Lukan Jesus*. BBB 73. Frankfurt: Hain, 1990.

Talbert, Charles H. *Literary Patterns, Theological Themes and the Genre of Luke-Acts*. SBLMS 20. Missoula: Scholars Press, 1974.

——— . "Shifting Sands: The Recent Study of the Gospel of Luke." *Int* 30 (1976):381–95.

——— . "Prophecies of Future Greatness: The Contribution of Greco-Roman Biographies to an Understanding of Luke 1:5–4:15." In *The Divine Helmsman: Studies on God's Control of Human Events, Presented to Lou H. Silberman*, edited by James L. Crenshaw and Samuel Sandmel, 129–41. New York: KTAV Publishing House, 1980.

——— . *Reading Luke: A Literary and Theological Commentary*. New York: Crossroad Books, 1982.

——— . *Acts*. Knox Preaching Guides. Atlanta: John Knox Press, 1984.

Talbert, Charles H., ed. *Perspectives on Luke-Acts*. Danville, VA: Association of Baptist Professors of Religion, 1978.

——— . *Luke-Acts: New Perspectives from the Society of Biblical Literature Seminar*. New York: Crossroad Books, 1984.

Tannehill, Robert C. "Israel in Luke-Acts: A Tragic Story." *JBL* 104 (1985):69–85.

——— . *The Narrative Unity of Luke-Acts: A Literary Interpretation*. 2 vols. Philadelphia: Fortress Press, 1986, 1990.

——— . "Rejection by Jews and Turning to Gentiles: The Pattern of Paul's Mission in Acts." In *Luke-Acts and the Jewish People: Eight Critical Perspectives*, edited by Joseph B. Tyson, 83–101. Minneapolis: Augsburg Publishing House, 1988.

Taylor, Vincent. *Behind the Third Gospel: A Study of the Proto-Luke Hypothesis*. Oxford: Clarendon Press, 1926.

Tiede, David L. *Prophecy and History in Luke-Acts*. Philadelphia: Fortress Press, 1980.

————— . " 'Glory to Thy People Israel': Luke-Acts and the Jews." In *Luke-Acts and the Jewish People: Eight Critical Perspectives*, edited by Joseph B. Tyson, 21–34. Minneapolis: Augsburg Publishing House, 1988.

Tinsley, E. J. *The Gospel According to Luke*. CBC. Cambridge: Cambridge University Press, 1965.

Trocmé, Étienne. "The Jews as Seen by Paul and Luke." In *"To See Ourselves as Others See Us": Christians, Jews, "Others" in Late Antiquity*, edited by Jacob Neusner and Ernest S. Frerichs, 145–62. Scholars Press Studies in the Humanities. Chico, CA: Scholars Press, 1985.

Tyson, Joseph B. "Acts 6:1–7 and Dietary Regulations in Early Christianity." *Perspectives in Religious Studies* 10 (1983):145–61.

————— . "Conflict as a Literary Theme in the Gospel of Luke." In *New Synoptic Studies*, edited by William R. Farmer, 303–27. Macon: Mercer University Press, 1983.

————— . "The Jewish Public in Luke-Acts." *NTS* 30 (1984):574–83.

————— . *The Death of Jesus in Luke-Acts*. Columbia: University of South Carolina Press, 1986.

————— . "The Gentile Mission and the Authority of Scripture in Acts." *NTS* 33 (1987):619–31.

————— . "Scripture, Torah, and Sabbath in Luke-Acts." In *Jesus, the Gospels, and the Church: Essays in Honor of William R. Farmer*, edited by E. P. Sanders, 89–104. Macon: Mercer University Press, 1987.

————— . "The Birth Narratives and the Beginning of Luke's Gospel." *Semeia*, 52 (1990):103–20.

Tyson, Joseph B., ed. *Luke-Acts and the Jewish People: Eight Critical Perspectives*. Minneapolis: Augsburg Publishing House, 1988.

Untergassmair, Franz G. *Kreuzweg und Kreuzigung Jesu: Ein Beitrag zur Lukanischen Redaktionsgeschichte und zur Frage nach lukanischen "Kreuzestheologie"*. Paderborner theologische Studien 10. Paderborn: Ferdinand Schonigh, 1980.

Uspensky, Boris. *A Poetics of Composition: The Structure of the Artistic Text and Typology of a Compositional Form*. Translated by Valentina Zavarin and Susan Wittig. Berkeley: University of California Press, 1973.

Van der Horst, P. W. "Jews and Christians in Aphrodisias in the Light of Their Relations in Other Cities of Asia Minor." *NedTTs* 43 (1989):106–21.

Van Unnik, W. C. "Luke-Acts, a Storm Center in Contemporary Scholarship." In *Studies in Luke-Acts*, edited by Leander E. Keck and J. Louis Martyn, 15–32. Nashville: Abingdon Press, 1966.

Veltman, Fred. "The Defense Speeches of Paul in Acts." In *Perspectives on Luke-Acts*, edited by Charles H. Talbert, 243–56. Danville, VA: Association of Baptist Professors of Religion, 1978.

Via, E. Jane. "According to Luke, Who Put Jesus to Death?" In *Political Issues in Luke-Acts*, edited by Richard J. Cassidy and Philip J. Scharper, 122–45. Maryknoll, NY: Orbis Books, 1983.

Wagner, Günter. *An Exegetical Bibliography of the New Testament: Luke and Acts*. Macon: Mercer University Press, 1985.

Walaskay, Paul W. *"And So We Came to Rome": The Political Perspective of St. Luke*. SNTSMS 49. Cambridge: Cambridge University Press, 1983.

Weinert, Francis D. "The Meaning of the Temple in Luke-Acts." *BTB* 11 (1981):85–89.

————. "Luke, the Temple, and Jesus' Saying about Jerusalem's Abandoned House." *CBQ* 44 (1982):68–76.

————. "Luke, Stephen, and the Temple in Luke-Acts." *BTB* 17 (1987):88–90.

Weiser, Alfons. *Die Apostelgeschichte*. 2 vols. Ökumenischer Taschenbuchkommentar zum Neuen Testament 5. Gütersloh: Gerd Mohn, 1981, 1985.

Weiss, Bernhard. *A Commentary on the New Testament*, Vol. 2. Translated by George H. Schodde and Epiphanius Wilson. New York: Funk & Wagnalls, 1906.

Weiss, Johannes. *Earliest Christianity: A History of the Period AD 30–150*. 2 vols. Translated by Frederick C. Grant. New York: Harper & Brothers, 1959.

Weizsäcker, Carl Von. *The Apostolic Age of the Christian Church*, Vol. 1. Translated by James Millar. London: Williams and Norgate, 1897.

Wilckens, Ulrich. *Die Missionsreden der Apostelgeschichte: Form- und traditionsgeschichtliche Untersuchen*. WMANT 5. Neukirchen kreis Moers: Neukirchener Verlag, 1961.

Wilcox, Max. "A Foreword to the Study of the Speeches in Acts." In *Christianity, Judaism and Other Greco-Roman Cults: Studies for Morton Smith at Sixty*, edited by Jacob Neusner, 1:206–25. SJLA 12. Leiden: E. J. Brill, 1975.

Wilshire, Leland E. "Was Canonical Luke Written in the Second Century?—A Continuing Discussion." *NTS* 20 (1974):246–53.

Wilson, Stephen G. *The Gentiles and the Gentile Mission in Luke-Acts*. SNTSMS 23. Cambridge: Cambridge University Press, 1973.

————. *Luke and the Law*. SNTSMS 50. Cambridge: Cambridge University Press, 1983.

————. "The Jews and the Death of Jesus in Acts." In *Anti-Judaism in Early Christianity*, edited by Peter Richardson with David Granskou, 1:155–64. Waterloo: Wilfrid Laurier University Press, 1986.

Wimsatt, W. K., Jr., and Monroe C. Beardsley. "The Intentional Fallacy." In *The Verbal Icon*, edited by W. K. Wimsatt, Jr., 3–18. Lexington: University of Kentucky Press, 1954.

Wuellner, Wilhelm. "Is There an Encoded Reader Fallacy?" In *Semeia* 48, edited by Edgar V. McKnight, 41–54. Atlanta: Scholars Press, 1989.

Zehnle, Richard F. *Peter's Pentecost Discourse: Tradition and Lukan Reinterpretation in Peter's Speeches of Acts 2 and 3.* SBLMS 15. Nashville: Abingdon Press, 1971.

Zeller, Edward. *The Contents and Origin of the Acts of the Apostles,* Vol. 1. Translated by Joseph Dare. London: Williams Norgate, 1875.

Zingg, Paul, *Das Wachsen der Kirche: Beiträge zur Frage der lukanischen Redaktion und Theologie.* Göttingen: Vandenhoeck & Ruprecht, 1974.

\

# Index of Modern Scholars

# Index of Biblical and Apocryphal References

211